UNDERSTANDING JEHOVAH'S WITNESSES

SECOND EDITION

OWEN MORGAN

UNDERSTANDING JEHOVAH'S WITNESSES

SECOND EDITION

OWEN MORGAN

CONTENTS

UNDERSTANDING JEHOVAH'S WITNESSES
SECOND EDITION

100 QUESTIONS FOR JEHOVAH'S WITNESSES

UNDERSTANDING JEHOVAH'S WITNESSES

SECOND EDITION

FOREWORD

If you were to take a World Religions class in high school, a handful of faiths would dominate the discussion: Christianity, Judaism, Islam, Hinduism, and Buddhism. If you're lucky, atheism and Humanism will also be mentioned.

But many religions, with hundreds of thousands of adherents (if not more!), fly under the radar. They're not big enough to warrant media coverage, be studied in school, or have buildings in your community. If people have heard the names of those religions, that's probably the extent of their knowledge.

I know what that's like because, raised as a Jain, no one knew anything about my religion. I was the first (and only) Jain my friends had met. I grew accustomed to explaining the basics of my faith to anyone who asked—questions they never had to answer about their religions. My entire life revolved around my family's religion, and yet it seemed to be a complete mystery to everyone else. I was lucky, though. Jainism has its flaws, but you'd be hard-pressed to find people who are traumatized by it. That's not the case with Jehovah's Witnesses.

Over the past few years, with the help of sites like YouTube and

Reddit, there has been a remarkable rise in former Jehovah's Witnesses speaking out about the religion. Far from being alone, they have found a community, shared their concerns, and formed networks to help others trying to walk away. (And my goodness, they have a lot to talk about.)

According to the Watch Tower Bible and Tract Society of Pennsylvania, there are more than 1.2 million Jehovah's Witnesses in the United States. They may be best known to casual observers for knocking on doors, sending handwritten letters, and setting up shop on busy street corners, hoping to speak with anyone willing to give them some time.

Yet, how many Americans know what they believe? I mean, really, truly believe? Perhaps they know about how Jehovah's Witnesses avoid blood transfusions, birthdays, and elections. Or that they attach a great deal of importance to the number 144,000. But I would bet most people know almost nothing about the faith. If they know anything, it's likely because someone close to them— perhaps a classmate or work colleague—is a member.

That's not unusual among more minor religions, but think about what that means when it involves a faith that harms so many people.

The rampant abuse in Kingdom Halls gets hidden even deeper in the shadows. The cruel, heartless act of disfellowshipping occurs in virtual secrecy outside the Jehovah's Witness bubble.

The general public ignores the most coercive elements of the faith, dismissing them as quirks of any small religion.

That unfamiliarity with the Jehovah's Witnesses allows its leaders to get away with much more.

My friend Owen Morgan has spent years documenting the Jehovah's Witnesses. His videos have given voice to ex-JWs while educating people like me who want to know more about the religion (but with the appropriate level of criticism). His videos are thoughtful because that's who Owen is; he doesn't need to exaggerate. Teaching you what Jehovah's Witnesses believe, why they believe it, and how they keep members in the fold is shocking enough. With this book, Owen introduces the religion—warts and all— to anyone willing to learn.

If you want a short summary of the faith, you can always go to Wikipedia. But suppose you're an outsider who wants to learn how the religion operates in practice and what believers fail to understand. You're in luck. Owen covers the faith's founding, failed prophecies, and future. He doesn't need to resort to cheap shots because telling the truth is often the most effective criticism. (As he writes in the book, "If it doesn't make sense to you, it's not you. It's them.")

This is a history and a memoir rolled into one. It's personal. And because Owen cares deeply about the subject, I know you'll care about it too.

Signed,

Hemant Mehta

PREFACE

If you're reading this as a Jehovah's Witness who's on the fence about remaining inside the religion, please read this book with open eyes and an open mind. My goal throughout this book is not to attack anybody. I simply want my story to be told. In the process, I hope to teach people about Jehovah's Witness culture and history. Ex-Jehovah's Witnesses are not "mentally diseased" or agents of Satan, as is claimed by the organization. I'm simply someone with an experience that must be described and understood.

When people hear the name Jehovah's Witness, they think of a smiley, happy group of people who love knocking on doors. But when you scratch the surface, you start to see what's underneath. I know what lies behind that smile because I had that smile myself. Not only was the religion damaging to me, but it was also damaging to everybody around me.

I would argue that most Jehovah's Witnesses don't even like knocking on doors. The organization is extremely controlling. In that type of environment, real smiles are rare. The religion even has a merchandise tagline: "Best Life Ever." The religion grinds people down. They smile because they've convinced themselves to do so.

I'd like to start by going through the organization's history chronologically. We'll start with the first president and founder of the movement, Charles Taze Russell, and move through each president as we discuss changes made through the years. As you'll come to find, different presidents had different priorities.

I'll tell my story after discussing the history and belief structure chronologically. The story should reveal the organization's deep-seated problems, which might otherwise be hard to quantify, identify, or vocalize.

Then, I'll discuss modern Jehovah's Witnesses. We'll discuss their current culture and hierarchy and some of the problems that any single member of the leadership could quickly and easily fix.

Growing up as a Jehovah's Witness, I remember the process of qualifying to become a member. It was arduous, difficult, and lengthy, and it included a great deal of memorization, much like a college course. There's even a test you must pass at the end before becoming a member, colloquially called the hundred questions. While telling my story, I hope to describe how to be a Jehovah's Witness.

I also want to tell the urban legends. Jehovah's Witnesses have bizarre urban legends about Smurf dolls standing up and walking right out of the Kingdom Hall, as well as demons possessing innocent Jehovah's Witnesses.

I've included a set of questions similar to Jehovah's Witnesses' baptism questions at the end of the book. The questions show that the religion's leaders do not hear God's voice; they are not uniquely in tune with him in a way others are not. The questions can be read and understood independently of this book.

I want to take you on a walk beside a Jehovah's Witness as we journey through the religion. I want to talk about what it was like to learn about the culture and how it felt to learn about the religious leaders' bad behavior. I want to explain what it was like to realize that the people at the top, the Governing Body, aren't God's mouthpiece on earth. This isn't Jehovah's chosen organization. Walk with me through my life as I learned to be a Jehovah's Witness, as the religion tried to take everything from me, and as I finally recognized the organization for what it is: a false religion.

I will not refer to Jehovah's Witnesses as a "cult" beyond this section. The word cult can make people feel like they're being attacked, even when they're not. I don't want to slander, attack, or demean anybody. I want to explain what the religion of Jehovah's Witnesses is and how it's been harmful to me personally, and to millions of others.

One dictionary definition of the word "cult" specifically requires the group to have a single leader that they worship. However, there's a movement to change that view. My definition is a little more complex than the dictionary definition. If I had to boil it down to a single term, I would choose "control."

Courts tend to use the term "undue influence." Undue influence happens when somebody is influenced into doing something without fully understanding the consequences. For example, society views children as innocent and unaware of the consequences of their actions. We give children more leeway for mistakes. If a five-year-old steals something from a store, they aren't usually arrested for petty larceny. Children aren't expected to have a fully formed understanding of morality.

Undue influence gives somebody an advantage to short-circuit another's moral system. Once the moral system is short-circuited, they're really no different than the five-year-old: both are trusting of authority figures, unaware of all consequences, and/or are convinced the results are worth the moral wrong. That doesn't mean a child or an adult should get away with harming others. Society should still be protected. However, undue influence should be considered when a cult member is judged in court or otherwise.

Should Jehovah's Witnesses be judged for shunning friends and family? It's impossible to fully understand what it's like to shun or be shunned until you're in the situation. Nobody expects it to come up. The thought barely crosses their mind before they're forced to face it. That's all part of undue influence.

Shunning is the ultimate punishment, but before shunning is considered, Jehovah's Witnesses use peer pressure. As we'll discuss, peer pressure can be so intense that it'll convince millions of people to avoid the Smurfs or yard sales for fear a demon might attach itself to the believer. Peer pressure is ultimately the controlling force behind everything in this religion.

Jehovah's Witnesses are rewarded for following instructions by receiving "privileges." Those privileges include setting up the sound system or adjusting the microphone for the speakers. Even though it's just labor for the organization, peers view members favorably for being granted the right to do that labor. The real reward is the jump in peer status.

Cults also sometimes control membership through the information they absorb. Jehovah's Witnesses have a TV show they release each month: JW Broadcasting. They also release Governing Body updates to their website and app. Jehovah's Witnesses are expected to watch everything released. If a political issue concerns the members, they'll let them know. Otherwise, they should stay away from the news. Members caught browsing "apostate" material (including any websites, books, videos, Facebook pages, or articles that might be critical of the organization) will be shunned for it.

Jehovah's Witnesses also use common language. For example, they don't say "oh my god" or "thank god." They say, "Thank Jehovah." They also have terms used to shut down critical thinking. When discussing the existence of Hell, they say, "Do you think a loving parent would put their child's hand on a hot stove as punishment for something?" They're trained to remember that story any time the subject of Hellfire comes up.

Jehovah's Witnesses are also taught to repeat the name Jehovah if they're in a challenging situation. If a young kid thinks there's a monster in their closet, repeating the name Jehovah will resolve it.

When I was young, my mom told me that a group of Bethelites, the most revered and respected Jehovah's Witnesses, went to see the movie "The Exorcist" in theaters. Bethelites live and work on a Jehovah's Witness compound. Shortly after the Bethelites went to the movie, Bethel was suddenly in complete chaos. They found guns in people's drawers, and Bethelites were getting drunk. When the higher-ups investigated and found out what happened, they removed the Bethelites and prayed over the Bethel location to restore Jehovah's presence. That's a common story told among Jehovah's Witnesses, and it builds fear to stop members from consuming taboo material.

Jehovah's Witnesses also use emotional control to keep members in line. Including things like preventing current members from talking to ex-members or encouraging a culture of distancing from the "bad" person before they're officially shunned. Even if the offense isn't technically worthy of shunning, like hanging around outsiders. This applies to children, parents, best friends, and any social net one may have built while being an active member.

Jehovah's Witnesses usually respond, "Families do all of that stuff, but they aren't a cult. My parents use control techniques to coerce me into getting good grades or taking out the trash. How is that any different? If I'm in a cult, everybody is in a cult." It's a good question. How are families different from cults?

Jehovah's Witnesses are correct when they say, "I influence my friend daily when I ask if he wants pizza. How is this any different?" The Influence Continuum, written by Steven Hassan, is a one-page model detailing the difference between destructive and constructive influence. According to the Influence Continuum, two types of influence are destructive and constructive. Constructive influence helps people be creative and form their own identity. Destructive influence depends on fear and guilt. Constructive influence has a system of checks and balances, while destructive influence holds absolute, unchecked authority. People can influence others without benefitting from the influence. That is just one way a family differs from the Jehovah's Witness organization.

Just like influence, there are varying degrees of radicalism and extremism. When does something go from being a regular social club to a cult? There's no good place to draw the line, so I choose to do what lawyers do when working with legal concepts: use a bright line rule.

A bright line rule is a line where a standard is placed. Kids can usually drive between sixteen and eighteen, but nobody can get a license at 12. When does it cross over from tipsy driving to drunk driving? In the United States, it crosses over at a .08 blood alcohol level. Are you more drunk at .079 than you are at .081? No, but the bright line is at 0.08.

I draw a clear line between constructive and destructive influence. If you're trying to take advantage of your friends to get free pizza, it is wrong to talk them into going to a restaurant. Intent is a big part of it, even if the influence isn't clearly and obviously destructive. Some things just can't be defined more clearly than that. As long as society agrees on where the bright line should go, putting down a random line is fine, just as we did with drunk driving.

If you noticed, I didn't provide a citation in this section. I decided to draw my own bright line for destructive groups. I'm not the ultimate authority on high-control groups or destructive religions. Although I am an expert on Jehovah's Witness culture, since I was a Jehovah's Witness for the first eighteen years of my life. This was my culture. I'm basing my ideas of high control groups on my own experiences. You can feel free to take it or leave it. So, let's start at the beginning.

CHAPTER 1
A HISTORY OF MISTAKES

et's discuss Jehovah's Witness history and beliefs in chronological order. The founder of the early Jehovah's Witness church, Charles Taze Russell, famously used Bible math to prophesy dates for when the end would come. The Bible math borrowed from the Millerites, another movement from the time.

Charles Taze Russell founded the Bible Students, which would eventually become Jehovah's Witness, in the 1870s. The parent company, what we now call the Watchtower Society, was created in 1881. William Miller popularized Russell's Bible math. The Millerite movement came and went before Russell was even born, but he still believed Miller was on to something. Miller used the math to calculate an end times date of 1844, which we now call the "Great Disappointment."

Russell's Bible Students were part of the Adventist movement sparked by William Miller. Adventism means the "arrival of an important person or thing." Adventists are different in that they believe Jesus will be here NOW. Lots of Christians believe Jesus will be here any second, but Adventists take it a step further. Sometimes, they even set dates.

Much of the Bible math used by Adventists like Millerites or Jehovah's Witnesses is based on the book of Daniel. Daniel was written in 164 BCE, but the book's setting is in the 500s BCE. Millerites and Jehovah's Witnesses base many math variables on King Solomon's temple. Let's take a moment to talk about the history of Solomon's Temple.

Solomon was the next king after David, sometime around 1000 BCE. He ordered a temple to be built in Jerusalem, the capital of Judea, which the Jews would use for worship. Judea, previously called Judah, was the sister nation of Israel around the time Daniel was set, 550 BCE.

In 597 BCE, King Nebuchadnezzar of the Babylonian empire, now modern-day Iraq, besieged the region around the nation of Judea. Nebuchadnezzar allowed it to function without his input as long as they paid tribute. Four years into Nebuchadnezzar's reign, the king of Judea refused to pay the tribute, and Nebuchadnezzar laid siege to the city. The city was taken, and many government leaders were taken to Babylon. Another government was formed, but Nebuchadnezzar returned in 586 BCE and destroyed Jerusalem and the Temple.

Nobody disagrees with that timeline except Jehovah's Witnesses. Every date and number in that timeline must be accurate for their beliefs to be correct. Let's discuss the movement that sparked Jehovah's Witnesses and how the Bible math was calculated.

THE VARIABLES

Adventists get many of their variables from what they call the day-year principle. The day-year principle is the belief that any time the Bible mentions a day, it could be switched out for a year. They got the idea mainly from two verses: Numbers 14:34 and Ezekiel 4:5–6. Numbers talks about the Israelites wandering the desert for 40 years, one year for each day spent in Canaan by Jewish spies. In the Ezekiel verse, God tells Ezekiel to lie on his left side for 390 days and his right side for 40 days, which is the number of years God will punish Israel and Judea. The day-year principle is the linchpin of the Adventist Bible math.

The variables consist of two categories: dates and numbers to add to the dates.

- **Variable 1: 606 BCE**—Nebuchadnezzar of Babylon destroyed the temple in 586 BCE. Jehovah's Witnesses incorrectly believe it was 606 BCE.
- **Variable 2: 536 BCE**—King Cyrus freed the Jews from Babylon in 538 BCE. William Miller thought it was two years later.
- **Variable 3: 457 BCE**—King Artaxerxes, I ordered the wall in Jerusalem rebuilt in 457 BCE. I can't verify whether that date is accurate or if the event even happened.
- **Variable 4: 538 CE**—William Miller believed Catholics named the first pope in 538 CE.
- **Variable 5: 70 weeks, or 490 days** - According to Daniel 8, atoning for sins would take Jews seventy weeks. Seventy weeks is 490 days.
- **Variable 6: 2,300**—Daniel 8 mentions 2,300 mornings and evenings. No context is necessary. It just says 2,300 mornings and evenings—simple as that.
- **Variable 7: 2,520**—In Daniel 4, Nebuchadnezzar dreamed that a large tree had been cut down and wouldn't grow back for "seven times." In the Bible, time usually means a year. Seven multiplied by 360 days, the length of a year at the time, comes out to 2,520.

- **Variable 8: 1,260**—Daniel 12 contains an apocalyptic vision in which a man holds a hand toward heaven and says, "It" would be for a time, two times, and half a time. The verse doesn't specify what "it" is, and "it" is irrelevant to Jehovah's Witness prophecy. One time, two times, and half a time add up to 3.5 years or 1,260 days.
- **Variable 9: Multiples of 7**—The number seven was significant to the Jewish people. For example, the seventh day of the week is the Sabbath.

How are 2,300 mornings and evenings connected to the reconstruction of Solomon's Temple? How can you apply the day-year principle to a verse that says, "mornings and evenings?" The answers are never provided, not by Miller, not by Russell, and not by modern Jehovah's Witnesses.

When the random numbers they chose didn't add up to anything, Jehovah's Witnesses and some Millerites claimed that something did happen. Jesus came back invisibly. The Bible verses used to get the variables honestly don't matter because they are meaningless to the prophecies they created. Still, we'll talk about the verses in more detail later.

CONSPIRACY MATH

Millerites thought 70 weeks, variable 4, foretold when Jesus would arrive. Miller took variable four and subtracted it from variable 3. That calculation got him to 27 CE. He made fabricated meaning to attach to it. He noted Jesus was on earth around that time, so he said the variables foretold the year when Jesus was baptized. Little did he know, Jesus was likely born around 3 or 4 BCE, not 1 CE.[1]

Variables 3 and 5 were used to arrive at 1843. Miller added 2,300 years to the date he believed Artaxerxes ordered Jerusalem to be rebuilt: 457 BCE. Two thousand three hundred years added to 457

BCE is 1843. The year came and went, and nothing happened. He said, "Oh, we forgot there was no year zero." He recalculated to 1844. It failed again, leading to the Great Disappointment.

The Great Disappointment is a good name for this failed prophecy, but it's a bit of an understatement. Homes were burned to the ground out of pure, unadulterated rage. Crops went unharvested. People sold everything they owned because they thought the end was here. Take a look at this excerpt from the book Sketches of the Christian Life and Public Labors of William Miller gathered from his memoir by the late Sylvester Bliss and from other sources:

> Some are tauntingly enquiring, "Have you not gone up?" Even little children in the streets are shouting continually to passersby, "Have you a ticket to go up?" The public prints, of the most fashionable and popular kind [...] are caricaturing in the most shameful manner of the "white robes of the saints," Revelation 6:1, the "going up," and the great day of "burning." Even the pulpits are desecrated by the repetition of scandalous and false reports concerning the "ascension robes," and priests are using their powers and pens to fill the catalogue of scoffing in the most scandalous periodicals of the day.

Even the children made fun of the Millerites for their failed prophecies. This shame led to the church's fracture into three main groups. The first group believed the Bible math was fake. The second group believed William Miller was correct—something really did happen in 1844: Jesus came back invisibly. The third group believed the Bible math was real, but William Miller had the variables wrong. Charles Taze Russell was from the third faction of the Millerite movement.

Today, Jehovah's Witnesses use variables one and seven to calculate 1914. They added 2,520 years, variable seven, from when Jerusalem was destroyed, and variable 1. That gets them to 1914. As mentioned, Nebuchadnezzar dreamed that a large tree was cut down and wouldn't grow back for "seven times" in Daniel 4. When the word "time" is used in the Bible, scholars and religious groups alike (including Jehovah's Witnesses) generally agree that a "time" is a reference to one year when used in the Bible. Seven times, or years, contain 2,520 days when using the calendar length used by the Jews at the time—360 days. Seven years multiplied by 360 days, which was the length of a year at the time, comes out to 2,520.

Except that Jerusalem fell in 586 BCE, not 606. When nothing happened in 1914, they used variable 8—a time, two times, and half a time—to extend it slightly longer. They added three and a half years to 1914. When it failed again, they claimed 1914 and 1918 were special years. 1914 was the beginning of the end, and 1918/1919 is when Jesus chose the Watchtower Society as his representation on earth. Jehovah's Witnesses have active prophecies that are based on these variables. They're essential to their theology.

Charles Taze Russell eventually used variable 9 to calculate the year 1874. As with the other dates he calculated, though, he used several "lines of evidence" to "prove" the date was correct. He used the verses from Daniel, jubilee cycles, and measurements from the Pyramid of Giza. Egyptians didn't use inches back then—they used cubits. A cubit is the length of the forearm, from the elbow to the tip of the middle finger. Since it varies from person to person, I'm sure you can see why that line of "evidence" was deeply absurd. But to Russell, God inspired the builders of the pyramid to put the correct number of "pyramid inches" in, a fraction of a cubit, to prove that Russell's dates were accurate 4,500 years after it was built. He was absolutely sure of it.

Charles Taze Russell died on Halloween night in 1916, and a pyramid statue was constructed at his gravesite in his honor.[2] Jehovah's Witnesses officially view Russell's Pyramidology as a doctrine of the devil. The Watchtower Society formally denounced the pyramid doctrine on November 15, 1928, twelve years after his death.

It is more reasonable to conclude that the great pyramid of Gizeh, as well as the other pyramids thereabout, also the sphinx, were built by the rulers of Egypt and under the direction of Satan the Devil...The Devil, by the use of the descendants of Ham, set up Egypt, or the land of Ham, as the first great world power. Then Satan put his knowledge in dead stone, which may be called Satan's Bible, and not God's stone witness. In erecting the pyramid, of course, Satan would put in it some truth, because that is his method of practising [sic] fraud and deceit.

JEHOVAH'S WITNESSES. THE WATCHTOWER. NOVEMBER 15, 1928. P. 344

Charles Taze Russell credited John Taylor and Charles Piazzi Smyth with saying, "The great pyramid is Jehovah's witness." At the time, the term Jehovah's Witness was uncommon and not generally used. The group wouldn't become Jehovah's Witnesses until long after Russell's death.

I'm sure it's becoming clear: they were conspiracy theorists. They were no different than the guy on the street corner screaming about a secret cabal of people operating in government, drinking the blood of children. People of the time viewed the founders of Adventism and Jehovah's Witnesses similarly.

EARLY FAILED PROPHECIES

The Watchtower Society, founded in 1881, is the parent company of the Jehovah's Witnesses. Although its official name wasn't the Watchtower Society when it was formed, the nickname stuck through the years. The Watchtower Society was and is basically just a publishing company that prints Bibles, books, and its magazine, *The Watchtower.*

Charles Taze Russell's first major prediction was in 1874. When it fell flat, it was a massive blight on his reputation. So Russell started what would be a long tradition that stands among Jehovah's Witnesses to this day: if he couldn't erase the mistake, he explained it away. He claimed something special really did happen in 1874: Jesus came back invisibly. It was the beginning of the end. Does that sound familiar?

When the new dates came and went, he used new variables to calculate what would most definitely be his final date and the end of the end: 1914. For sure, this time. Though 1874 and 1914 were the most well-known, there were other failed predictions: 1798, 1799, 1843, 1844, 1874, 1878, 1881, 1913, and 1914, to name a few.

Every single prophecy failed. He was a conspiracy theorist.

1914: ANOTHER FAILED PROPHECY

1914 is a significant year for modern Jehovah's Witnesses. They've built their entire theology around it. They believe that Jesus returned to earth invisibly in 1914. It's calculated using the variables 2,520 from Daniel 4 and 606 BCE, the (incorrect) date that Solomon's Temple fell. The verses are about Daniel in Babylon. Nebuchadnezzar had a strange dream, so he called the magicians and enchanters to shed some light on what his dream meant— including Daniel.

Nebuchadnezzar's dream was about a large tree. It was cut down with bands around its base to prevent it from growing again. Nebuchadnezzar was changed into a wild animal, and seven times passed over him. The day-year principle turns "seven times" from Daniel 4 to 2,520 years. That means Russell had a variable. Now, he needed to find a starting point.

Charles Taze Russell decided to start counting from when Jerusalem fell, 606 BCE. 606 BCE plus 2,520 years puts the end of the age firmly at 1913. Since there's no year zero, that brings it to 1914. Russell believed the start of World War I confirmed his math was correct. Using that logic, he assumed Jesus returned to Earth in October 1914. Modern Jehovah's Witnesses still believe the "First World War" logic.

The first significant problem with the math is that Jerusalem wasn't destroyed in 606. That might have been the assumption when Charles Taze Russell made the calculation. Scholars have known since at least 1929 that it took place in 586. Second, what does Jesus have to do with the temple falling? What does that have to do with some arbitrary number found in the book of Daniel?

HOW WE KNOW 1914 IS INCORRECT

We know that Solomon's Temple fell in 586 BCE because of an ancient Babylonian tablet: VAT4956. Ancient Babylon is an extremely well-documented time. Thanks to the Babylonians' use of clay tablets and meticulous record keeping, it's one of the best-preserved civilizations from the ancient world. The Babylonians even dated some writings by listing the positions of the stars on some tablets.

The VAT4956 tablet tells us which year of Nebuchadnezzar's reign they were in at the time of writing. It provides thirty positions of the moon and five positions of the planets to use as a timestamp.[3] By running some calculations to determine when the planets and moon would be in those positions, we have a precise time for when the tablet was written—and more traditional dating methods back it up. Beyond a shadow of a doubt, the tablet reveals that the thirty-seventh year of Nebuchadnezzar's reign was in 567 BCE. Traditional scholarship tells us when Nebuchadnezzar laid siege to the temple, but 2 Kings 25:1 lays it out, too.

> And it came to pass in the ninth year of his reign, in the tenth month, in the tenth day of the month, that Nebuchadnezzar king of

Babylon came, he and all his army, against Jerusalem, and encamped against it; and they built forts against it round about.

2 KINGS 25:1

Nebuchadnezzar's 37th year is an anchor point that shows us that the year the temple fell was 586 BCE. This is just one of 14 pieces of evidence used by ex-Jehovah's Witness Carl Olof Jonsson to find the date of the temple's destruction in his book titled The Gentile Times Reconsidered: Have Jehovah's Witnesses Been Wrong All Along About 607 BCE?

The temple's destruction is relevant to more than just Jehovah's Witnesses. It's a pivotal moment in Jewish history. This date is undisputed by everybody except for Jehovah's Witnesses.

JEHOVAH IS NOT GOD'S NAME

The name Jehovah has always been a core belief of the Watchtower Society. After Charles Taze Russell died, Joseph Rutherford took control of the Watchtower Society. He was the second president and served from 1917 to 1942. Rutherford started pushing the name Jehovah in 1926. At a convention in Columbus, Ohio, in 1931, Rutherford announced a big change. He was changing the group from the Bible Students to Jehovah's Witnesses after Isaiah 43:10:

You are my witnesses, says the Lord,
    and my servant whom I have chosen,
    so that you may know and believe me
    and understand that I am he.
    Before me no god was formed,
    nor shall there be any after me.

ISAIAH 43:10

One glaring problem with this is that Jehovah is not God's name. The real name of God in the Bible is Yahweh.[4]

The tetragrammaton is the set of four letters that refer to God's actual name: YHWH. Vowels didn't exist in the ancient Hebrew language. Native speakers just understood which vowels should be inserted. Modern scholars believe the name was pronounced Yahway.

So, where did the name Jehovah come from? Ancient Jews, preservers of the old text, had a superstition about speaking the Holy Name. Jews have a long tradition of publicly reading the Torah. Saying the holy name in public would be a disaster.

Over time, the Hebrew language gained vowels. The vowels are represented by a series of dots and squiggles, which can be inserted into writing without the need to rewrite the text altogether. When vowels were added, the preservers and copiers inserted the vowels for the word Adonai, which means Lord.[5] The tetragrammaton, YHWH, was combined with the vowels from the word Adonai, AOAI, to produce the name YAHOWAH. It was intentionally difficult to pronounce in the language. The preservers wanted people to stop and think instead of accidentally reading the name.

As YAHOWAH moved through European regions, it morphed into something that roughly sounded like "Jehovah." Some European languages at the time, like German, pronounced Y's like J's and W's like V's. That's how the name changed from Yahweh, in its original pronunciation, to Jehovah. Jehovah's Witnesses insist that Jehovah is a more accurate English translation.[6] It's not more accurate; it's less accurate.

Yahweh started as a Canaanite god. Canaanites were a group of people who lived in the same area as the Jews and had their own set of gods. People had a god for everything. Canaanites had a creator god named El, which simply means god. El was considered the supreme god. El created a set of gods under him, collectively called the Elohim, which is the plural form of El. The Bible doesn't necessarily talk about the Canaanite gods when it says Elohim or El —this explanation just shows the origins of the gods and their names.

By the way, when you hear the term "pagans" in the Old Testament, this group of gods is part of that broad non-Jewish (and eventually non-Christian) category. Below is a list of some Canaanite gods you might recognize. Each god in the list is mentioned in the Bible.[7,8]

- **Ba'al**—a storm god associated with fertility
- **El**—God of creation, husband of Asherah
- **Asherah**—queen consort of El (Ugaritic religion)
- **Anath**—virgin goddess of war and strife, sister and putative mate of Ba'al Hadad
- **Molech**—putative god of fire, husband of Ishat
- **Yahweh**—also called Yah. In the oldest biblical literature, he possesses attributes typically ascribed to weather and war deities.

Scholars have offered educated guesses that Yahweh might have been a war god.[9] There isn't enough information to know for sure. One thing we can be sure of, though, is that he was in the Canaanite pantheon. The Israelites and Canaanites obviously shared some culture and theology.

The Israelites chose one God as their own and made an agreement with him: "If you protect us, we will worship you and only you." The agreement can be found in the Ten Commandments—you shall worship no other gods before me. It's unlikely that Israelites even claimed to be monotheistic for centuries. They just liked Yahweh the most.

Scholars agree that, at best, about ten percent of the ancient world could read or write. To preserve their history, Jews had a tradition of using oral storytelling, poems, and songs, which were repeated regularly by the common people, the illiterate.

In the centuries after Jesus came, Jews had all but worked the tetragrammaton out of standard editions of what would eventually become the Old Testament.[10] In most places, it was replaced with the name "LORD." In some Bibles, the early pages mention that the word LORD in all capitals was used to replace the Holy Name.

Jehovah's Witnesses decided to run with the wrong name and stuck it everywhere—even where it didn't belong. Instead of inserting the correct words, they replaced "LORD" in their translation of the Bible, the New World Translation. The New Testament didn't contain a single instance of the name Yahweh. The word most used to refer to God in the New Testament was KURIOS, which means Lord.[10] Jehovah's Witnesses inserted the name Jehovah all over the New Testament anyway.

Jehovah's Witnesses are spectacularly wrong about the Holy Name and dead set on remaining wrong. As a result, just hearing the name Jehovah makes me cringe. Particularly when Jehovah's Witnesses replace the word "God" with the name "Jehovah" in common sayings, such as "Oh my Jehovah" or "Thank Jehovah for this or that." It can be difficult for some ex-Jehovah's Witnesses to stomach.

The Watchtower Society is dead set on calling members "one of Jehovah's Witnesses" instead of "a Jehovah's Witness." Throughout this book, I'll call them "a Jehovah's Witness" instead. They aren't witnesses to Jehovah because Jehovah isn't real. God's name in the Bible was Yahweh, not Jehovah.

Jehovah's Witnesses aren't historically or doctrinally correct about much, but the Hellfire and Trinity teachings are exceptions to the rule. Jehovah's Witnesses have believed that the Hellfire and Trinity teachings were wrong since the beginning. If they're historically inaccurate, where did those two teachings come from? The answer might surprise you, so let's talk about it.

THE APOCALYPSE OF PETER

Hellfire is a doctrinal belief that the Watchtower Society has rejected nearly since its founding.[11] Many people credit Dante's book "The Divine Comedy" as the source of the modern Christian idea of Hell, but the Apocalypse of Peter came first. It likely dates to around 100 or 150 CE, roughly the same time as the Book of John.

The word "apocalypse" literally means "revealing" or "explaining." The book of Revelation can also be called "The Apocalypse of John." Apocalyptic writing, like science fiction or fantasy, was a style at the time. There are even some apocalyptic writings outside of the Bible. It all follows a similar formula. The writer sees a bizarre, vivid vision that makes no sense. Then, an angel comes in to explain what it meant. The explanation usually ends with God's people being vindicated in some way.

There was debate over whether the Apocalypse of Peter or the Apocalypse of John (the book of Revelation) should be included in the Bible. Obviously, John's apocalypse won out at the end of the day. That might have been for the best. The book of Revelation is terrible, but the Apocalypse of Peter is worse. Much worse.

This apocalypse flows in a very similar pattern to Daniel and other writings in the apocalyptic genre. Peter is given a vision. In this apocalypse, the vision is of the afterlife. It portrays Hell as a place where sinners receive a punishment similar to the sin they committed. Here's a short list:[12]

- Blasphemers are hung by the tongue.
- Women who adorn themselves for the purpose of adultery are hung by their hair over a bubbling mire. The men who had adulterous relationships with them are hung by their genitals next to them.

- Venomous creatures and numberless worms torment murderers and their allies.
- Mothers who committed infanticide have their breast milk congeal into flesh-devouring animals that torment both parents. (Their dead children are delivered to a caretaking angel called Temlakos.)
- Rich people who neglected the poor are clothed in rags and pierced by a sharp pillar of fire.
- Sorcerers are hung on a wheel of fire. It's an extraordinarily vivid and graphic description of Hell, but Jehovah's Witnesses accurately believe that Hell is a later creation. It's not something Jesus himself accepted.

According to Jehovah's Witness doctrine, when you die, you're just dead. The candle snuffs out. No torture, no suffering, no being hung from your twig and berries.

THE TRINITY

Like the doctrine of Hellfire, Jehovah's Witnesses don't accept the Trinity. They've held this position from the beginning. Jesus didn't believe he was God.[13] He thought he was a messenger of God. The concept of the Trinity didn't appear until centuries after Jesus died. Jesus' divinity was suggested to deal with the fact that he'd died. Jesus' death was not originally part of the plan.[14] He expected to form a real, literal kingdom—the Kingdom of God, not to be confused with the Kingdom of Heaven. The Kingdom of God would stand for the rest of eternity on earth.

The book of John, written in 100 CE at the earliest, lightly suggests that Jesus might have been God but doesn't describe the Trinity doctrine. Early Christians later formed the doctrine by trying to come up with explanations to fill theological holes they didn't understand.

Jehovah's Witnesses have always used those correct positions to build public trust for other religious ideas. For example, Jehovah's Witnesses believe Jesus died on a stake rather than a cross. When people find out they were correct about the Hellfire doctrine, they trust that they're correct about the stake, too. But he did not die on a stake. The cross was the most common method of execution at the time. Demonizing the cross wouldn't be worked into the belief system until 1936 under the next president of the Watchtower Society, Joseph Rutherford. Let's talk about the Rutherford era.

CHAPTER 2
THE 144,000

THE ANOINTED CLASS

n the intervening years between 1874 and 1914, Charles Taze Russell published a series of writings titled "Studies in the Scriptures." The final part of the six-part series was titled "The New Creation," and it was published in 1904. In part six, he postulated that there were two classes of Christians: one group called the Anointed and one called the Great Crowd. His basis for the belief can be found in Revelation chapters 7 and 14. Before discussing his reasoning, though, let's talk about what it means to be anointed, why the number 144,000 is relevant to Jehovah's Witnesses, and what they believe about the Rapture.

Many traditional protestant denominations believe there will be a rapture. However, every Christian denomination I've personally investigated has misinterpreted the meaning and intent behind the verses used to establish the doctrine of the Rapture.

The verse commonly used to support the modern understanding of the Rapture is 1 Thessalonians 4:13–18. However, the original context of the verse doesn't imply a modern understanding of the Rapture—it was intended to quell fears that Jesus wasn't coming back.[1,2]

According to the biblical narrative, the kingdom of Israel controlled the entire levant area under the reign of King David. The Jews were determined to remain culturally separate from those whom they viewed as invaders. As a result, Jews were the target of persecution throughout the generations. The Jewish scriptures talk about a messenger of God who will unite the kingdom of Israel and the surrounding area under a single kingship. He'd be a political leader who takes control and forms his own empire in the name of God. This political leader was called the Son of Man in the Old Testament (Daniel 7:13–14). The Son of Man was supposed to be "a coming judge" of the earth. Jesus' followers believed him to be the Son of Man, though Jesus didn't seem to believe it himself.

When Jesus died, the apostles were confused. They didn't know what to say or do. Their beliefs were shattered. In an attempt to explain what had just happened, they claimed he would return to fulfill his role as the Son of Man. Remember, the Son of Man is the political leader of Israel. Since Jesus never took on the role of a political leader, he hasn't fulfilled the position of Son of Man yet.

The fact that Jesus hasn't fulfilled his role as the Son of Man has opened the door for a plethora of religious groups to claim that their leader is really the Son of Man—Jesus came to deliver a message as the son of God, and they have come as the Son of Man to lead God's people (usually Christians) to the promised land and spark Armageddon. I just described the basis for the belief that other modern-day people might be the Messiah. Not literally Jesus, but the person who will finish what Jesus started: the Son of Man.

Paul, posthumously named an apostle, effectively formed the culture and beliefs of the early Christian church. He didn't become a Christian until about four years after Jesus died, never met Jesus, and knew little about his actual life or teachings. As the de facto leader of Christianity in its earliest days, Paul attempted to explain the errors and problems with what he saw. Why did Jesus die before becoming King? Paul claimed that he died as a redeemer, a savior, and a sacrifice for our sins.1 He said that belief in Jesus is a prerequisite to making it into the Kingdom of God, as he said in Ephesians 2:8–9. He claimed that Jesus would return, and soon—in the lifetimes of the church members.[3]

… And time went on. Church members died. Jesus never came, though they kept waiting for him. The congregations started to get nervous and ask questions, so in response to those fears and anxieties, Paul said that the ones who die before Jesus returns will have a special role to fill. When Jesus comes down from the clouds, those who've died will rise up out of their graves and meet him in the sky to escort him back to earth.[4]

> For the Lord himself shall descend from heaven with a shout, with the voice of the archangel, and with the trump of God: and the dead in Christ shall rise first. Then we which are alive and remain shall be caught up together with them in the clouds, to meet the Lord in the air: and so shall we ever be with the Lord.
>
> *1 THESSALONIANS 4:16–17*

Charles Taze Russell used the concept of the Rapture combined with some other doctrines to conclude that only 144,000 Christians, called "the Anointed," would be raptured to heaven with Jesus. The rest, which he called the great crowd, would stay on earth for a sort of Garden of Eden 2.0. Additionally, Russell believed that when a member of the 144,000 died, they would instantly go to heaven to become joint heirs to the throne to rule over the earth for eternity. That belief is still held by Jehovah's Witnesses today.

THE ANOINTED 144,000

Not only do Jehovah's Witnesses currently believe that the Anointed people shoot straight to heaven, but they also believe that the Anointed can directly commune with God.[5] That doesn't mean they directly hear his voice. They believe their hearts are in tune with God's heart in a way nobody else experiences. As a result, they're uniquely qualified to "lead the flock." Jehovah will be able to guide them more effectively than non-Anointed people.

The 144,000 Anointed also take communion as Jesus instructed just before he died. Ordinary members of the church, the Great Crowd, do not. The Anointed receive communion once per year on Good Friday. The tradition is called the Memorial. Jehovah's Witnesses calculate the day out with the calendar used in Jesus' time. It's different from what we have now, so the date of the Memorial changes from year to year. There's a variation of about three weeks. Sometimes it's in mid-March; sometimes it's in mid-April.

People at the very top of the organization's hierarchy must be Anointed. It's controlled by a Governing Body, like a board of directors, and every other role is filled by what the Governing Body calls "helpers." Helpers are simply there to take instructions, fulfill commands of the Anointed Governing body members, and learn how to lead in their place when the organization's hierarchy is broken by the United Nations directly before the end. We're already supposed to be in the end, but let's not focus on the details.

Even the president of the Watchtower Society is a Governing Body helper, only there to fulfill their wishes. When I explain that to people, the next question commonly asked is, "Who decides who's Anointed?" Here's the answer: You just know. There's nothing more profound to it.

Jesus didn't say how often his followers should take communion, which left it open for interpretation by people like Jehovah's

Witnesses. I personally believe that Jesus meant it should be done regularly by anybody who considers themselves a follower of Jesus. I also don't believe Jesus literally turned anything into his skin or his blood. I think Jesus meant that as a metaphor, and in my opinion, that's pretty obvious. It's astounding that some denominations—not Jehovah's Witnesses, but some—believe the wine and bread literally turn into his flesh and blood.

I've only ever seen one person claim to be anointed at the Memorial. His name was Maurice, and I was about six years old. Anointed Jehovah's Witnesses are exceedingly rare. Jehovah's Witnesses' self-reported numbers over the years reveal that there were over 25,000 in the late 1940s. 2016 was the largest percentage increase in Memorial partakers since 1948.

Jehovah's Witnesses' self-reported numbers show that there were 21,150 "Memorial partakers" in 2022. They also claimed a total memorial attendance worldwide of 19,721,672. Contrast that with their reported total publishers, 8,699,048, and it starts to become clear how much Jehovah's Witnesses pump up the Memorial. They have about 20 million people on the periphery at any given moment.

That means the rate of people taking communion is between 1 in 1,000 and 1 in 2,000. The average congregation size is 72. The median congregation size is likely much larger. I would guess that the low numbers are weighing the average down. My little congregation in West Virginia had 114 people when I was young and grew to about 140 over eight-ish years. Most new attendees were children of existing members. Every congregation I've ever visited has had at least 100 members. That means there's roughly one Anointed person in every 14 congregations. Either way, there are absolutely more than 144,000 people who claim or are believed to be part of that group—for example, Jehovah's Witnesses also believe that the apostles are part of the Anointed 144,000.

TAKING COMMUNION

Jehovah's Witnesses hold the Memorial service in their church building or Kingdom Hall. They actually hate the term church. You'll never hear a Jehovah's Witness refer to themselves or their meeting places as churches. I'm just using the term for simplicity.

The Memorial takes place on Nisan 14, which is the night Jesus was executed. Members bring as many friends and family as they can muster. It's presented as the only holiday they celebrate, though they don't give each other gifts. It's just like every other day except for the special service.

The Governing Body, a group of nine men as of the writing of this book, sends a letter to each congregation telling them to announce to the membership when the Memorial will take place each year. The congregation receives a box of small, one- to two-page "invitation" pamphlets for family and coworkers to invite them to the Memorial. Jehovah's Witnesses don't typically have friends to whom they can give the invitations because they aren't supposed to have friends outside the religion. However, they give invitations to people they regularly interact with, like coworkers or non-Jehovah's Witness family members.

Everybody who is interested in the religion should attend the Memorial. That includes people who are actively being shunned—grandparents or parents who never joined, coworkers, anybody you can find. Shunning remains in effect throughout the Memorial for people who left the religion after being baptized or people who are critical of the religion to any degree.

Jehovah's Witnesses also have the "special talk" on the Sunday before the Memorial. The Governing Body supplies outlines for every talk given from the stage. A brand-new talk outline is provided once per year and presented at the "special talk" meeting.

The Memorial, like every religious service, is coordinated by elders. Each congregation has six to twelve elders to coordinate, administrate, and manage the entire congregation. Elders take on different roles and have helpers called Ministerial Servants. Ministerial Servants are one step below elders and revered and respected within the congregation as particularly spiritual. Positions of authority within the church are also limited strictly to men.

The Memorial starts after sundown. Usually, sundown arrives at around 7:00 PM during that time of year. The elders arrange for unleavened bread and wine to be brought to the Kingdom Hall on memorial night. Unleavened bread is bread that's been made without yeast. It's kind of like pita bread or a cracker. My congregation made their own bread. Jehovah's Witnesses have a tutorial video on their website for how to make it at home. According to Jehovah's Witnesses, the lack of yeast symbolizes purity. Wine that contains no additives is typically purchased for the same reason.

The Memorial begins with a song from the Jehovah's Witness songbook. After the song is sung and a 30-second to 2-minute prayer is given, a "brother" (as they refer to each other) on stage invites the rest of the congregation to sit by raising his head after the prayer and saying, "You may be seated." After that, one particularly spiritual person stands on stage and describes the scene— Jesus stands with his apostles on his final night. He takes the wine and says, "This is my body. Eat this in remembrance of me."

The helpers, usually the "most spiritual" men in the congregation, stand at the end of each row of chairs and pass the bread to the first person. The unleavened bread makes its way to the Elder on the other side. They move to the next row and do it again. Sometimes, Kingdom Halls can be filled beyond capacity for the Memorial service. If that's the case, the brothers will bring the bread and wine to the people standing in the back so everybody has an opportunity to observe and pass it on. It doesn't matter if they're a Jehovah's Witness or not.

After the bread has been passed to every person in the congregation, the helpers sit down, and two more helpers stand up and pass it to the ones who just passed it to everybody else. Every person in the building must have the Emblems passed to them, even if they're the ones doing the passing.

After the bread has been passed, it's placed on a table on stage, and the helpers retrieve the wine. Next, the same process takes place with wine. The Elder giving the talk on stage says, "This is my blood. Drink this in remembrance of me." Once again, every person in the congregation, including the helpers, is given a chance to pass the wine to another person. The reason each and every person must have an opportunity to have the bread and wine passed to them is because Anointed members of the religion must have a chance to eat the bread and drink the wine. They say if there's any doubt in your heart, any hesitation at all, you aren't Anointed, and you shouldn't partake of the Emblems. Nobody has to sign a form before eating the food or agreeing to anything special. They don't even have to tell anybody they believe they're anointed. They tell them by eating the bread. However, it's reserved for active, baptized Jehovah's Witnesses.

After everybody has an opportunity to partake of the bread (the wine comes later), the Elder on stage continues to tell the story of the night Jesus died. After about an hour, the talk ends, and the Elder gives a closing prayer. Everybody bows their head. The Elder gives a personal and heartfelt prayer, not recited by rote. Typically, the prayer consists of copious amounts of "thank you" and "we love you, Jehovah"—again, not God's name.

At the end of the prayer, everybody raises their heads and solemnly and quietly converses for about 10 to 15 minutes as some make their way to their cars. Nobody has to stay and talk if they don't want to. It just makes you look extra spiritual, which gives you a better chance of receiving more "privileges," like setting up the sound system, giving talks written and approved by the Governing body from the stage, or passing microphones around for the question and answer section of Sunday meetings. If you're looking for a wife, this is a must.

THE PANDEMIC

Surprisingly, Jehovah's Witnesses took Covid very seriously. They encouraged their members to get vaccinated, socially distance, and avoid meeting with older people in person. They even switched to fully online meetings. It was an opportunity to see how the congregations would perform if people weren't allowed to meet in person anymore. They came up with a contingency plan for pandemics, war, bans, and even for members being jailed.

However, when brainwashing is unplugged, people wake up from what they just experienced. That's precisely what happened when Jehovah's Witnesses began holding their meetings on Zoom. The leaders claimed that the dwindling membership was further evidence of the end. They used the following verse:

...and because of the increasing of lawlessness, the love of the greater number will grow cold.

MATTHEW 24:12, NWT (JEHOVAH'S
WITNESSES' TRANSLATION)

Before the latest edition of their translation of the Bible, the verse was translated as "the greater number will cool off." When I was young, my mom quoted that verse whenever we received news of falling membership or a disfellowshipping. It almost became a mantra.

Jehovah's Witnesses obviously take the Memorial very seriously, and everybody must observe it and have an opportunity to eat from the Emblems. So, how did they handle the Memorial during the pandemic? The following is a quote from their website about how the Memorial was handled when they couldn't show up in person.

Jehovah's people could not attend the Memorial in person when this pandemic struck. But that did not prevent them from observing the Memorial.

> Congregations with access to the Internet held the Memorial by videoconference. But what of the millions who had no access to the Internet? In some countries, arrangements were made to broadcast the talk on television or radio. In addition, branches recorded the talk in over 500 languages so that even those in remote areas could observe the Memorial. And faithful brothers arranged for the recordings to be delivered to those who needed them.
>
> JEHOVAH'S WITNESSES. "JEHOVAH BLESSES OUR EFFORTS TO OBSERVE THE MEMORIAL". JW.ORG.

All Jehovah's Witnesses are expected to observe the Memorial and have the bread and wine passed to them, even if that means holding it in front of them and observing the plate alone for a moment. They could make it at home or buy the communion Emblems, but they must observe the Memorial.

Their contingency plan for when they're jailed is also interesting. I can't imagine toilet wine is an acceptable analog for Jesus' blood. The following quote is from the same article. It talks about a man named Artem who sat in a 183-square-foot prison cell with five other people.

> Despite being imprisoned, he was able to collect some items to use as Memorial emblems, and he planned to give the Memorial talk for his own benefit. But his cellmates smoked and cursed a lot. What did he do? He asked them if they could refrain from cursing

and smoking for just one hour. To Artem's surprise, his cellmates agreed not to smoke or swear during the Memorial. Artem says, "I offered to tell them about the Memorial." Although they said that they did not want to hear about the event, after seeing and hearing Artem observe the Memorial, they asked him all about it.

"JEHOVAH BLESSES OUR EFFORTS TO
OBSERVE THE MEMORIAL."

My mistake—maybe toilet wine is acceptable. Hopefully, he didn't consider himself Anointed and have to drink it.

In all seriousness, I imagine grape juice and normal leavened bread would be perfectly acceptable in a pinch. This is one case in which Jehovah's Witnesses believe that "best efforts" are good enough. It's likely what they call "a conscience matter." If you can't get what you need to observe it, it is what it is. You'd better be prepared to defend your best efforts to Jehovah when the time comes. Best efforts might or might not seriously include toilet wine. They leave it up to you to decide how you think Jehovah will feel about it.

Jehovah's Witnesses resumed in-person Memorial services in 2022. They hadn't had an in-person memorial service since early 2019. Lockdowns didn't happen until March 2020, but the United States started taking the pandemic seriously in late February. Jehovah's Witnesses took it very seriously from the very beginning. While some other denominations continued to hold church services throughout February and March 2020, Jehovah's Witnesses took it deadly seriously nearly immediately and switched to Zoom.

KINGDOM HALL CRASHING

From time to time, Ex-Jehovah's Witnesses participate in crashing Memorials. When the wine is passed to them, they stand and publicly drink the wine right before they start yelling out all of the inconsistencies and problems within the religion. Kingdom Hall crashers will commonly talk about Jehovah's Witnesses' mishandling of child sexual abuse cases.

There are many videos of Memorial crashers on YouTube. When the Memorial crasher sips the wine, you can hear an audible *gasp* from the crowd of Jehovah's Witnesses. They think the emblems are sacred and special because they're part of a sacred ceremony ordained by Jesus himself. When somebody drinks the wine, they believe Jesus' sacred ceremony has just been disrespected. I don't think "Memorial crashing" is a productive method of reaching people. Jehovah's Witnesses will often literally cover their ears when Memorial crashers start talking. Everything they hear hits a wall formed by the Watchtower Society.

When I was young, there was an apostate yelling out at one of their yearly conventions. Jehovah's Witnesses use the word apostate to refer to somebody who is opposed to the religion, whether disfellowshipped or simply critical of the doctrine or leadership. Like the Memorial, these conventions are typically quiet, solemn times. Speaking is strictly forbidden. Whispering to the person next to you is acceptable if it's something relevant to the topic being addressed.

When an apostate stood up and yelled during this convention in the 1990s, a group of elders surrounded him, locked arms with each other in a circle, and walked out of the arena with him in the center of the circle. Being a strictly pacifistic, non-violent group, that's as extreme a measure as they'll take. Nowadays, they simply try to usher the person out without touching them. If that doesn't work, they call the police. I don't believe in violence to any degree, either. Maybe I picked that up from them.

Typically, the Memorial takes place without Memorial crashers. I've only ever seen it happen on video—never in person. The tactic isn't used much among ex-Jehovah's Witnesses anymore because most realize the tactic locks people into their beliefs and positions even deeper by exacerbating their persecution complex. The Memorial usually goes off without a hitch.

HOW 144,000 IS CALCULATED

Charles Taze Russell built his "understanding" about the 144,000 on Revelation chapters 7 and 14.

> Do not harm the earth or the sea or the trees, until we have sealed the servants of God on their foreheads. And I heard the number of the sealed, 144,000, sealed from every tribe of the sons of Israel…

REVELATION 7:3–8

This section of the book of Revelation is written in an apocalyptic style, like the book of Daniel. When something is written in the apocalyptic genre, you can bet Jehovah's' Witnesses will find a way to misinterpret it.

Apocalyptic writing focused on problems people were facing in that time and place. For example, Revelation clearly referred to a city built on seven hills throughout the book. References to the number seven are all over the place. The city of seven hills is the name ancient people sometimes used for Rome.[6] The appearance of the seven is a profound mystery to theologians today, who seem to believe it must have a secret meaning. The text doesn't confuse scholars. Even evangelical scholars understand that there was a secret meaning—a meaning understood by readers of the time. It simply refers to the Roman Empire.

Regarding Russell's belief in the 144,000 from Revelation 7:3–8, how do Jehovah's Witnesses rationalize the fact that it specifies people from the tribes of Israel? How could gentiles possibly be included in the equation?

12,000 from the tribe of Judah were sealed, 12,000 from the tribe of Reuben …

It proceeds to list all 12 tribes of Israel. Reuben, Asher, Judah, Levi, et cetera.

According to the March 15, 2010, Watchtower, p. 24, paragraph 5, they use John 3:3 to justify their belief that this is figurative by pointing out that the Bible occasionally intended "the tribes of Israel" to be figurative.

> I make a covenant with you, just as my father has made a covenant with me, for a kingdom, that you may eat and drink at my table in my kingdom, and sit on thrones to judge the twelve tribes of Israel.
>
> *JOHN 3:3*

That seems flimsy at best. Now look at Revelation 14:1, the next verse used to justify their belief in the 144,000.

> Then I looked, and behold, on Mount Zion stood the lamb, and with him 144,000 who had his name and his father's name written on their foreheads…
>
> and they were singing a new song before the throne and before the four living creatures and before the elders. No one could learn that song except the 144,000 who had been redeemed from the earth. It is these who have not defiled themselves with women, for they are virgins. It is these who follow the lamb wherever he goes. These have been redeemed from mankind as first fruits for god and the Lamb, and in their mouth no lie was found, for they are blameless.
>
> *REVELATION 14:1, 3–5*

If it doesn't make sense to you, it's not you. It's them. The reasoning doesn't make sense to anybody. They're picking verses at random and applying dates with no regard to context, just as they did to calculate the year 1914. The justification for the belief that 144,000 Jehovah's Witnesses will go to heaven is based on pretty much nothing. These verses in Revelation were right in the middle of apocalyptic writing. Finding single sentences to pluck out randomly and combining them with other chapters, books, and eras isn't reading the Bible. It's creating a new book entirely, in my opinion.

What about the other people on the earth? What happens to the Great Crowd when the 144,000 are raptured to heaven? They use Revelation 7:9 to explain what will happen to the other believers. "After this I looked, and there before me was a great multitude that no one could count, from every nation, tribe, people and language, standing before the throne and before the Lamb" (Revelation 7:9).

In Jehovah's Witness theology, the Great Crowd will remain on earth, eventually living in a paradise the way God originally intended. That'll play out after Armageddon. There will be a seven-year period of tribulation leading up to Armageddon in which Jehovah's Witnesses will be terribly persecuted.

From here, Jehovah's Witness "eschatology," or belief about the end of the world, follows a very specific timeline. Let's break it down.

- **1914**—Jesus came to earth invisibly to mark the "beginning of the end."
- **1918**—Jesus stayed on earth for a period of three and a half years. Obtained from Daniel 12:7.
- **???**—The end of the end. Still waiting.

Charles Taze Russell believed 1874 was the beginning of the end, and 1914 was the end of the end. Jehovah's Witnesses noticed nothing happened in 1874 or 1914, so they shifted it up. Jehovah's Witnesses dropped the year 1874 and claimed 1914 was the beginning of the end. I'm not sure why the end needs a beginning. I thought the beginning preceded the middle, and the end was at the end. I'm unsure how the end isn't inherently the end on its face.

THE FAITHFUL SLAVE

Today, Jehovah's Witness leaders call themselves "The Faithful and Discreet Slave." It effectively means they uniquely have a mandate to lead Jehovah's people. All members of the Faithful Slave must be Anointed.

I can't pinpoint an exact date for when they started using the term "Faithful Slave," but I know for sure it was at least earlier than the 1950s. That's the first mention I could find in their literature. That's not completely trustworthy, though, because they erase things from their history when it's inconvenient to their current set of beliefs or their reputation.

The term "The Faithful and Discreet Slave" refers to Potiphar's servant, Joseph, from Genesis 39:4–6. The story of Joseph in the Book of Genesis is a dark one. Joseph's brothers hated him, so they sold him into slavery in Egypt. Eventually, he made his way to the upper echelons by being a "faithful slave" to his master, Potiphar. According to the Biblical narrative, even when Potiphar's wife flirted with Joseph, he rejected her advances.

> Joseph found favor in his eyes and became his attendant. Potiphar put him in charge of his household, and he entrusted to his care everything he owned. From the time he put him in charge of his household and of all that he owned, the Lord blessed the household of the Egyptian because of Joseph. The blessing of the Lord was on everything Potiphar had, both in the house and in the field. So Potiphar left everything he had in Joseph's care; with Joseph in

charge, he did not concern himself with anything except the food he ate.

GENESIS 39:4-6

The parables to support the idea that there's a "slave class" comes from Matthew 24:45–47.

Who really is the faithful and discreet slave whom his master appointed over his domestics, to give them their food at the proper time? Happy is that slave if his master on arriving finds him doing so. Truly I say to YOU, He will appoint him over all his belongings.

MATTHEW 24:45–47 (NWT)

A more accurate translation can be found in the NRSV translation. Jehovah's Witnesses treat the Faithful and Discreet Slave as a proper noun, but the NRSV shows that it's more of a descriptor than a title.

Who then is the faithful and wise servant, whom the master has put in charge of the servants in his household to give them their food at the proper time? It will be good for that servant whose master finds him doing so when he returns. Truly I tell you, he will put him in charge of all his possession.

MATTHEW 24:45–47 (NRSV)

Interestingly, Jehovah's Witnesses chose to morph it into a title and trade the word "wise" for the word "discreet" before applying the title to themselves. In fact, as far as I can tell, the Jehovah's Witness translation of the Bible is the only one that translates it as "discreet" rather than "wise."

When I was young, I heard the term "Faithful and Discreet Slave" and thought they were using the word "discrete" with an E-T-E at the end rather than "discreet" with an E-E-T. The two words have the same root word but follow different lingual chains. The ETE variant comes from the Latin word discretus and evolved from late middle English. It means "individually separate and distinct."

The EET variant, which Jehovah's Witnesses use to refer to their leadership, comes from the root word discretion. That eventually evolved into the old French word discreet and finally into the English word "discretion." Discretion, or the form of the word that's used by Jehovah's Witnesses, "discreet," means to be careful and circumspect in one's speech or actions.

Jehovah's Witnesses believe that the faithful slave, the primary leader of the religion, must be one of the Anointed 144,000. Today, the Faithful Slave is effectively interchangeable with the term Governing Body. Technically, though, it refers to the leadership of the Jehovah's Witness religion, whoever that happens to be. As of the time of writing, the Governing Body has nine people, all of whom consider themselves Anointed and take communion at the yearly Memorial. As joint heirs to the throne and having dominion over all of creation, Jesus can commune with them directly. He apparently chooses to commune with the nine men on the Governing Body.

This is a quote directly from the July 15, 2013, Watchtower, under the article "Who really is the faithful and discreet slave?"

"The faithful and discreet slave": A small group of anointed brothers who are directly involved in preparing and dispensing spiritual food during Christ's presence. Today, these anointed brothers make up the Governing Body.

Jehovah's Witnesses have a history of claiming a position of authority that they don't deserve through Bible math that doesn't make sense. The math doesn't even add up correctly. My interpretation of the situation can be summed up in five words quoted from Deuteronomy 18:22—"You need not be afraid."

"YOU NEED NOT BE AFRAID"

The Watchtower Society's history is one of failed prediction after failed prediction. There are dozens of them. Even the modern rendition of the Watchtower Society has failed predictions under their belt. The January 1, 1989, Watchtower, p. 12, should prove that unequivocally and beyond a shadow of a doubt:

"...He was also laying a foundation for a work that would **be completed in our 20th century"**

JEHOVAH'S WITNESSES.
THE WATCHTOWER. JANUARY 1, 1989. P. 12.

That kind of thing has happened throughout the Watchtower Society's history. Even a single failed prediction should be all you need to discard the organization as a false religion. One verse has freed many people from the invisible shackles the Watchtower Society uses to bind its members.

When a prophet speaks in the name of the LORD, if the word does not come to pass or come true, that is a word that the LORD has not spoken; the prophet has spoken it presumptuously. You need not be afraid of him.

DEUTERONOMY 18:22

That verse in Deuteronomy is about God appointing a single person with whom he'll communicate as a prophet. If somebody pretends to speak for God when they aren't, they're sentenced to death. How can you tell they're not speaking for God? If the "word does not come to pass or come true," they lied.

I personally don't believe in the death penalty. I think life is the most precious thing in the universe. At the very least, the Watchtower Society should lose its credibility as God's "chosen organization" on earth as of 1919. The Kingdom Halls should be so empty they can't afford to keep the doors open anymore.

Up to this point, I get why people would excuse the mistakes away and see the good in this organization. But before dismissing my portrayal of the leadership, let's talk about the tone and personalities of the people at the very top of the organization since its inception.

I posit that the leadership today and in its infancy acted cynically and calculatedly. I propose they used people for their own benefit—certainly, not somebody Jesus would hand-pick as his representative on earth. Next, let's talk about Rutherford, possibly the most corrupt but certainly not the only corrupt leader in Watchtower history.

CHAPTER 3
HOSTILE TAKEOVER

WATCHTOWER LEADERSHIP

The company, colloquially known as the Watchtower Society, was originally named Zion's Watch Tower Tract Society until 1896 when the Bible Students owned it. In 1896, under Charles Taze Russell's leadership, it was renamed the Watch Tower Bible and Tract Society. The second president, Joseph Rutherford, changed the name of the religion from the Bible Students to Jehovah's Witnesses in 1931. Nathan Knorr took over in 1942. Under his leadership, the company name was again changed to Watch Tower Bible and Tract Society of Pennsylvania in 1955.

Nathan Knorr's vice president, Fred Franz, was the last extremely important Watchtower Society president. After Fred Franz, the organization's structure changed to give the Governing Body more power and influence. Today, the president is just a Governing Body helper who follows the instructions of the Governing Body to the letter. The following list shows each president of the Watchtower Society since its inception:

- 1881–1916—Charles Taze Russell
- 1917–1942—Joseph Rutherford
- 1942–1977—Nathan Knorr
- 1977–1992—Fred Franz
- 1992–2000—Milton George Henschel
- 2000–2014—Don Alden Adams
- 2014– ?—Robert Ciranko

When Joseph Rutherford came along, he completely transformed the organization into something he could bend to his will. He stripped the board of power and took it for himself. It remained that way under Rutherford and under Knorr, the third president. Rutherford made so many organizational changes that it would be impossible to cover all of them, but we'll cover the most groundbreaking changes chronologically.

1917: THE POWER STRUGGLE

At its heart, the Watchtower Bible and Tract Society was little more than a printing press for many years. They printed (and still print) journals, Bibles, and other religious materials. Being a large, non-profit, tax-exempt religious organization, they've always had a complicated relationship with the government. Joseph Rutherford decided to join the Watchtower Society as legal counsel in 1907. In addition to his role as legal counsel, he acted as a traveling representative for the Bible Students under the leadership of Charles Taze Russell. Three months after Russell died, Joseph Rutherford was elected president of the Watchtower Society (January 6, 1917). He ran unopposed.[1]

According to Tony Willis in his 2006 book *A People For His Name*, contemporary leaders in the organization accused Rutherford of closing nomination votes immediately after he was nominated as a candidate. He was the only candidate in the race, and nobody else could join. That was the first step in his hostile takeover. An article titled "Light After Darkness" and dated September 3, 1917, contained the following quote from F. G. Mason regarding Rutherford's hostile takeover:

TO WHOM THIS MAY CONCERN:—

Deeply regretting the trials and trouble brought upon the Church by the high-handed usurpation of dominion over the affairs left by the Will of Brother [founder Charles Taze] Russell and the decree of the Charter of the [Watchtower] Society placing the management of its affairs in the hands of the Directors; and being in possession of several facts pertaining to the unjust and unbusinesslike methods being followed by the present Management, it is with love toward all, "out of a pure heart," that I offer my protest against the action of those in charge in illegally disposing of four of the Society's Directors (each, with one exception, having been our dear Pastor's choice for many years in faithful service to the Church, and each having been named by him to be used and continued), while permitting others to continue to govern without even the assent of the shareholders.

MASON, F. G. *LIGHT AFTER DARKNESS.*
SEPTEMBER 3, 1917. P.15

Here's the historical context behind what we just read: The board of directors thought Rutherford was moving in an "autocratic" direction and attempted to limit his powers. Rutherford fired four of the board members and replaced them with people loyal to him. He consolidated his power and said that the work of the Watchtower Society required "the direction of one mind." That phrase never has happy campers on the other end.

Rutherford's behavior caused what he referred to as a "storm." The storm led to about 15 percent of the organization leaving and creating their own splinter groups. Many called themselves some variation of the name "Bible Students." The Bible Students wasn't just a religion—it was a movement. Some formed their denominations based on the teachings of Charles Taze Russell and considered Rutherford's teachings to be false doctrine.

And with that, Rutherford had successfully completed his hostile takeover. He was sour about his predecessor for obvious reasons. This was the first major schism in the church. Rutherford felt he needed to stamp out any record of his predecessor's fingerprints on the organization. Shortly after taking control of the organization, he made a big announcement: 1925 was the new date for when the end would come.[2] With that announcement, he continued Charles Taze Russell's age-old practice of making false end-times predictions. But the Watchtower Society still had an open prophecy: 1918, which eventually turned into 1919. They had to find a way to deal with the existing prophecy when it failed.

1919: JESUS, TAKE THE WHEEL

Jehovah's Witnesses consider 1919 to be the year when Bible Students were chosen as Jesus' representatives on Earth. Adopting that prophecy effectively established them as Earth's supreme, unquestioned authority. After the organization changed from the Bible Students to Jehovah's Witnesses, there were many splinter groups. One could consider Jehovah's Witnesses a splinter group because it deviated heavily from Charles Taze Russell's teachings and the teachings held in 1919. Either way, Jehovah's Witnesses now claim that they were chosen by Jesus to represent him on Earth, even though he didn't choose Jehovah's Witnesses—he chose the Bible Students. Let's talk about why they believe that.

When 1914 came and went, Charles Taze Russell noted that Jesus never returned as he claimed he would. He looked for some significant event that took place in 1914, and he found it. World War I started in October 1914, so they reworked the prophecy to add three and a half years to October 1914—another variable from the book of Daniel. The month and year are essential here because Jehovah's Witnesses eventually changed and stretched dates, then pretended they didn't.

> ...And I will grant my two witnesses authority to prophesy for one thousand two hundred and sixty days, wearing sackcloth.

> *REVELATION 11:3*

Revelation 11:3 talks about the two witnesses—a particularly mysterious and confusing part of the book of Revelation. Revelation was written in the apocalyptic genre, just like Daniel. This type of language is standard for the genre. It doesn't mean it's some far-off prophecy intended for thousands of years in the future. The book of Revelation was written for people of the time. It seems cryptic and confusing to us because modern Christians don't have the cultural context that the people of the era and region had. Revelation was not cryptic to the ones reading it when it was written. It made perfect sense.

Much of Protestant Christianity views the "1,260 days" verse as describing the end of days. In modern Protestant Christianity, the Tribulation is expected to last seven years. The last half of those seven years, 1,260 days, is how long the antichrist will rule over the Earth before Jesus sets things right again. For Jehovah's Witnesses, the verse gives the religion's leadership a mandate to govern.

The modern Jehovah's Witness organization still reveres 1918 as a significant date. Today, they believe that Jesus returned in 1914, roved around the Earth looking for an organization that matched God's expectations of a church, and finally chose the Bible Students as his chosen organization, thus giving them a mandate to speak on God's behalf.[3]

Doctrinally, not only did Jesus come to Earth to search for an organization that matched God's expectations, but he also took over "the throne" in 1914. As a result, anybody who dies as an Anointed person goes straight to heaven, starting in 1914.

As we've seen, the formula for this religion seems to work like this: something significant happens. Go back to another point of some significance. Count the amount of time between the two events. Find a number in the Bible. Make the number fit.

For the 1919 prophecy, Jehovah's Witnesses start from their date of 1914 and add 1,260 days from Revelation 11:3. For some reason, Jehovah's Witnesses believe that the 1,260 days listed in Revelation mean literal days instead of years. They used the day-year principle for just about every other mention of days in the Bible. At a minimum, they converted days to years for their prophecies about 1844, 1874, and 1914. That's assuming we're leaving Miller's calculations out of it. I guess using days or years is a selective process—go with whichever is most convenient.

They started counting the 1,260 days/3.5 years/42 months from December 1914. The fact that they began in December is important. Jesus supposedly came to Earth in October 1914—not December—because that's when World War I started. They pretended he came in December because it was convenient for the rest of the prophecy. This is a prime example of Jehovah's Witnesses stretching dates that simply don't match up.

The two witnesses from Revelation are supposed to parallel "the Faithful and Discreet Slave" being chosen by Jesus. Jehovah's Witnesses' prophecy about the two witnesses places Jesus' return to Earth in October 1914. Those two missing months, October 1914 to

December 1914, throw off their prophecy completely. The result is that Jehovah's Witnesses believe Jesus left Earth in 1918, but the Faithful Slave was chosen in 1919.

They chose 1919 because something significant happened at the time—in their little world, anyway. The board of directors of "The Society" was arrested—their words, not mine. According to the formula, if something significant happens, you move the date up to account for it.

> Modern historical evidence shows that during the world war of 1914–1918, the dedicated, baptized, anointed remnant of Jehovah's Christian witnesses were brought into Babylonish captivity.
>
> JEHOVAH'S WITNESSES. *THE WATCHTOWER.* DECEMBER 1, 1972. PP. 724–725

> Shortly after the arrest, the Society's administrative staff members were also arrested. On June 21, 1918, they were sentenced to 20-year prison terms. The preaching of the good news came to a virtual standstill."
>
> JEHOVAH'S WITNESSES. *PROCLAIMERS OF GOD'S KINGDOM.* P. 211

Let's recap. Everything in this list is still currently and actively believed by Jehovah's Witnesses. Understanding and agreeing with it is a prerequisite to joining the religion.

- **1914**—Jesus takes the throne.
- He roves around the Earth looking for an organization that represents him for exactly 3.5 years.
- **1918**—Jesus finds the Society—a "clean" organization representing Jesus properly—marked by the Society's board being arrested on June 21, **1918**—3.5 years after December 1914 (not October?).
- **March 26, 1919**—Jehovah releases the board from "captivity" just as he released Jews from Babylonian captivity.

They view the 1918 arrest as a parallel to Jewish exile in Babylon. The exile was supposed to be a punishment for idolatry and disobedience to God, so I'm not sure how that part parallels with the arrest unless it was a sign that Jesus was unhappy with the Society's board of directors. Why did they even pick the Jewish exile as a point of comparison? How are they related at all? This is like choosing a verse from Revelation, Daniel, and Numbers and combining them into a brand-new set of verses.

Come to think of it, that's precisely what they did here.

According to modern Jehovah's Witnesses, Jehovah released them from captivity because they were "cleansed," "wholly theocratic," 2 and providing "spiritual food at the proper time." Jehovah's Witnesses refer to 1919 as the year that Jesus chose the Faithful and Discreet Slave.

When he arrived to inspect the "slave" in 1918, Christ found a spirit-anointed remnant of faithful disciples who had been using this journal [the Watchtower] and other Bible-based publications to provide spiritual food at the proper time since 1879. He acknowledged them as his collective instrument, or slave, and in 1919, entrusted them with managing all his earthly belongings.

JEHOVAH'S WITNESSES. *THE WATCHTOWER.*
APRIL 1, 2007, P.22

The organization at that time was in no way "clean," "wholly theocratic," or "pure." To list just a few things they did or believed at the time that the organization now views as pagan, influenced by Satan himself, and worthy of shunning:[23]

- Use and believe in the cross.
- Celebrate birthdays and Christmas.
- Every active Jehovah's Witness goes to heaven when they die, not just the 144,000 Anointed.
- The Pyramid of Giza was actively a legitimate method of arriving at the year 1914.
- "The last days" started in 1798—originally prophesied by William Miller.
- The 1800s were the worst period in human history. After all, the last days started in 1798.
- Blood transfusions weren't banned.
- Jesus should be worshiped, too, not just Jehovah.
- Armageddon occurred in 1914.
- The Faithful and Discreet Slave was simply Charles Taze Russell.
- Jesus appeared on Earth in 1874 and began ruling in 1878.

If you notice, 1798 is on the list. That's an old "prophecy" from the Millerite movement. It was calculated using the 1,260-year variable from Daniel 12:7. The verse refers to a time, two times, and half a time. They assume it was referring to real, literal days to get them from 1914 to 1918, but in this case, they believed it was 3.5 years' worth of years, using the day-year principle. The calendar used by Jews was, of course, 360 days long. Three hundred sixty days multiplied by 3.5 years adds up to 1,260. They believe Catholicism started persecuting Christians in 538 CE. 1260 + 538 CE = 1798 CE. Again, they're picking these variables and dates out of thin air and finding where they fit. When nothing happens, they claim it just took place invisibly.

This list isn't complete, but it's a sample of how the organization at the time was deeply pagan and part of broader Christendom—in the eyes of Jehovah's Witnesses, at least. The Watchtower Society of today would look at the Bible Students, the actual group that was picked by Jesus in their eyes, as a false religion that the Great Beast will destroy in the end.

1925: "MILLIONS NOW LIVING WILL NEVER DIE"

After his takeover, Rutherford announced a new end-times prophecy: Millions now living will never die. Rutherford was obsessed with the same Bible math. He started talking about his fabricated 1925 prophecy in a series of public lectures starting in February 1918.2

His basis for claiming 1925 was when the end would really for sure be here this time is revealed in these two quotes from his books, which he published leading up to 1925:

> Seventy jubilees of fifty years each would be a total of 3500 years.
> That period of time beginning 1575 before A.D. 1 of necessity

would end in the fall of the year 1925, at which time the type ends and the great antitype must begin.

…

Seventy times 50 is 3,500. The whole period would therefore have been 3,500 years from the time the Jews entered Canaan until all the types would have been fulfilled. As they entered Canaan 1,575 years before Christ there would be 1,925 years of types after Christ, or 1925 A.D.—Rutherford, Joseph.

JEHOVAH'S WITNESSES. THE WAY TO
PARADISE." JW.ORG. P. 223

He calculated 1925 by adding up jubilee years, which is the exact method Russell used to arrive at some of his calculations. Again, one would think these people would learn from their mistakes and stop naming specific dates. Not only do they keep naming dates, but they even use the same methods as previous failed prophecies. I don't understand why they keep doing this.

As mentioned, the number seven was special to Jews. The seventh day of the week is the Sabbath. It's important not to work on the Sabbath, including not lighting a fire. In our modern era, that means not turning on a light switch, adjusting the thermostat, driving a car, or even pressing an elevator button. Every hospital elevator in Manhattan, New York City, stops at every floor on the sabbath day so Jews who live in the area won't put God's favor at risk by pressing the elevator button. Similarly, the seventh week, the seventh year, and the seventh set of seven years were very important to them.

In Rutherford's mind, seventy jubilees of fifty years each would total 3,500 years. Beginning in 1575 BCE and adding 3,500 puts you firmly at 1925. Why did Rutherford start in 1575 BCE? It seems that it was simply a convenient anchor date for some event. In this case, the event was when the Jews entered Canaan.

Did he realize that our timekeeping abilities haven't always been top-tier and, as a result, calendars have lost entire weeks, months, years, decades, and even centuries? Did he realize there was absolutely no way to be sure he was using the correct starting points? If he realized that, he likely wouldn't have prophesied about numerology in the first place.

Rutherford eventually published the lectures in booklet form in 1920 and announced elaborate prophecies leading up to 1925.2 His first book after the "Millions now living will never die!" booklet was titled "The Harp of God" (1921). The cover's inscription reads, "Proof Conclusive that Millions now Living will never Die." His second book was a children's book titled The Way to Paradise, in which he continued to make strange, prophetic claims about 1925.

Before continuing, I would like to credit jwfacts.com, a website run by Paul Grundy that has exposed the history of the religion since long before I joined the movement. I want to offer a special "thank you" to JW Facts and Paul Grundy personally for compiling detailed information about many of these subjects and even making the original materials available for download in PDF or image form. On that note, the book Millions Now Living Will Never Die (1920), by Joseph Rutherford, is downloadable in searchable PDF format on the JWFacts article titled "1925 - Millions Now Living Will Never Die!"[22]

Some of Rutherford's claims about 1925 included the end of false religion, the earth's restoration to a paradise, and the resurrection of the dead. The proclamations he laid down in the book are key teachings of Jehovah's Witnesses today.

After Rutherford started his tour of speeches in 1925, The New York Times published an article about "Russellites" and their track record of false predictions.

NEW DATE FOR MILLENNIUM [sic]

Russellites Now See It Coming on Earth in 1925.

"If Moses was to descend upon the earth today he could very probably solve most of the distressing problems of the day. But I have not the slightest doubt but that Moses would be clapped into jail, just as we were," said Alexander Hugh MacMillan, at the closing session of the convention of the International Bible Students' Association, yesterday afternoon in the Academy of Music, Brooklyn. The speaker said he wanted to warn all the sinners to prepare for the millennium, which is to arrive in 1925.

"Moses and Abraham will be here then," he declared, "and we shall be associated with the holy ancients when the Kingdom of God is upon the earth. These ancients will help to restore main to a proper civilized condition."

"THE NEW MILLENNIUM". *THE NEW YORK TIMES*. JUNE 2, 1919. P.20

In the book The Way to Paradise, Rutherford claimed that Jerusalem would become the world's capital and God's favor would return to the Jewish people in 1925. He also called back to Russell's Pyramidology when he wrote the following:

The Bible and "The Bible in Stone" [the Pyramid of Giza] give the date 1914: for the beginning of the great change. History proves that the ouster proceedings began promptly on time. Prophecy indicates that 1925–1926 will see the greater part of the ousting completed. All the world's statesmen are dreading the next few years.

RUTHERFORD, JOSEPH. *THE WAY TO PARADISE*. P. 171

He eventually denounced Russell's Pyramidology, but that didn't happen until 1928. Regardless of the starting point and the date Jesus came to earth, Rutherford's prophecies failed miserably, just like his predecessor's.

1925: THE BEARD BAN

Jehovah's Witnesses have had a long-standing rule banning them from having beards. It seemed like an odd rule to… well, everybody. Jesus is wearing a beard in every magazine and book that they print. What could their reasoning possibly be for banning beards when their lord and savior has one himself?

The Society's official reason for banning beards was that they symbolized rebellion. The Society said people in the hippie movement commonly wore beards, and Jehovah's people were neither rebellious nor political. Except beards had been banned long before the hippie movement came along. So, what was the real reason? Why were beards forbidden for so long? The reason traces back to Joseph Rutherford's attempt to snuff out any record of his predecessor.

William J. Schnell was born in 1905 and joined Jehovah's Witnesses in the 1920s. He gave his prime years to the Society, only to get nothing in return—the story of countless others, including myself. After leaving the organization, he wrote a book titled 30 Years a Watchtower Slave, which describes the moment things took a turn for beards within the organization. The scene is described to us in the following passage. The events described happened around 1925:

An amusing incident took place at the time of the Judge's [Rutherford's] visit. The Director of our German branch, as had many before him, had grown a large beard, patterned after Charles T. Russell's beard. The Judge did not want anything at all to remain which might remind him of Russell - not even the cultivation of a beard. So, sitting at the table for dinner one night within my earshot, the Director asked the Judge for one more large rotary press. The Judge said nothing for a while, merely ate. So, suddenly he looked up, his eyes pinned severely on the Director's huge beard and said, "I will buy you the press if you take that thing off," pointing to the beard. It surely shocked the Director's sensibilities, but he meekly heeded the warning and soon shamefacedly appeared minus the beard.

SCHNELL, WILLIAM J. 30 YEARS A WATCHTOWER SLAVE. 1971. PP. 51–52

As an "apostate"—that is, one who is critical of the organization—I can understand the skepticism of current Jehovah's Witnesses about such an account. However, the Watchtower Society affirmed the report in one of its yearbooks.

Yearbooks are a record-keeping device for Jehovah's Witnesses. They record significant events and are given to members at the yearly conventions or ordered at their local Kingdom Hall.

Sometimes, the yearbooks contain information the Society would prefer to erase, in which case members are instructed to burn it. However, the 1974 yearbook is still on their website. The following article can still be pulled up through a simple search:[4]

But more equipment was needed. For that reason Brother Balzereit asked Brother Rutherford for permission to buy a rotary press. Brother Rutherford saw the necessity and agreed, but on one condition. He had noticed that over the years Brother Balzereit had grown a beard very similar to the one that had been worn by Brother Russell. His example soon caught on, for there were others who also wanted to look like Brother Russell. This could give rise to a tendency toward creature worship, and Brother Rutherford wanted to prevent this. So during his next visit, within hearing of all the Bible House family, he told Brother Balzereit that he could buy the rotary press but only on the condition that he shave off his beard. Brother Balzereit sadly agreed and afterward went to the barber. During the next few days there were several cases of mistaken identity and some funny situations because of the "stranger" who was sometimes not recognized by his fellow workers.

JEHOVAH'S WITNESSES. 1974 YEARBOOK. PP. 97–98

That's quite a charitable interpretation of the event. No matter what Rutherford's intent was, that was the source of the 1925 beard ban. This is another prime example of an organization desiring people to act a certain way and pushing them into doing it without outright saying it. When the culture forms adequately, it is officially codified if there's minimal pushback.

In mid-December 2023, Jehovah's Witnesses reversed their position on the beard ban and officially allowed them again. Governing body member Stephen Lett delivered the announcement. He blamed the original ban on the hippie movement and effectively said the hippie era had passed, so it was safe to come out of the beard closet again. Mustaches, on the other hand, have always been acceptable within the religion.

1927: EVOLUTION IS WRONG

The first instance of the Watchtower Society's attempt to counteract evolution seems to be in 1927. Dates are hard to pinpoint, but Rutherford wrote about evolution in his 1927 book Creation. As time passed, the Watchtower Society became more and more literal in their interpretations of the Bible. Even parables are taken literally by modern Jehovah's' Witnesses. When it's convenient, though, they believe there's some hidden secret meaning behind what's written. The Watchtower Society decides which cases should be literal and which shouldn't.

Jehovah's Witnesses mostly take the Book of Genesis literally—but not entirely. Many of its writings were copied from even older stories, like the Epic of Gilgamesh. The following example illustrates the point of the book of Genesis.

A scorpion wants to cross a river but can't do so alone. It asks a frog to take it across. The frog says, "If I take you across, you'll sting me." The scorpion says, "If I sting you, you'll drown, and I'll die too, dooming us both." The frog reluctantly decides to take the scorpion to the other side. Halfway across, the scorpion stings the frog. As the frog sinks, he says, "Why'd you sting me? Now we're both going to die." The scorpion responds, "Because I'm a scorpion, and that's what scorpions do."

That's a modern parable told to children today. It has talking animals, fantastical characters, unrealistic scenarios, and a moral lesson—much like the book of Genesis. The story of the frog and the scorpion was never intended to be taken literally. It was meant to convey a point: bad people do bad things, even when it's not in their best interests.

The Book of Genesis is not intended to be taken literally. It is from the antiquities genre, which is simply a set of parables and campfire stories that attempt to explain the world around them in a way that allows the listeners to derive some meaning while simultaneously being entertained. Though it's written as a historical narrative, antiquities genre writing contains a collection of cultic lore, anecdotes, genealogies, and individual stories. The genre doesn't differentiate between fact, legend, and myth.

Jehovah's Witnesses are in an unusual category of Christians known as Old Earth Creationists. That means they accept or reject parts of Genesis seemingly at random. They accurately believe the earth is 4.5 billion years old, and they think dinosaurs roved around the planet millions of years ago, but they don't accept evolution. Their website says the following about dinosaurs:[5]

> The Bible describes sea and land animals as being created during the fifth and sixth days, or epochs, of creation. Thus, the Bible allows for the appearance and existence of dinosaurs over a lengthy period.
>
> JEHOVAH'S WITNESSES. "WHAT DOES THE BIBLE SAY ABOUT DINOSAURS?" JW.ORG.

They subscribe to the Gap Theory, a Christian doctrine that postulates that the six days of creation weren't literal days but epochs. I don't know how they justify believing that plants came before the sun. As aforementioned, some things are literal, and some are figurative. The Watchtower Society determines which is which.

They also believe Adam and Eve were real, literal people. If he was the second generation on Earth, I'm not sure who Cain should have married. Those little details are seldom addressed, and when they are, the answers are unsatisfactory. Answers in Genesis, creators of the Creation Museum and led by Ken Ham, believe Cain married his sister.

Jehovah's Witnesses use a thought-stopping story to explain sin.

It goes like this: Imagine a bread pan. The pan is used to produce loaf after loaf. One day, the pan is dented. Every loaf produced in the pan from that moment onward has that dent. The dent represents sin. In Jehovah's Witnesses' eyes, God couldn't have created a new mate for Cain because the dent wouldn't be in the bread pan. He must have married one of his sisters.

Like Adam and Eve, Jehovah's Witnesses believe Noah was a real, literal person, and his ark held millions of species of life. Jehovah's Witnesses believe the ark was a simple, rectangular box, unlike most other denominations. However, as they claim, it would have capsized if it had been rectangular.

Genesis 6:19 says Noah brought two of each animal on the ark, but Genesis 7:2 says he brought seven clean animals and two unclean. Jehovah's Witnesses explicitly believe the Genesis 7:2 version.

My dad refused to be part of any religion for many years. He finally started to investigate Jehovah's Witnesses about eight years before I was born. According to him, the first question he asked Jehovah's Witnesses was, "Why were the dinosaurs here?" They answered, "I think they were here to act as fertilizers. Giant creatures wandering around, eating and dying everywhere was the perfect fertilizer for a garden."

My dad told me that story when I was very young. In retrospect, the heart of his question was clear: Do you accept that dinosaurs existed millions of years ago? The organization called "Answers in Genesis" and its public face, Ken Ham, have their own unique interpretation of Genesis. It leads them to officially believe that Adam and Eve slapped a saddle on the backs of dinosaurs and rode them. The Creation Museum, created by Answers in Genesis, has animatronic dinosaurs with saddles without a lick of irony.

My dad didn't seem willing to accept that line of thinking, which is the current leading belief among standard evangelical

Christianity. He did, however, accept Jehovah's Witnesses' position on evolution. Jehovah's Witnesses have opposed evolution for at least a century, and opposition to it is a core doctrine. I rejected evolution until I learned how it works at about 22 years old.

1929: RUTHERFORD'S MANSION

Joseph Rutherford had a mansion called Beth Sarim, Which means House of Princes. This subject is important to me personally. It might seem like a little thing to others, but it finally woke me up to what was happening around me.

In 1929, Joseph Rutherford built a mansion. This was openly discussed in some old Jehovah's Witness literature, but Jehovah's Witnesses presumably view it as a stain on their history because they let it fall to the side and now pretend it never happened.

Unfortunately, they can't entirely erase their old books from existence. The book The Golden Age from 1930 shows a copy of the deed to the House of Princes. Rutherford had it deeded to Bible characters, believe it or not. A copy of the deed was printed in Watchtower Society publications of the time, and a scan of the deed from the literature can be found in the accompanying citation to JWFacts. Here's what the property deed said:[6]

> NOW THEREFORE this trust is created and said trustee shall hold the title to said property in trust for the use and benefit of the following named persons, whose names appear in the Bible at the book of Hebrews, chapter eleven, verses one to forty, to wit: Abel, Enoch, Noah, Abraham, Isaac, Jacob, Sara, Joseph, Moses, Rahab, Gideon, Barak, Sampson, Jephthah, David, Samuel.

The deed is strange enough and certainly sufficient to make somebody stop and think about what they're doing, but having it deeded to Bible characters isn't the end of the story. Rutherford also decided to stay in the mansion himself, presumably to "keep it warm" for the Bible characters to whom it was deeded.

Another property was purchased next door to Beth Sarim, named Beth Shan. There's a Hebrew word spelled sha'an, which means "undisturbed." That's my best guess at what the name was intended to convey. House of the undisturbed. Its purpose was twofold. It served as a burial place for Joseph Rutherford and as an Armageddon shelter when the end came. Rumors spread about it being a sort of bomb shelter, and the Watchtower Society eventually had to address it in a 1940 Watchtower article.

> Some unreliable person is responsible for the circulation of a report that Beth-Sarim is being enlarged as a place of security and that this is being built by the Society. There is absolutely not one word of truth in the report. Those who are interested in the Theocracy would better be circulating the kingdom message rather than false imaginations of others.

JEHOVAH'S WITNESSES. *THE WATCHTOWER*. JUNE 1, 1940. P. 162

This article serves as an example of what the Watchtower Society does when unwanted rumors spread. They address the rumors directly. Throughout this book, I will argue that Jehovah's Witness culture is a far more robust control mechanism than rigid doctrine. If some cultural quirk or belief forms and the Watchtower Society thinks it's useful, they keep it.

1930S: POLITICAL INVOLVEMENT IS BANNED

Jehovah's Witnesses have had a firm "no politics" policy since the early days. It doesn't seem like it had a hard start date. Various political activities were gradually banned, one after another. Today, it's such a firm stance that the Watchtower Society is willing to have their own people killed or even bribe government officials so they don't have to take part in government or politics to any degree.

In the 1930s, Jehovah's Witnesses chose to take a stand on the pledge of allegiance. I believe people shouldn't have to say the pledge of allegiance if they don't want to. However, Jehovah's Witnesses died as a result of their decision to force members not to say the pledge of allegiance. Instead of starting slow and telling their members they should avoid it where it's safe or fighting the court battle before issuing the command to their membership, they told them to stop saying the pledge of allegiance—full stop.

Jehovah's Witness believers were just as fervent then as they are now. They would do anything for this organization, even refuse to say the pledge of allegiance, knowing that non Jehovah's Witnesses in the community would beat them half to death—or even beat them to death completely—in retaliation for stepping outside the norm.

The case that established people's right not to say the pledge of allegiance was West Virginia State Board of Education v. Barnette. Two young sisters named Gathie and Marie Barnette refused to say the pledge in school one day. The school tried to force them to, and Jehovah's Witnesses filed suit against the local board of education.

The suit was extremely influential in American law. Not only did it establish that people have the right to express themselves how they want, but it was a landmark case in establishing that the government can't compel speech. As a result of that court battle, the U.S. government is not allowed to force anybody to say anything they don't want to say—except in unique and special cases, such as testifying under oath. Even when testifying under oath, though, the Fifth Amendment guarantees our right not to incriminate ourselves.

When I was young, Gathie Barnette attended my congregation.

She married Boyd Edmonds, which made her Gathie Edmonds when I knew her. I went to her house many times. She and Boyd lived in a log cabin. I lived about three miles from her. She had pictures around her living room of her fighting for civil rights in 1943. From time to time, lawyers or reporters would call and ask her about the battle.

Jehovah's Witnesses have historically fought and won civil rights battles, which is highly respectable. However, those battles were utterly self-serving. They don't care about other people's pain or suffering. They care about their ability to worship the way they want to worship. Helping others is inconsequential.

Jehovah's Witnesses have faced (and lost) a seemingly never-ending string of lawsuits for the way they handled cases of child sexual abuse. The Watchtower Society's lawyers fought for their right not to disclose lists of names of possible predators or victims.[7] I'm not sure how that furthers the goals of civil rights, but it certainly furthers the objectives of the Watchtower Society. They never cared about civil liberties. They cared about their own selfish goals.

In 2005, Hurricane Katrina hit Louisiana. There was mass devastation. It did $125 billion in damage. It was horrific. Luckily, Jehovah's Witnesses stood ready to help in any way they could. They gathered a group together. I wanted to go, too, but I was too young.

The group from my congregation traveled to Louisiana to help build new houses...for other Jehovah's Witnesses. They weren't there to help other people, to provide food, financial aid, or housing for anybody except for other Jehovah's Witnesses.

Jehovah's Witnesses do not help outsiders. It's part of their culture, and they remain completely separate from the rest of the world. The Hurricane Katrina plan to help Jehovah's Witnesses but not others wasn't remotely surprising. The surprising decision would have been to find Jehovah's Witnesses assisting outsiders when they arrived.

Tax-exempt status within the United States was intended for organizations that provide some benefit to society. It was assumed that churches would provide some sort of public good, so churches receive tax exemption by default. Jehovah's Witnesses, though, don't improve broader society. They provide for other Jehovah's Witnesses only. In my opinion, tax-exempt status should require proof that the organization contributes meaningfully to society.

Jehovah's Witnesses' strict stance on political activity has brought terrible pain and suffering for countries that have mandatory conscription laws. Some countries, like Israel, require everybody to join the military at 18 years old. That's caused many problems for Jehovah's Witnesses in those countries, and it's revealed yet another deep hypocrisy within the religion.

Fred Franz, the fourth president, had a nephew named Ray Franz. Ray served on the Governing Body for many years but abruptly left in the early 1980s. He left because he was appalled by the behavior of the Watchtower Society. His book Crisis of Conscience gave valuable insights into how the Governing Body works and some of the more questionable decisions and behaviors in the organization's upper echelons.

In Ray Franz's book, he talks about the "no-politics" rule being applied unevenly. Paul Grundy broke down the issue on his website, JWFacts. Grundy's article on the issue includes original documents and excerpts from *Watchtower* magazines.[8] Malawi required its citizens to hold a political card. The Watchtower Society directly forbids them from doing so. After Ray Franz's revelation, the ex-Jehovah's Witness community found evidence in old literature to affirm his claims. The Watchtower magazines from around that time describe the results in pretty clear terms:

It is because Jehovah's Witnesses refuse to buy the Malawi Congress Party card. This card declares the holder to be a member of the ruling political party of Malawi. But for Jehovah's Witnesses to buy a political card and thus join a political party would be an open denial of what they believe and stand for.

JEHOVAH'S WITNESSES. *AWAKE!* AUGUST 8,
1976. P. 5

The Watchtower Society refused to allow their members in Malawi to hold a political card—something that's wholly trivial and meaningless. Simply having the card meant nothing. It didn't indicate your feelings about the country's political positions. But Jehovah's Witnesses are nothing if not sticklers. The members can't even have the facade of cooperation with political parties. They must always remain 100 percent completely and totally neutral, no matter what.

For some of our dear sisters, the persecution was especially harrowing. Many were the reports of rape, mutilation, and beating of Christian women. The sadistic attackers spared nobody. The elderly, the young, and even some pregnant sisters were put through such cruel ordeals. Some suffered miscarriages as a result. Once again, thousands were forced to flee their villages. Many found refuge in the bush. Others went into temporary exile in neighboring Mozambique. By the end of November 1967, the brutal wave of attacks on Jehovah's Witnesses had claimed at least five more lives...The vicious attacks claimed many lives. In Cape Maclear, at the southern end of Lake Malawi, bundles of grass were tied around Zelphat Mbaiko. Petrol was poured on the grass and set alight. He was literally burned to death! Sisters also suffered terribly. Following their refusal to buy party cards, many were repeatedly raped by party officials. In Lilongwe, Sister Magola, along with many others, tried to flee the trouble. However, she was pregnant and could not run very fast. A mob, acting like a pack of wild dogs, caught up with her and beat her to death. At the campus of Bunda College of Agriculture, just outside of Lilongwe, six brothers and one sister were murdered and their bodies were horribly mutilated.

JEHOVAH'S WITNESSES. *1999 YEARBOOK.*
PP. 182,189

The Watchtower Society's decisions matter. The calls they make are the difference between people living and dying. The Watchtower Society viewed those people's lives and the dignity, safety, and mental health of the women in Malawi as a sacrifice that the Watchtower Society was willing to make.

This situation is horrific enough as is, but when you remember that the Bible never condemns political involvement in any way and that the Watchtower Society used the verse that says you should "live in the world, but be no part of it" as paper-thin reasoning for their anti-political involvement policy; it makes the situation that much worse.

At the same time the Malawi situation was happening, Mexican Jehovah's Witnesses faced a similar problem. Military conscription was mandatory. Refusing to join the military or do some kind of community service in Mexico lands a person in prison.

Despite the Watchtower Society's hard-line approach to Malawi Jehovah's Witnesses, they held a different standard for members in Mexico. They told Mexican Jehovah's Witnesses that it was permissible to bribe officials to purchase a "Cartilla" card, similar to the Malawi card. The double standard held by the Watchtower Society directly led to death for Jehovah's Witnesses who were lucky and worse for those who weren't.

The Watchtower Society intentionally included that story about Malawi in the yearbook as part of its strategy to shape the culture. The Society plays the same songs in every Kingdom Hall worldwide on the same day. It also has question-and-answer sections in the same books and magazines every week worldwide.

The Watchtower Society forms the culture fully and completely. They specifically and directly told Jehovah's Witnesses that Beth Shan was not an Armageddon bunker because they didn't want that rumor to spread. When they don't want a rumor or a piece of culture to exist, they kill it.

The Bible—Old Testament and New Testament—never requires human sacrifice. There are a few arguable examples of when God might or might not have expected it, like Jesus or Abraham and Isaac. Either way, it wasn't a regular part of worship.

Despite that, the Watchtower Society expects—no, demands that Jehovah's Witnesses suffer through literally anything, up to and including rape and murder, to appease the Society. Remember, Jehovah never demanded political neutrality—the Society did.

Are they really God's chosen organization on earth? Still, after everything they've done? If you still feel they are Jehovah's chosen organization, maybe the next section will change your mind. After Rutherford leaned into his anti-politics position, he did something deeply disturbing.

JEHOVAH'S PEOPLE AGREE WITH HITLER

Joseph Rutherford revealed his true character when he wrote a letter to Hitler, effectively agreeing with his decisions and praising him. Jehovah's Witnesses were terribly mistreated during the Second World War. Many holocaust museums have a "Jehovah's Witnesses" section. Jews were forced to wear a gold star, political prisoners wore a red triangle, and Jehovah's Witnesses wore a purple triangle. The purple triangle is a source of pride and unity among Jehovah's Witnesses today.

However, Joseph Rutherford attempted to work with Hitler before the Second World War. In the early 1930s, the Watchtower

Society produced a publication titled *Declaration of Facts*, which was given to Jehovah's Witnesses in and around Germany. A copy of it was sent to Hitler, along with a personal letter from Joseph Rutherford.[9]

Hitler began his rise to power and his persecution of Jews in the early 1930s, and it turned into genocide as time marched forward.[10] Before the killing began in full, Jewish shops were vandalized. People stopped speaking to them. They had "JEW" written on their storefronts and homes. The intensity stepped up on April 1, 1933. Germany scheduled a Jewish boycott for that week, and the world was horrified by the imagery coming out of the country.

Though Hitler was a confirmed Catholic and spoke positively about Christianity regularly, he had a strained relationship with other power structures, such as the institution of Catholicism and the Protestant Church. He took control of the Protestant Church by rigging church elections to put one of his men—Ludwig Müller—at the top. Since he couldn't do that with Catholicism, he persecuted Catholics to push the Pope into a treaty.

This moment in history was a tipping point. Hitler had just taken power two months before the April 1 boycott. The world disliked him, and he was polarizing in Germany, too. He was appointed, not elected. If power structures such as the Catholic and Protestant churches had challenged his authority, they might have been able to prevent what came next. Instead, the Pope signed a treaty with him—a concordat—granting Catholics protection and power in society. They seized the opportunity to gain concessions from the new authoritarian German government, like the authority to control the educational system. The Vatican was the first major government to lend Hitler credibility. They threw innocents under the bus by doing so.

Hitler and the Catholic Church had a friendly and close relationship from that moment. Jehovah's Witnesses had an adversarial relationship with Catholicism nearly since the beginning, and that worked against them. I believe it was one of the reasons they were banned in Germany. Another reason for the ban is that both Jehovah's Witnesses and the Nazi movement are totalitarian systems. Power struggles are inevitable when totalitarian systems come in contact with each other. For more information, check out my book, *Was Hitler an Atheist? How Hitler Exploited Religion to Seize Power*. My books can be found at owenmorgan.com.

After the ban, Joseph Rutherford went on a media tour praising Hitler and agreeing with Nazi ideology to regain his favor. Joseph Rutherford chose to take a stand and chose the wrong side. That should tell you all you need to know to decide if Jehovah picked the Watchtower Society as God's chosen organization in 1919, with Joseph Rutherford in control as president since 1917.

A document titled *Declaration of Facts* was released at a convention held in Germany in the Wilmersdorfer Tennishallen—a sports hall. Rutherford chose not to remove the swastika flags during the convention, and the service opened with a song set to the tune of the German national anthem.

Jehovah's Witnesses answer to these accusations in a *Watchtower* article from 1998:

[Critics] claim that representatives of the Watch Tower Society tried unsuccessfully to curry favor with the new government and that, at least for a time, they endorsed the racist ideology of the Nazis, which eventually led to the murder of six million Jews.

It is possible, however, that there were flags on the building's exterior. A Nazi combat troop had used the hall on June 21, the Wednesday prior to the convention. Then just the day before the convention, crowds of young people along with units of the SS (Schutzstaffel, originally Hitler's Blackshirt bodyguards), SA, and others celebrated the summer solstice nearby. So Witnesses arriving at the Sunday convention might have been greeted with the sight of a building decked with swastika flags.

JEHOVAH'S WITNESSES. *THE WATCHTOWER.*
JULY 8, 1998. PP. 10-11

We have a copy of the *Letter to Hitler,* and the Watchtower Society independently confirmed its existence in the 1974 Yearbook of Jehovah's Witnesses. The *Declaration of Facts* was publicly available.

It is falsely charged by our enemies that we have received financial support for our work from the Jews. Nothing is farther from the truth. Up to this hour there never has been the slightest bit of money contributed to our work by Jews.

JEHOVAH'S WITNESSES. *DECLARATION OF FACTS.* 1933.

Joseph Rutherford decided to put his hatred of Jews on record.

The Jews entirely reject Jesus Christ and emphatically deny that he is the Savior of the world sent of God for man's good. This of itself should be sufficient proof to show that we receive no support from Jews and that therefore the charges against us are maliciously false and could proceed only from Satan, our great enemy.

JEHOVAH'S WITNESSES. *DECLARATION OF FACTS.* 1933.

Joseph Rutherford played right into the fears and hatred fabricated and pushed by the Nazi party. It doesn't appear that he was trying to get on Hitler's good side only to spare his people the pain of persecution—which, by the way, would have still been forbidden

—but he appears to have aligned himself against Jews, thus aligning himself with the Nazi cause.

If a Jehovah's Witness denies Jehovah to save his own life, his life is forfeit in Jehovah's eyes. Under no circumstances should a Jehovah's Witness ever deny Jehovah. That's what I was taught as a young Jehovah's Witness through the 1990s and the 2000s. I must tell the truth, or I'll die in Armageddon.

> The greatest and the most oppressive empire on earth is the Anglo-American empire. By that is meant the British Empire, of which the United States of America forms a part. It has been the commercial Jews of the British-American empire that have built up and carried on Big Business as a means of exploiting and oppressing the peoples of many nations.
>
> JEHOVAH'S WITNESSES. *DECLARATION OF FACTS.* 1933.

If Joseph Rutherford said this publicly, you can imagine what the letter to Hitler said. Luckily, we also have photocopies of the original letter in German. The citations in this section lead to the JWFacts article on the subject. It's a secondary source, but it contains all original documents.

These documents would be lost to time if not for diligent ex-Jehovah's Witnesses dedicated to finding old literature in their homes and making the materials available to others. The *Letter to Hitler* and the *Declaration of Facts* are both available under the article titled "Letter to Hitler & Declaration of Facts." Take a look at some quotes from the English translation of the *Letter to Hitler*:

> The Brooklyn headquarter of the Watchtower Society is pro German in an exemplary way and has been so for many years.

RUTHERFORD, JOSEPH. *LETTER TO HITLER.*

1933.

He said it was pro-Germany. It was not completely neutral, but it favored one political side. He said that the Watchtower Society's board of directors was arrested in 1918 for refusing to allow the Watchtower to be used as anti-German war propaganda.

For that reason, in 1918, the president of The Society and seven members of the board of directors were sentenced to 80 years in prison, because the president refused to use two of the magazines published in America under his direction for war propaganda against Germany.

RUTHERFORD, JOSEPH. *LETTER TO HITLER.*

1933.

To this day, Joseph Rutherford is deeply respected by modern Jehovah's Witnesses despite everything he said and did—the same person who praised Hitler and told him he agreed with his actions against Jews. Here's another line from the letter:

The conference of five thousand delegates also noted - as is expressed in the declaration - that the Bible Researchers of Germany are fighting for the very same high ethical goals and ideals which also the national government of the German Reich proclaimed respecting the relationship of humans to God, namely: honesty of the created being towards its creator.

RUTHERFORD, JOSEPH. *LETTER TO HITLER.*

1933.

He said Hitler was fighting for high ethical goals and ideals. If Jehovah's Witnesses were aware of this and connected the dots for when the Watchtower Society claims to have received Jesus' mandate to lead, they would leave. Even if this was Joseph Rutherford's attempt to put a puff in Hitler's petticoat to avoid negative blowback against Jehovah's Witnesses in Germany, it was still unacceptable.

CHAPTER 4
PAGANISM

WHAT IS PAGANISM?

n the Old Testament, the Israelites lived in the same area as the Canaanites. Everyone coexisted, but the Jews didn't want their people to intermix with the Canaanites or their gods. "Pagan originally meant anybody who wasn't Jewish, and after Jesus came and died, it meant anybody who wasn't Christian. It's that simple.

Under the definition used by Jehovah's Witnesses, practically everything is of pagan origin. This effectively means anything that isn't of Jehovah's Witness origin, but only when convenient. Unless otherwise specified, everything in this section is an active doctrine to this day, including the Christmas ban and the ban on certain types of dancing.

The following is a short list of things banned within the religion for having some ties to paganism:[1]

- Christmas, Easter, birthdays, New Year's Eve, Valentine's Day, Mother's Day, Father's Day, Halloween, Dia de los

Muertos (a Mexican tradition), and every other holiday for their own reasons

- Carnivals (Jehovah's Witnesses. *Awake!*. March 8, 1973, pp. 5–8)
- Lent (Jehovah's Witnesses. *Awake!*. March 8, 1973, pp. 5–8)
- Olympics—This is banned because the games are kicked off by lighting a torch. It's of Greek origin rather than of Christian origin, which makes it pagan in the eyes of Jehovah's Witnesses.
- Weddings—Throwing rice, throwing the bouquet, wedding marches.
- Rosary, Star of David, astrology.
- Symbols on graves such as fish, anchor and dove, and peacock.
- Democracy—theocracy is the only acceptable form of government.
- Mazes and labyrinths.
- The cross.
- Hell—Jehovah's Witnesses believe this is of pagan origin, but it is not. The doctrine of Hellfire is of Christian origin.[2] We'll discuss this in more detail later.
- Immortality of the soul—Jehovah's Witnesses think only angels and Anointed people have immortal souls. They believe that immortality implies incorruptibility. Humans with everlasting life can still be corrupted and, thus, can still be killed. (Jehovah's Witnesses. Watchtower. April 1, 1984, pp. 30–31)
- Clerical celibacy, the Trinity, saying "bless you."
- Philosophy—specifically Taoism, Confucianism, Greek philosophy, materialism, and Platonic philosophy.
- Offering incense to the dead, bowing to a picture of a deceased one.

- Throwing soil into a grave, throwing flowers into a grave.
- Drawing halos on religious figures.
- The Twist and other forms of dancing.
- The following is a list of things that have pagan roots but are acceptable anyway:
- bride's veil
- Bridesmaids having the same color as the bride, or even white.
- Wedding ring—acknowledged pagan roots but deliberately ignored.
- Toasting, wedding cake, calendars, using flowers at a funeral.
- Piñatas—technically not banned but heavily discouraged.
- Disfellowshipping—initially believed to have pagan origins. Still, the practice was implemented within five years of releasing an article condemning it as pagan.

WHAT'S ALLOWED AND WHAT'S BANNED?

Bride's veil—allowed

Jehovah's Witnesses acknowledge that they believe the veil has a connection to paganism in a Watchtower from 1969:

> To some in Germany, a white gown signifies virginity. Others there believe that it prevents evil spirits from recognizing the bride. In Japan some view the white gown as a symbol of mourning; the bride 'dies' to her parents and remains with her husband until death.

JEHOVAH'S WITNESSES. *THE WATCHTOWER*. JANUARY 15, 1969. PP. 57–61

In the very next sentence, they excuse the wedding veil as acceptable anyway.

However, to many people worldwide, the white dress is simply a quaint tradition with no particular meaning. A Christian bride need not think that a white gown is essential or that it is universally forbidden.

In Jehovah's Witnesses' minds, bride's veils are acceptable. For now, at least. We'll see if that changes in the future.

DANCING—HEAVILY RESTRICTED

Jehovah's Witnesses have even addressed dancing. In the 1960s, there was a fear-mongering campaign over dancing. Jehovah's Witnesses always have some input on political issues, and members are expected to adopt those positions. However, having political positions of your own is banned.

Here's what Jehovah's Witnesses have had to say about dancing:

Many of the news reports will likely have a few words about the origin of a new dance, and this is true of The Twist. Time magazine, for instance, commented:

The Twist at first was an innocent enough dance; it has since been largely discarded in favor of such refinements as 'The Roach' and 'The Fly.' But the youngsters at [a certain New York nightclub] [sic] have revived The Twist and parodied it into a replica of some ancient tribal puberty rite. The dancers scarcely ever touch each other or move either feet. Everything else, however, moves. The upper body sways forward and backward and the hips and shoulders twirl erotically, while the arms thrust in, out, up and down.

JEHOVAH'S WITNESSES. *THE WATCHTOWER*. JULY 1, 1962. PP. 409–414

Later in the article, they use The Twist as an example of an unacceptable dance because of its connection to paganism.

In this example we have found that the dance craze mainly involves bodily gyrations and that the words used to describe them are "frantic," "sensual" and "erotic." You have also learned what kind of persons developed the dance and that it is basically an imitation of some pagan tribe's dance, involving gestures of a sexually suggestive nature.

Mazes and labyrinths—banned

Jehovah's Witnesses believe that mazes and labyrinths are of pagan origin. Here's a quote from a 1999 issue of *Awake!*:

Large floor mazes were laid in other medieval French and Italian cathedrals and churches, including those at Amiens, Bayeux, Orléans, Ravenna, and Toulouse. The one at Reims was destroyed 200 years ago, and the Mirepoix Cathedral's maze features a central Minotaur.

Regarding the incorporation of labyrinths into prominent religious buildings, one authority writes: "The pagan labyrinth was adopted by the medieval Christian church and adapted for its own use by including Christian symbolism in the design."

JEHOVAH'S WITNESSES. *AWAKE!*. DECEMBER 22, 1999. PP. 20–24

Based on this magazine, the mazes and labyrinths they describe are of Christian origin, not pagan. Why do Jehovah's Witnesses believe that things of Christian origin are pagan? Greece had some conception of the doctrine of Hellfire, but the doctrine, in its current interpretation, didn't come from Greece. It came from the Apocalypse of Peter, a Christian writing. In the same way, mazes and labyrinths have been used throughout history by a multitude of cultures. Why do they call it pagan when modern practices, traditions, and concepts were born out of Christianity?

The cross—banned

Their reasoning rests upon the word used to describe it: the Greek word Stauros, which means an upright pole. However, we have descriptions of crosses used to execute people. One such description can be found in the epistle of Barnabas. In that book, it's likened to somebody standing upright with outstretched arms or like a ship's mast. It was a cross, not a stake.[3]

I could get behind the idolatry aspect, but that's not even Jehovah's Witnesses' primary complaint with the doctrine. Jehovah's Witnesses use the JW.ORG logo everywhere—on their books, pens, magazines, stickers, buttons, pins, necklaces, and even earrings. If that's not idolatry, then I don't know what it is.

Starting in 1919, Jehovah's Witnesses claimed to be God's mouthpiece on earth. Either God gave them special insight into his desires when they were chosen, or he didn't. Either God's moral commands change, or they don't.

It's active doctrine unless a Jehovah's Witness belief is specifically denounced. The November 1 *Watchtower* from 1950 is a great example.

Reference to the original languages in which the Bible was written will show beyond a question of doubt that Christ was never hung on any pagan cross. Hence, the use of the word "cross" in the English-language Bibles is a mistranslation. On this, the…

JEHOVAH'S WITNESSES. *THE WATCHTOWER.*
NOVEMBER 1, 1950. PP. 425–427

The Watchtower quotes its own Bible translation to back up the claim. The article continues:

…is a mistranslation. On this, the New World Translation of the Christian Greek Scriptures, in its appendix, on pages 768-771, in commenting on Matthew 10:38, where the Greek word σταυρός (stau·ros′) first appears and which is translated "cross" in most Bibles, states:

This is the expression used in connection with the execution of Jesus at Calvary. There is no evidence that the Greek word stau·ros′ used here meant a 'cross' such as the pagans used as a religious symbol for many centuries before Christ.

This article is still considered a valid doctrine. Not only can it be found in old magazines, but it can still be found on Jehovah's Witnesses' own website as of the writing of this book. Why do Jehovah's Witnesses quote their own publications as evidence of their claims about the cross? Why do they do it in other instances? Why should we trust the organization to give us honest and complete interpretations of works they don't cite? In many cases, Jehovah's Witness literature doesn't even name the source, let alone correctly cite the source. Why should we believe a word out of the mouths of the Governing Body or writing department?

Here's another piece of evidence that it was a cross rather than a stake: John 20:25 clearly indicates that multiple nails were used—one through each arm. Why would multiple nails be used if his hands were crossed over one another?

So the other disciples told him, "We have seen the Lord!' But he said to them, 'Unless I see the nail marks in his hands and put my finger where the nails were, and put my hand into his side, I will not believe."

JOHN 20:25

Jehovah's Witnesses get downright indignant about the verse in *The Watchtower* from April 1, 1984.

Much time and trouble have been wasted in disputing as to whether three or four nails were used in fastening the Lord. Nonnus affirms that three only were used, in which he is followed by Gregory Nazianzen. The more general belief gives four nails, an opinion which is supported at much length and by curious arguments by Curtius. Others have carried the number of nails as high as fourteen.

JEHOVAH'S WITNESSES. *THE WATCHTOWER.* APRIL 1, 1984. PP. 30–31

If you notice, the last sentence uses weasel words. That means they don't specify their source. "Others have carried the number"— what others? Who? Which people specifically say that? Do they have the credentials to make that kind of claim? If these "others" really did claim that, why didn't Jehovah's Witnesses give us their names?

I have no idea what they're talking about, but knowing they like to cite their own publications as evidence of claims, I don't trust a word they say. The point is that Thomas wanted to see the holes in the nails—plural, multiple nails. It's a pretty unavoidable conclusion: Jehovah's Witnesses are incorrect.

Birthdays—banned

As with Christmas, Jehovah's Witnesses find a reason not to celebrate birthdays. Evidence for their claims is paper thin. According to Jehovah's Witnesses, Jesus didn't celebrate his birthday. Of course, they couldn't know that because they weren't there. Just because it isn't mentioned in the gospel accounts doesn't mean it didn't happen.

Jehovah's Witnesses claim that every birthday account in the Bible ends negatively. If that's the standard, then I should point out that every account in the Bible about dogs is also negative.[4] Do Jehovah's Witnesses keep the same standard for dogs as they do for birthdays? Of course, they don't. They have invalid and ridiculous reasons for not celebrating every holiday commonly observed in the United States and elsewhere. Why?

In my opinion, they ban holiday celebrations because they want to separate their people from society even more than they already are. They want their people to stand out and be different. They don't want them to fit in with broader society.

In elementary school, I wasn't allowed to celebrate birthdays with the other kids. On Valentine's Day in fifth grade, in art class, everybody made a paper pouch with art supplies and hung it on the side of their desk. Then, everybody made Valentines for others in the class. Everybody was supposed to get one. As a Jehovah's Witness, I was forbidden from participating in holiday celebrations.

Jehovah's Witnesses separate their members from society altogether. They use asinine and backward reasoning, which is selectively applied in some situations but not others. Selectively finding pagan origins in practically everything ramped up heavily under Joseph Rutherford, but it didn't stop there.

Nathan Knorr was Joseph Rutherford's vice president. When Rutherford died in 1942, Knorr took control of the organization, which only worsened under his leadership. This is the end of the Rutherford era, but as with Russell, his effect on the religion still permeates the organization today. Next, let's discuss the changes made under Nathan Knorr.

Christmas—banned

Jehovah's Witnesses celebrated Christmas for years, including when Jesus picked the Bible Students as his chosen representatives on earth in 1919. Joseph Rutherford didn't ban Christmas until 1928, nine years later. Christmas was (and is) condemned by Jehovah's Witnesses as a pagan tradition.

What caused the Bible Students to stop celebrating Christmas? Richard H. Barber gave this answer: "I was asked to give an hour talk over a [radio] hookup on the subject of Christmas. It was given December 12, 1928, and published in The Golden Age #241 and again a year later in #268. That talk pointed out the pagan origin of Christmas. After that, the brothers at Bethel never celebrated Christmas again."

JEHOVAH'S WITNESSES. *1975 YEARBOOK.*
P. 147

Again, this publication is still searchable on its website. I wonder why Rutherford labeled so many activities as pagan.

Their book, Jehovah's Witnesses—*Proclaimers of God's Kingdom*—which members call "The Proclaimers Book"—discusses Christmas celebrations on page 198.

When Jehovah's Witnesses cast aside religious teachings that had pagan roots, they also quit sharing in many customs that were similarly tainted. But for a time, certain holidays were not given the careful scrutiny that they needed. One of these was Christmas.

JEHOVAH'S WITNESSES. *PROCLAIMERS OF GOD'S KINGDOM.* P.198

They claim that they abandoned pagan practices after being chosen by Jesus as God's one and only organization in 1919. Yes, there are pictures of Christmas trees in the Watchtower Society headquarters. Jehovah's Witnesses celebrated Christmas at their headquarters until 1926.

The leadership knows their members will never investigate any deeper. They'll accept anything they tell them without doing the research. In fact, any time members do independent research, they're told to drop the matter or be disfellowshipped. So, what's the real reason they don't celebrate Christmas? Look at this quote from a book published in 2014 titled God's Kingdom Rules! It's the replacement for the deprecated Proclaimers book.

The article "The Origin of Christmas" in [old Jehovah's Witness book] The Golden Age of December 14, 1927, noted that Christmas is a pagan celebration that focuses on pleasures and involves idol worship. The article made it clear that the celebration was not ordered by Christ and concluded with this pointed statement about Christmas: "The fact that the world, the flesh, and the Devil are in favor of its perpetuation and observance ... is a final and conclusive argument against its celebration by those who are dedicated wholly to the service of Jehovah." Not surprisingly, the Bethel family did not celebrate Christmas that December—or ever again!

JEHOVAH'S WITNESSES. *GOD'S KINGDOM RULES!.* 2014. P. 102

I find it interesting that every holiday Jehovah's Witnesses don't celebrate has a different justification—yet they're all banned. What a strange coincidence. Did they find a questionable practice for literally every single holiday? That seems unlikely.

As it turns out, Christmas is almost certainly not of pagan origin. The prevailing belief is that Saturnalia was a celebration of the sun god in the early days of Christianity. Christians latched on to the celebration to spread Christianity far and wide. However, we might not be getting the whole picture because we only hear from the elites of the time—the very few people who were even capable of reading and writing. Additionally, Saturnalia wasn't celebrated on December 25th. It was celebrated from December 17th to 23rd. The festival of the god Sol Invictus, a much lesser-known celebration, occurred on December 25th.

A competing (and, in my opinion, much more plausible) idea is called Calendar Theory.[5] The early church came up with the idea that Jesus was conceived on the same day he died. They believed he was on earth, in fetus form or otherwise, for precisely 34 years. If that theory is true, he was conceived on the Friday before Easter—Good Friday. Nine months from that point on the Gregorian calendar is December 25th.

Contrary to popular belief, the Christmas tree is likely of Christian origin.[6,7] As aforementioned, most people in antiquity were incapable of reading. To communicate the Bible stories to the masses, people put on plays to act them out. The Adam and Eve story included a tree on stage called a paradise tree.

During the medieval era, Christians began going into the forest, cutting down evergreen trees, and putting them up in their homes. The Christmas tree and Christmas itself were likely not of pagan origin. Some non-Christian traditions and cultural practices might have entered the celebration, but the basis for it was Christian.

Even finding reason to believe Christmas was of pagan origin (whatever that means), it seems like they could at least participate in the gift-giving aspects, the Jesus aspects, or any other parts of the holiday that don't have pagan origins. They conveniently find a reason to avoid every single holiday—not the pagan portions, all of it.

MICHAEL JACKSON'S FIRST CHRISTMAS

Michael Jackson grew up as a Jehovah's Witness. His entire family was involved when he was part of the Jackson Five. Michael Jackson's family didn't appear to have been in good standing with the religion.

Michael Jackson is odd. Nobody could tell if he was as creepy as people thought. He was accused of heinous things, child sexual abuse being among those accusations.

Having grown up as a Jehovah's Witness, the "creepiness" or "weirdness" vibe that Michael Jackson exuded from every square inch of his body is the exact "weirdness" vibe that I personally displayed when I finally re-entered society after being completely isolated from the age of 12 to 16. Adapting to society after living in a perfect Jehovah's Witness bubble will do strange things to your mind. The odd personality Jackson had is part of the Jehovah's Witness package. He was deeply entrenched in the religion in his formative years, just like I was.

Fox released a set of home movies with Michael Jackson and Liz Taylor celebrating Michael's first Christmas together. It was December 25th, 1992. Liz Taylor decked out Neverland Ranch, Michael Jackson's home, in Christmas gear.[8] It had lights, trains, and tinsel everywhere. In the video, Liz says it took her five years to convince him to celebrate Christmas.

By 1992, Michael Jackson was on the periphery of the religion. Though he was no longer directly involved, something buried deep in him still made him recoil at the thought of celebrating Christmas. Liz likely knew the standard criticisms of Christmas from Jehovah's

Witnesses because she didn't bother justifying its ties to Jesus' birth or its religious value. She simply said that it's a celebration of love.

On Christmas morning, Liz Taylor walked down the hall and knocked on his door. He had no idea she had planned it. She had stayed up all night decorating the house for Christmas morning without him even realizing it. When he came out of his room, he saw presents and asked, "Can I open them?" She said, "Sure!"

He said he remembers being excited but feeling guilty at the same time. He said, "I remember going in the bathroom and crying later. I felt that I had done something wrong. I was raised not to ever celebrate it."

An innocent and beautiful expression of love to family and friends turned into a dark, painful sadness that led to crying in the bathroom. That's what the religion does to countless people around the world, and it's unacceptable.

As is common with Jehovah's Witnesses while celebrating their first Christmas, they don't know how it's supposed to work. They've never seen it. It's a little thing, but you wouldn't even realize how important those little cultural things are to fit into the rest of society. When somebody talks about making peppermint bark or cookies on Christmas Eve, there's a schedule, a routine. They get the dough, sit together and spread it out, cut cookie shapes, and put it in the oven...little steps add up to a larger process that Michael Jackson and I didn't understand.

When are you supposed to open presents? What goes in a stocking? When is the stocking supposed to be opened? Did the stocking also come from Santa? Who are the presents officially considered to be from? What is mistletoe, and how is it relevant to the Christmas celebration?

Missing everything and not understanding any of it makes you feel like an outsider in society. Of course, Christmas isn't the only holiday Jehovah's Witnesses don't celebrate. They don't celebrate any of them, citing different reasons for each. Considering the totality of the little cultural things you miss by not celebrating holidays or being around outsiders makes you strange and different. You know the difference is there, and so does everybody else.

Everybody realizes you're odd, and you don't know how to explain that to them. It would take…well, an entire book to explain why you're so strange. After leaving the religion, I used to say and do very odd things. They were normal for Jehovah's Witnesses, but everybody on the outside—which was now everybody in my life—could see them. It was like I entered "uncanny valley." Nobody could quite pinpoint what was strange, but something was.

When I saw those gears turning in people's heads, I would tell them, "I'm sorry. I know I'm kind of strange. I grew up in a cult." That was the shortest and quickest explanation I could offer. Inevitably, the other person would ask, "Oh. Which cult was it?" I would tell them, "Jehovah's Witnesses." Without fail, the other person would start to argue about whether Jehovah's Witnesses were a cult. After a few instances of that, I simply refused to tell them which one. I would just say, "A deeply damaging one," or something to that effect. It would take too long to explain, and I don't feel the need to talk every person I meet into accepting the damaging qualities of Jehovah's Witnesses.

That's why I feel for Michael Jackson. Everybody viewed him as strange, but I understood him perfectly. Like me and countless others, Michael Jackson lost his childhood. He didn't know what it was like to be normal. He wanted to experience life from the start since he didn't get to the first time around. I was like him for a while until I entered normal society for the first time. In my opinion, Michael Jackson's bizarre personality was a direct result of isolation brought on by Jehovah's Witnesses, as well as the general isolation suffered as a result of fame.

Michael Jackson isn't the only famous Jehovah's Witness. Serena Williams is an active Member, and Prince was active until his death. Charlemagne Tha God's entire family is affiliated with the religion. He still seems to believe it, though he isn't an active member.

Selena, Biggie, Ja Rule,22 Dave Mustaine, and Childish Gambino all grew up as Jehovah's Witnesses or had devout family members who did. In an interview with The Daily Beast, Childish Gambino discussed his affiliation and described what it was like in school as a child.

> Being a Jehovah's Witness was interesting. I think it amplified my own alienness. I was always the odd one out, and Jehovah's Witnesses don't celebrate Christmas, you don't say the Pledge of Allegiance, and when you have Jewish kids in the class who don't celebrate Christmas everyone understands, but when you say you're a Jehovah's Witness they say, "So…You come to my door at 9 a.m. and wake my family up?"[9]

Donald Glover understands. His success and pain, as with Selena and Ja Rule, is shared among all of us. There's something unique about feeling the pain of hatred directed at you personally. It's an experience impossible to describe. If you know the feeling, you know it.

Dave Mustaine has an entirely different viewpoint from me regarding society, religion, politics, and just about everything else. Despite that, Mustaine knows. He understands. He was there. He went to meetings and probably knocked on doors. We both know what it's like to be chased by dogs. We both know what it's like to have our lives restricted and put into a box. Regardless of Mustaine's politics or religious views, he and the broader ex-Jehovah's Witness community understand each other in ways others simply can't.

My parents were dirt poor when I was young. They filed for bankruptcy when I was eight. We had nothing to our names. They asked the congregation for help, and the congregation came through. They gave us money, food, clothes, and school supplies.

The congregation bought my backpack for me that year. They helped my family more than anybody could have asked. Despite that help, they would rather see me dead in a ditch now that I'm on the outside. Whether they admit it, that's official doctrine. If they see me on the street, they won't look in my eyes. They won't give me the time of day. They'll pretend I'm a ghost.

When somebody gives you school supplies when you're young because your parents didn't have enough money to buy them, there's a unique connection to that person. They understand your life better than most. When you see that person in a grocery store, and they refuse to look in your eyes, it hurts. That was my first experience with real persecution. It's a pain that must be experienced to be fully understood.

Pain is the goal, of course. Jehovah's Witnesses are unlikely to watch "30 Rock" or listen to Donald Glover's albums. He's dead to them. I don't have to explain the feeling to Childish Gambino. He knows.

Though it comes with intense persecution, the chains that once held him down don't hold him anymore. He succeeded despite the Watchtower Society's best efforts. Freedom of mind is more important than anything else. Despite the hatred that comes from active Jehovah's Witnesses, I'm free. Donald Glover is free. Selena is free. We don't have to be alien people anymore.

The type of experience Jehovah's Witnesses put us through literally causes a form of PTSD called RTS: Religious Trauma Syndrome. I unexpectedly started experiencing symptoms of PTSD, which were directly from Jehovah's Witnesses. I still have nightmares about being shunned regularly. It used to be on a nearly nightly basis. I started having trouble talking to people I didn't know, like I did when I was a Jehovah's Witness. I still can't approach somebody with whom I'm unfamiliar.

RTS isn't simply the result of leaving a religion. It's the result of deep mental and emotional trauma brought on by losing your entire support group—everybody you ever knew or loved. It's something that's typically only suffered by people from high control groups and often isn't recognized or diagnosed. If you think you might have it, ask a professional about it.

CHAPTER 5
THE PREACHING WORK

NATHAN KNORR—THE THIRD PRESIDENT

Nathan Knorr, born in 1905, started showing interest in what was still called the Bible Students at age 16—1922. By this point in the Watchtower Society's history, Rutherford had already announced his end-times prediction for 1925.

Knorr was Joseph Rutherford's vice president from 1941 to Rutherford's death in 1942. He was president from 1942 to 1977. While president, he created several training programs—some still existing—heavily related to Jehovah's Witnesses' door-knocking campaigns. He was also responsible for the shunning policy, which we'll discuss soon. Let's look at a chronological record of Jehovah's Witnesses' beliefs under Nathan Knorr, starting with his training programs.

THE PREACHING WORK

When I was a member of the religion, the Theocratic Ministry School was a program aspiring Jehovah's Witness men (and only men) could join. Since I left in 2007, the Theocratic Ministry School has been discontinued and replaced with the "Our Christian Life and Ministry" meeting. I'm unfamiliar with it, but I've been told it's very different from the Theocratic Ministry School. It used to take place during the midweek meeting—for me, it was Wednesday night.

The goal of the Theocratic Ministry School was to create a system in which members could learn doctrine and public speaking. After joining the program, members were given a large red book with tips on creating an outline, how to maintain eye contact with a crowd, suppressing nervousness, and more. In contrast to other educational programs by Jehovah's Witnesses, The Theocratic Ministry School was conducted by peoples' home congregations.

Nathan Knorr also started Gilead, which is still in operation today. Gilead essentially trains people—including women, in this case—to be full-time evangelists. Married couples can go through Gilead, but they aren't allowed to have children until after they attend. In other contexts, having children is neither encouraged nor discouraged. It's up to each couple. Abortion is banned, but birth control is perfectly acceptable. Gilead turns out missionaries and Special Pioneers. We'll talk about them in more detail in the next section.

School for Kingdom Evangelizers, or SKE, is a pseudo-school for Jehovah's Witnesses in good standing. It's a two-month course—tuition-free. In fact, Jehovah's Witnesses offer everything for free. This gives the appearance that money flows from the organization to the membership rather than the other way around. In reality, it flows from membership to leadership in less obvious ways, like through manual labor.

They used to charge for magazines, but all literature has been free since at least 2000. I was born in 1989 and remember knocking on doors in the 1990s. I don't ever remember paying for literature. Maybe I wasn't paying attention when my parents were paying for it, or maybe there was a program to give literature to low-income families. However, there was a time when Jehovah's Witnesses used to ask for payment at doors to help pay for the literature they passed out. They carried little money bags with zippers on the top for payment collection. I was either not born yet or too young to remember people using money bags regularly.

Commonly, women aren't allowed to participate in any special "privileges," but any baptized Jehovah's Witness in good standing is permitted to attend SKE, women and married couples included, just like with Gilead. Again, they aren't allowed to have children until after they attend. Ministerial Training School (MTS), not to be confused with the Theocratic Ministry School (TMS), was the predecessor to the School for Kingdom Evangelizers. SKE is available to women, but MTS is not. Both SKE and MTS effectively produce ultra-invested indoctrinated drones.

Ex-Jehovah's Witnesses have a shorthand for referring to members' degree of investment. If you ever find yourself in an ex-Jehovah's Witness space, you'll likely recognize some of these acronyms. PIMO means "physically in, mentally out." It means the person officially attends meetings and knocks on doors, but they no longer believe it. They're likely keeping up appearances to maintain relationships. I was POMI for years—physically out, mentally in. I had been disfellowshipped but still believed it. Now, I'm POMO. Ex-Jehovah's Witnesses refer to the extreme, indoctrinated drones as PIMI or ultra PIMI—physically in, mentally in.

If a Jehovah's Witness isn't ultra-PIMI when they attend SKE, they certainly will be by the time they leave. After being accepted into SKE, they move to a training site where they live full-time. The site is completely self-sustaining, and even the food is produced by Watchtower Farms.

Sometimes, SKE participants will learn a new language at the live-in school. Learning a second language is a big deal among Jehovah's Witnesses. Everybody is encouraged to do so. Though SKE didn't exist when I was a member, the culture encouraged people to learn new skills that could be useful to the organization. I learned ASL—American Sign Language—because there weren't any other useful languages to learn in my area of rural West Virginia.

In addition to learning a new language, SKE members intensively learn doctrine, public speaking, and door-to-door sales techniques. They're then sent back to their home congregation to act as a Watchtower Society beacon—particularly loyal to the organization. According to the Jehovah's Witness website, graduates are "usually sent back to their home congregation."

The live-in locations where Gilead and SKE take place are colloquially and collectively called Bethel. Bethel means "House of God." The term refers to any branch of Jehovah's Witnesses headquarters, including bookbinding, printing, audio/visual production, and school sites.

Outside of the special schools already mentioned, when a member applies and is approved to attend Bethel, they don't know which role they'll fill until they arrive. They're typically put into a slot for which they're exceptionally skilled—artists are sent to the art department, writers to the writing department. Women go to the laundry and maid service department (I'm only partly joking). Women are allowed to do any non-leadership job in Bethel. Still, somebody has to do laundry, dishes, and cleaning for the governing body and other members of Bethel.

Like other Jehovah's Witnesses, Bethelites also go door-knocking, known as "going in service." Historically, Service has been considered a requirement to survive Armageddon, but their beliefs have waffled over the years. Bethelites are not exempt from that expectation. Going in service is about the only time Bethelites ever leave the compound. They can leave if they want, but everything is provided on-site.

Jehovah's Witnesses like to point out how valuable their training programs are to the membership. I have to agree—it is extremely valuable to learn public speaking through the Theocratic Ministry School or a second language at SKE. Unfortunately, complete sacrifice is expected from the organization. It's effectively a deal with the devil—you get something in return, but what you get is not worth what you gave to get it.

PAID PREACHERS

Gilead doesn't just produce ultra-PIMI beacons. It also trains missionaries and Special Pioneers. These positions are extremely uncommon, and the ratio of missionaries to standard Jehovah's Witnesses is very low. Since its inception in 1943, about 8,000 Gilead graduates have graduated.

If a member has ever been reproved, disfellowshipped, or marked, their application to Gilead is unlikely to be accepted. If somebody reaches that level, they're nearly guaranteed to remain loyal to the organization. However, a member of the Governing Body defected from the organization in the 1980s, so we shouldn't discount any possibilities.

Jehovah's Witness missionaries are entirely different from Mormon missionaries. Mormon missionaries commonly spend one or two years in an unfamiliar area and must pay for their trip upfront before going. For Mormons, this is like a rite of passage; almost all go through a missionary period with the church.

Jehovah's Witness missionaries are sometimes relocated to dense cities where they can have the most impact. On rare occasions, they'll send them to foreign countries to get a foothold in developing communities.

Missionaries are paid a monthly stipend. This information is extremely difficult to find independently, but from what I can tell, in the mid-2000s, Special Pioneers were paid $600 per month to get about 130 hours per month—32 hours per week. Around this time, the minimum wage was $5.50 per hour. Their hourly pay averages out to $4.60 per hour.

In the mid-2000s, Bethelites were paid $80 monthly, but their housing and food were paid for. Based on the information I could find, Special Pioneers and missionaries are likely paid minimum wage for 32 hours per week wherever they go. They certainly need another job on top of that. People in urban areas couldn't afford to live off minimum wage for 32 hours per week.

WHAT IS "GOING IN SERVICE?"

"Going in service" or "witnessing" is the term Jehovah's Witnesses use to refer to knocking on doors. Specifically, these terms describe devoting time to "giving a witness," or talking about Jehovah, to people around a particular neighborhood or area. "Cart witnessing" is a newer form of spreading the message that has overtaken door-knocking in many areas. They have small carts filled with Jehovah's Witness literature that they can try to impose on passers-by.

Schoolchildren are responsible for accessing people within gated communities. Their classmates might live in gated communities otherwise closed off to Jehovah's Witnesses, so children are expected to "work" the school like a territory. This obviously leads to being heavily ostracized by peers, which is a useful side effect of the religion, intentional or not.

Since I left the religion, "cart witnessing" has become more common. Few people appreciate somebody knocking on their door, especially at 9 a.m. on a Saturday. I can't tell you how many people I very obviously woke up. That isn't conducive to a friendly environment.

The Society came up with the idea of cart witnessing to counter the possibility that they were being bothersome in a neighborhood. Cart witnessing also gives them a chance to access people to whom they might not otherwise have access.

Standard times to knock on doors are Saturdays at 9:00 a.m. or Sundays around 1:00 p.m. Some congregations have meetings on Sundays from 10:00 a.m. to noon, and some have meetings from 6:00 p.m. to 8:00 p.m. People commonly find a time for service that works around the Sunday meeting schedule.

"Cart witnessers" don't have to adhere to strict times like traditional door knockers tend to. Before cart witnessing was popular, people would go to dentist's offices and hospitals and place the magazines on the other magazine stacks.

The carts Jehovah's Witnesses commonly use are supplied through the Watchtower Society or one of their third-party affiliate companies. Third-party companies sell Jehovah's Witness gear like convention badge holders and embossed Bibles. The carts fold up neatly and fit into a bag. They typically contain a variety of books, but mostly the books that Jehovah's Witnesses are pushing at any given moment—the latest book released at a convention or a book explicitly tailored to non-believers as an introduction to the beliefs and doctrine, such as the book *"What does the Bible really teach?"*—which has been a popular one for a long time.

Cart witnesses often stand on the street corner smiling for hours at a time. Remember, this isn't a pleasant experience for most of them. They could be at home building model airplanes or learning to play an instrument. Instead, they're out on a street corner, trying to get people to accept their little books.

I never knew anyone who went in service because they enjoyed it. They're effectively door-to-door salesmen. It's a job that pays nothing except in extraordinary circumstances. They do it because they believe the Society needs them to, and it might help save people from eternal death—including themselves.

For the more fervent members of the religion, there is a role known as "pioneer" and another called "auxiliary pioneer." These aren't to be confused with Special Pioneers, who require graduation from the Gilead training school. Anyone in good standing, including women, can participate in pioneering or auxiliary pioneering.

The numbers have changed slightly since I was involved, but an auxiliary pioneer agreed to give fifty hours of service per month when I was a member. That's about 12 1/2 hours per week. A pioneer agreed to get seventy hours of service per month for 12 consecutive months, or 17.5 hours per week. A Special Pioneer gets 130 hours per month, or 32.5 hours per week, and receives a (very) small stipend. The other types don't receive any money at all.

Being a pioneer, auxiliary or otherwise, is typically an unofficial requirement for moving up the religious ladder. Pioneers are given priority when people apply to live and work on their compound. The more time they invest in pioneering, the more likely they are to be accepted for higher roles within the organization.

Saturday is a typical day for all Jehovah's Witnesses to go in service. When I was involved in the religion, my book study group met at the group leader's house for a 15-minute planning session to determine who would go with whom.

To my knowledge, book studies have been renamed service groups. Service groups split the congregation into groups of about 30 people each—micro congregations that can function as autonomous units when the world crumbles and the United Nations takes on the role of the Great Beast of Revelation. Each service group is led by a couple of elders and some ministerial servants. Ministerial servants are like deacons; they're simply assistants to the elders.

To qualify to go in service, you must petition the elders in the congregation to become an unbaptized publisher. That's the first step on the road to baptism. In 2022, Jehovah's Witnesses reported a total of 8,699,048 publishers.[1] I'm assuming that number includes both unbaptized and baptized publishers.

A baptized congregation member must be present for an unbaptized publisher to be allowed to go in service. A baptized male will take the lead over the woman if he is present. He is permitted to go in service with women if one of those women is his wife, and he's never left alone with any of the other women. If a child was born into the religion, they can go door-to-door with their parent, whether they're an unbaptized publisher or not. I handed out my first tract when I was two years old—before I can remember.

On Saturdays, I would wake up at about 7:30 AM. I would shower, brush, and put on my suit. All Jehovah's Witnesses dress formally—suits for men and dresses for women. Color and style are optional, with a couple of exceptions. First, nothing flashy. Dress clean and well, but no unusual colors or extremely expensive suits. Modesty is important. Second, as ex-Governing Body member, Tony Morris often said, no pants that are too tight. Tony Morris claimed that homosexuals within the fashion industry are desperate to make men wear tight pants. He was fired in early 2023, but since the Governing Body hasn't denounced it, it's still doctrine as of 2024.

KNOCKING ON DOORS

After putting on my suit, I would grab my service bag—which was different from my meeting bag—and we would all get in the car and drive to the Kingdom Hall or the service group leader's home. When we arrived, the conductor for the service group would say a short prayer and note who brought a car (vans were preferred, as they could hold more people). He would then divide people into groups of four to six, depending on how many people fit in the car.

A baptized group leader always decides when breaks are taken and who goes to specific houses. Adult males are preferred. If an adult male is not available—that is to say, if a car group must be all women—that's okay, but there can't be a male of any age with the group of women unless it's the unbaptized child of one of the women. Women are subservient to the lowest-ranking male, no matter what their age. If a ten-year-old male is baptized but isn't old enough or competent enough to lead, another male must be present to assist in the leadership and teach the boy.

The male in charge of the group also must be related or married to one of the women in the group. He can't go door to door or be left alone with a woman roughly his age under any circumstances. They're complicated rules, but they're instinctual for most service overseers.

If a woman must lead the service group with a baptized male present, as in the case of a ten-year-old child, she has to wear a head covering. The head covering is effectively a hijab. It's commonly an improvised item like a doily, napkin, or tea towel. The hijab shows subservience and reverence to her superior—no matter his age or circumstances.

The hijab rule applies to more than just going in service. If a woman's husband, father, or grandfather is present but incapable of leading a group in some spiritual matter, she must wear the hijab. Spiritual matters include preparing for service, family worship, or studying with a prospective member, even if he's incapable because of dementia or another type of disability. Even if he's occupied with his own "book study" at the same time, even if he can't lead because he's too young, she must show subservience if she is the only one available to take the lead and a baptized male is present. Truth be told, though, women aren't often in this type of position. My mom wore a hijab a few times when I was growing up because she was reading Jehovah's Witness literature with me when my dad was in the other room. The woman must also be sitting in situations where a hijab is necessary.

After arranging the car groups, the service overseer will make sure each car group has a territory map, and they'll send them on their way. They usually hit the road by 9:15 AM and knock on their first door by 9:30 AM or 10:00 AM. My congregation hadn't adapted to computers yet, so they would keep track of houses by printing out small territory maps. The small maps would be about 4x6 in size. They'd be laminated; if somebody asked to be put on the "do not call" list, their address could be listed on the back of the card. The house would be overlooked for about ten years or so. After some time, the house would be rechecked to see if the person still lived there and wanted to be on the do-not-call list.

Territory maps are checked out and, when completed, are put in the back of the stack. By operating this way, every house in the United States would eventually be visited, regardless of how many Jehovah's Witnesses lived in any given area. Kingdom Halls likely still use this method, especially in more remote areas.

Here's an essential point: You don't have to be mean to Jehovah's Witnesses. They have a hard time as it is. Nobody wants to be out there pounding pavement and cramming religious literature down people's throats. Don't harass them, don't mistreat them, don't laugh at them. Instead, say, "Can you please put me on the 'do not call' list?" It's that simple. They won't bother you again—at least not for ten more years.

When the car group reaches the territory, the group's leader splits people into groups of two and gives them a list of houses to hit. Typically, each set of two people will hit about five houses and meet back at the car when they're done. Most people probably won't answer. If they do, they'll likely say, "Not interested." Jehovah's Witnesses bring in almost nobody through door-knocking efforts. See the section "Conversion Rates" for more information.

If one group takes longer to finish their section than the others, they continue to the next street instead of returning to the car. Jehovah's Witnesses reach into their bag, grab a small tract or a Watchtower magazine, fold it up, and stick it in the door if nobody answers.

Each month, Jehovah's Witnesses were expected to fill out a small sheet that detailed how many hours they put in, how many magazines they placed, how many books were placed, and how many return visits they had. I intended to supply an image of the old service slip I used, but the Watchtower Society has a ruthless reputation regarding copyright laws. It's simple to find through a Google image search for "Jehovah's Witness field service report." I filled one of these little slips out every month for years. If I forgot to turn it in, the service overseer would chase me down, even going so far as to call me to find out how many hours I'd put in. As of 2023, normal Jehovah's Witnesses aren't expected to fill out service reports anymore. Only pioneers, Special Pioneers, and missionaries.

Many people lie on these reports. Personally, I preferred not to lie outright. I wasn't "going in service" on Saturdays or Sundays, so I'd added up how many hours I spent talking about Jehovah to people around me. Coworkers, classmates, and others. If I talked about the religion at all, I counted it. Conveniently, my calculations showed my hours almost always added up to precisely ten hours per month—the minimum number required to be considered "active" within the religion.

Not going in service isn't against the rules—you won't get disfellowshipped for never going in service. You will, however, be culturally shunned by your peers. Regardless of how consistently you make the meetings (it should be 100%), if a member isn't going in service, people will be cautious about inviting them to events or chatting with them.

As mentioned, the service report is no longer required. I'm not sure how they gauge "active" and "inactive" anymore, but I'd imagine it's probably based on how many meetings the member attends. I suppose it's possible that the title "inactive" doesn't exist at all anymore. I'm sure we'll get the answers to our questions as the membership culture slowly forms and changes with the guidance of the religion's leadership.

Jehovah's Witnesses usually start Saturday service at 9:00 AM and take a bathroom and lunch break around 12:00 or 1:00 PM. They typically have a common place they like to go for lunch. When I was a Jehovah's Witness, we went to Tim Hortons—a donut shop. The culture dictates that somebody else will pay for their food in service if somebody doesn't have the money to pay for it. Sometimes, one person will pay for everybody anyway to show "brotherly love."

Good Jehovah's Witnesses will head back out after their short lunch break. Depending on how "good" or "bad" they are, they might start counting time from when they arrive at the Kingdom Hall, or even when they leave the house. "Good" Jehovah's Witnesses start counting when they arrive at the territory. It could take up to 30 extra minutes to arrive in the territory they'll be working.

Sunday meetings in my congregation end at noon. The congregation gives people 30 minutes to chat with others before starting the service meeting. By 1:00 p.m., Jehovah's Witnesses are usually out the door and headed toward a territory map. They'll usually knock on doors from 1:00 p.m. to around 4:00 p.m., another three-hour block.

Suppose a Jehovah's Witness does three hours every Saturday, 9:00 AM to noon, or even 9:30 AM to 12:30 PM; that adds up to about 12 hours per month. To get a minimum of ten hours per month, you can go in service for three Saturdays or Sundays per month. Some people come to the Kingdom Hall on the fourth Saturday anyway and get a group together to clean. Wiping baseboards, dusting the literature counter, cleaning the bathrooms, etc.

An alternative to going door-to-door, commonly used by people with disabilities, is letter writing. Letter-writing campaigns were also particularly useful during COVID-19. Unlike many other fundamentalist religions, Jehovah's Witnesses took COVID very seriously. They reasoned, "If people are concerned with COVID and we're there knocking on their door, it might make us look bad." Completely sound logic. I, for one, am happily surprised that they took it so seriously.

Disabled people have always participated in letter-writing campaigns, but the leadership started a letter-writing campaign when COVID-19 hit. I assume the Governing Body wasn't sure if this was "the end of the end." It seemed like they were leaning that way for a while because pestilence is one of the signs of the times. Their propensity to assume the end will be here at any given minute led them to heavily imply that this might be members' last opportunity to save people before the end arrives. Jehovah's Witnesses eventually continued their door-to-door effort, but letter writing counts as time to maintain a member's "active" status. Find a phone book, write a handwritten letter about how great Jehovah is, and mail it to the addresses in the book.

Exploiting emotional vulnerabilities seems to be a common tactic of the religion. If there's a way to exploit somebody emotionally, they do. For example, Jehovah's Witnesses commonly do "social media witnessing" on Twitter and Facebook. I've watched it happen personally. A close friend was pregnant and deeply excited about having a baby. Sadly, when the birth came, the baby was stillborn. It was crushing. She was hyping up the pregnancy for the entire nine months. She had to go to Twitter to tell her followers what happened, a profoundly devastating event made even worse by the necessity to explain what happened.

Within a couple of days of her tweet, a Jehovah's Witness showed up on the tweet to post a link to the Jehovah's Witness article about losing somebody you love. He apparently searched the term "dead baby" or "stillborn" and posted a link to the article on each of the tweets from the search results. Needless to say, it's a highly predatory practice that is encouraged by the Watchtower Society. When I challenged the Jehovah's Witnesses' tactics, they blocked me and moved on to the next search result.

There's a bulletin in the back of the Kingdom Hall. The bulletin lists disabled or otherwise homebound members of the congregation. Each week, those homebound members are supposed to receive a visit from a car group to "offer encouragement." They'll commonly offer to do some chores for them, like cleaning the house or doing dishes. The time spent at the homebound peoples' homes is sometimes counted as time in service, depending on how desperately the person needs hours.

HOW MANY PEOPLE CONVERT?

I'll use 2018 as the base year for conversion rates because it happened before COVID-19, and Jehovah's Witnesses still reported certain statistics. In 2018, they reported a total of 2,074,655,497 hours of field service.2 That number almost certainly includes letter-writing campaigns and simply discussing the religion with coworkers. In the same year, 281,744 people were baptized.[2]

I would guess most baptisms were likely children of existing members—not adults whose door-knocking or letter-writing campaigns had converted. Even assuming that all baptisms were brought in by field service, that means one Jehovah's Witness has to knock on doors for about 7,363 hours to bring in a single convert. Even that number is extremely generous.

Assuming that extremely generous number is accurate, and assuming most Jehovah's Witnesses get the standard ten hours per month, it takes one Jehovah's Witness 61 years to convert somebody to the religion.

Optimistically, a lucky pioneer (840 hours/year) might bring in one person every ten years or so. That includes bringing their own children to baptism. For every family of four who gets baptized, a pioneer preached for 40 years without bringing a single person to baptism. My mom pioneered practically her entire adult life and never got anybody baptized except her own four kids—who are all disfellowshipped or disassociated now.

THE WATCHTOWER AND AWAKE! MAGAZINES

The Watchtower Society has published the *Watchtower* magazine since its early days. They started printing the *Awake!* magazine on October 1, 1919, under the name *The Golden Age*. It was renamed to *Awake!* on August 22, 1946. It derived the name from Romans 13:11: "It is time for you to awake out of sleep: for now is salvation nearer to us than when we first believed."

The articles in *Awake!* magazine commonly appealed more to the outside world, while the Watchtower magazine was intended to target believing Jehovah's Witnesses who already understood the religion's doctrine. *Awake!* magazine was produced twice monthly until it dropped to monthly issues in January 2006. In January 2016, it was reduced even further to one issue every two months; in January 2018, it was reduced to three issues per year. As of 2022, they print one issue per year.

Jehovah's Witnesses split the *Watchtower* into a study and public edition in 2008. The study edition is heavily targeted toward believing members who already clearly understand doctrine and culture. They are never handed out to non-members. Reading this book will give you the context necessary to understand *The Watchtower* study edition. The study edition is not hidden from the public by any means—at least, not yet. It's currently accessible on their website. The fact that it exists, however, means that this group has a method of communicating directly with the membership and keeping that information hidden from broader society.

Watchtower and *Awake!* have traditionally been 32 pages long each, but in 2013, the public edition of the *Watchtower* was reduced from 32 pages to 16 pages. Jehovah's Witnesses have, however, traditionally printed bound volumes of their *Watchtower* and *Awake!* Magazines, a compilation of every magazine produced for the year, from January to December.

For most of my childhood, the *Watchtower* had two monthly issues and was 32 pages long, meaning that bound volumes were usually around 384 physical pages, or 768 numbered pages. Sometimes, when a *Watchtower* or *Awake!* magazine is quoted, the bound volume will be referenced rather than the specific issue of the *Watchtower* or *Awake!*

JEHOVAH'S WITNESSES' LITERATURE

In addition to the *Watchtower* and *Awake!*, Jehovah's Witnesses release detailed explanations of doctrine or breakdowns of apocalyptic literature like Daniel or Isaiah. Sometimes, they re-release updated copies of the same book.

A literature counter stands at the back of the Kingdom Hall, typically near the door. They tend to hold at least a few of the most requested books, Bibles, and *Watchtowers* in reserve. Somebody works the literature counter before and after meetings. Any elder can access the counter if somebody needs something during off hours. If somebody forgets their Bible at home, or they don't have the week's *Watchtower* (both of which are BIG problems), an elder can grab an extra for anybody who wants it.

Everything behind the counter is completely free. When I was a member, each family had a box reserved behind the literature counter and a standard order of magazines they were likely to place throughout the month. Suppose somebody is looking for a specific book that is still in print. In that case, the literature counter worker can order it, and the Watchtower Society will deliver it with their next shipment of magazines.

Each year, they release new literature at their conventions. At the end of the assembly day, if Jehovah's Witnesses have a brand-new book to release, they'll make it available to anybody who wants one (it's free) as they walk out the door. Grab one from a box as you go. They also have a book titled The Daily Text, now called Examining the Scriptures Daily. It's a reasonably small book that releases a brand-new copy each year, and for every day in the calendar, you can flip to the month and day to find a message the Watchtower Society wants people to think about for the day. The following is an example of a *Daily Text* entry.

SUNDAY, JANUARY 22

Jesus gave way to tears.—John 11:35.

In the winter of 32 C.E., Jesus' good friend Lazarus got sick and died. (John 11:3, 14) The man had two sisters, Mary and Martha, and Jesus loved this family very much. When Martha heard that Jesus was coming, she rushed out to meet him. Imagine the surge of emotions as she said: "Lord, if you had been here, my brother would not have died." (John 11:21, 32, 33) Jesus was surely moved to tears on seeing how Mary and Martha were affected by the death of their brother. If you have lost a loved one, Jehovah understands how you feel. Jesus is "the exact representation" of his Father. (Heb. 1:3) When Jesus wept, he reflected his Father's emotions. (John 14:9) If you are enduring the loss of a loved one, you can be sure that Jehovah not only notices your grief but also feels deeply for you. He wants to heal your broken heart.

—Ps. 34:18; 147:3. w22.01 15 °5–7

Jehovah's Witnesses used to release yearbooks that contained interesting or noteworthy changes or events in the religion. However, they stopped doing so in 2017 and started releasing "Service Year Reports" instead. These reports are only a few pages long and can be found on their website. They contain statistics about total hours spent in field service, newly baptized members, etc.

THE SILVER SWORD: JEHOVAH' WITNESSES' BIBLE

Jehovah's Witnesses' Bibles come straight from the Watchtower Society in various sizes and colors, but when I was young, my mother ordered a specially embossed and colored Bible. Traditional, standard colors for Jehovah's Witness Bibles (when I was young) were maroon and black. Bibles came in two sizes: pocket-size and full-size. The pocket size still contained all the same books and information; it just had a smaller text.

Every family member should have their own copy of the Bible. I had a copy I commonly used, but my family of six (two parents, four children) always had a few Bibles around the house in case we had taken ours out of one of our bags and forgot to put it back. I commonly had two Bibles—one for my service bag and one for my briefcase.

In 2013, Jehovah's Witnesses released a newer edition of their New World Translation, primarily in light gray. Since it was mostly light gray unless requested otherwise, the 2013 edition of the New World Translation became known as "The Silver Sword."

JEHOVAH'S WITNESSES' BAGS

Jehovah's Witnesses generally have two bags: one for meetings and one for door-knocking. Women will have the same type of design for each. Men tend to use briefcases for meetings. I was gifted a briefcase when I was baptized. Presumably, the reason is twofold:

one, it looks professional and nice while being perfect for storing items; two, when a man moves up the religious ladder, he'll gain access to a book that's not supposed to be accessed by anybody—even his own wife.

The *Elder's Manual* must NEVER be left in a room without you unless it's in a locked case. Elders are not permitted to show or discuss its contents (or even its existence) with their wives. It is top secret. Of course, copies are very easy to find online. If you've made it this far, you already know some of the worst things in the *Elder's Manual*.

The briefcase will usually contain a Bible, the latest magazines being discussed at the Sunday meeting, some pens, a notebook for taking notes, and maybe some candy (like cream savers—those were the best). That's about it unless you want to carry some book you're reading with a "return visit"—somebody who's invited you back to their house to discuss the religion further. Jehovah's Witnesses publish books like the practice is going out of style, so there's always something new to put in the bag to read.

The service bag will contain ten or so sets of magazines to be placed. Sometimes, Jehovah's Witnesses run campaigns where they try to push certain specific books for some period—maybe a month. The service bag will also contain a Bible, a notebook, some pens for notetaking, and candy out of the wazoo. Whoever has candy is the most popular person in the car. It'll also contain a set of small sheets of paper, about the size of a field service report, with a breakdown of which houses the members visited and their level of interest.

At each house, you give the person the book, magazine, or whatever you're "placing" at that moment. At the end of the 30-second presentation, you ask the householder if they would mind if you returned to give them the newest copy of the magazines. If they say they wouldn't mind, it becomes a return visit. You're expected to return to their house every week or two to give them the latest magazines.

I'm sure I don't need to point this out, but most return visits aren't interested in the religion at all. They're simply too friendly or too socially anxious to turn somebody down. That leads to a perpetual cycle of receiving magazines that'll just go in the trash anyway.

SPECIAL PRODUCTS

Jehovah's Witnesses need specially designed products. The products aren't always directly produced and sold by the Watchtower Society, but sometimes they are. Jehovah's Witnesses supply things like Bibles and literature. They also supply carts used for cart witnessing. There are a few other organizations that sell useful Jehovah's Witness goods and services, like the service of having a copy of the Jehovah's Witness Bible embossed with names or having a zipper added to the Bible so it doesn't fly open at inopportune times. It's not a feature that ever appealed to me, but it must appeal to somebody, or they wouldn't offer it.

Most companies that sell Jehovah's Witness-specific goods, services, and materials are typically affiliated with Jehovah's Witnesses in some strong way. These companies sell anything a Jehovah's Witness might need, including briefcases, go bags (for when Armageddon starts), and a variety of pens, pins, and stickers with the Jehovah's Witness logo on them. Etsy is also booming with all the goods a Jehovah's Witness might need.

PRACTICING PRESENTATIONS

When I was young, Jehovah's Witnesses distributed Kingdom Ministries to everybody who had achieved the rank of "unbaptized publisher." Kingdom Ministries were released monthly. In addition to basic relevant announcements, they contained suggested presentations, about 30 seconds long, specific to the most recent magazines. Presentations weren't scripted; they were improvised. They just gave examples.

The one role women could have in the meetings took place during the midweek meeting—Wednesday nights for me. Women can serve as an example but can't teach anybody anything. The meeting conductor would pick two women and have them demonstrate the proper method of presenting the magazines each week. The women would read through the presentations and practice them before demonstrating in front of the congregation.

If possible, Jehovah's Witnesses should complement the householder. If they have a beautiful and well-loved yard or garden, point it out and find a way to relate it to the magazine's most recent edition.

> You have a lovely garden. Did you know the Bible says the entire earth will be like that again one day?

A compliment to their intelligence and attention goes a long way. If there are kids' toys in the yard, you might say,

> Children can be such a blessing. You know, Jesus loved children, too. Have you ever seen the advice the Bible offers about raising children?

Maybe that's why I'm so good at improvising conversation as an adult.

We've touched on expectations to remain a member of the religion, but we haven't talked about shunning offenses. Shunning wasn't part of the religion until Nathan Knorr's leadership in 1952. Let's talk about what it takes to be shunned by Jehovah's Witnesses.

CHAPTER 6
THE SHUNNING BEGINS

PUNISHMENT IN THE CHURCH

Jehovah's Witnesses did not practice shunning until Nathan Knorr formally incorporated it into the religion in 1952. Today, they have a few punishment tools in their toolbox. Since they can't legally jail people, they find other control methods. They engage in a standard set of control methods, such as thought-terminating cliches or limiting information by banning certain websites or Facebook pages. If members break one of the rules, they use the following strategies to control their membership: reproof, marking, and disfellowshipping.

If you break any of the rules—and there are many—you will be taken from the life you once enjoyed and be kicked out for the rest of your life. Even slightly bending the rules in a way that doesn't reach the disfellowshipping level will get a member pre-shunned. Your friends and family won't want to be in your life. There's nothing technically wrong with being friends with you; they just... don't want to be anymore. They keep their distance. Sometimes, punishment is private; sometimes, it's public. It depends on which level of discipline is being received and how public the offense is.

There are a variety of thoughts or behaviors that can get you socially ostracized within Jehovah's Witnesses without being full-blown shunned. For example, when I was about ten, my brothers got the tips of their hair frosted. It was a popular style at the time. They were reproved for it.

Reproof is a process by which Jehovah's Witnesses punish members for breaking a rule, but the elders believe the person is "repentant," which means the elders trust that they're sorry and don't intend to do it again. Reproof means losing "privileges" in the congregation. That means the person can no longer move up the social ladder and show how spiritual he is. He can't give talks from the stage, help set up the sound system, or hand out magazines or other literature at the desk in the back of the Kingdom Hall. There is nothing. He holds a status lower than the lowest-ranking male in the congregation.

If the person is unmarried, dating and marriage are almost certainly completely out of the question until the punishment process is complete. If the "offense" was bad enough, reproof might or might not include a ban on going in service, and possibly even participating at the meetings by giving answers during the question-and-answer section.

Any baptized individual, including women, is subject to these rules. People who never got baptized won't be invited to events or befriended by other Jehovah's Witnesses. People are expected to keep their distance if somebody in the congregation has been reproved. Remember, every friend or family member you have is part of the religion. They aren't considered friends or family members if they aren't part of the religion.

Disfellowshipping happens when an offense occurs, but the judicial committee doesn't believe the person is repentant. In both cases, shunning takes place. The judicial committee's decision depends entirely on how well you can convince them you're sorry. Obviously, befriending the elders and their family members can be very valuable to a young Jehovah's Witness.

If there's wrongdoing, a "judicial committee"—a group of three elders—will investigate the situation and ask pointed questions about what happened. If they believe you're sorry, they'll reprove you. You'll be disfellowshipped if they don't think you're sincere in your repentance. However, reproval is also used for lesser offenses.

If you watch R-rated movies, you could be reproved but not necessarily disfellowshipped (unless there was nudity). If you were in a car alone with somebody of the opposite sex, no matter the circumstances, it's assumed you slept with the person. If you convince the committee that you didn't and repent for being alone with them, you might be reproved instead of disfellowshipped. Lying is a disfellowshipping offense. If it's a one-time thing that isn't very serious, it would warrant reproof rather than disfellowshipping.

If the offense worthy of reproof was very public, like describing an R-rated movie to everybody in the Kingdom Hall, an announcement would be made. Otherwise, it's kept private. Losing privileges alone would make it obvious to other Jehovah's Witnesses. Everybody would likely know exactly what happened. Gossip spreads like wildfire in Jehovah's Witness circles.

If they decide to make the reproof public, one of the three elders from the judicial committee convened to determine your guilt will stand up on stage during the public announcements section of the mid-week meeting and announce, "Owen Morgan has been reproved." The announcement is similar to disfellowshipping —"Owen Morgan is no longer one of Jehovah's Witnesses."

Each week, a section of the meeting is devoted to "local needs." Sometimes, the "local needs" talk follows the standard cookie-cutter outlines the Society provides. If somebody is being "disciplined," the elders will give a talk based on the outline about R-rated movies, wearing beards, being alone in a room or a car with somebody of the opposite sex, or a woman not respecting the "loving arrangement" of being considered inferior to the lowest-ranking male in the congregation, or any number of other things worthy of reproval. The elders don't even have to announce why the person was reproved. All the members must do is listen closely to the local needs talk.

When I was about 12, a woman named Liz was disfellow-shipped in my congregation. Before the meeting ended, I already knew why: she had cheated on her husband. It was even justified to me through whispers.

…He wasn't a Jehovah's Witness—she joined, and he didn't.

…He cheated on her, and in retaliation, she cheated on him. That's what he gets.

The justifications came from my mom, who got them from somebody else. They probably passed through my mom's filter. My dad had cheated several times, and she was still very bitter years later—understandably. My mom would never break a rule, but she was ready to jump on any bandwagon to defend somebody who got one over on a cheater. The whispers will be much more malicious and hateful if the person is viewed unfavorably.

Liz had a 14-year-old daughter and a 19-year-old niece at the same Kingdom Hall. Everybody wondered how her daughter and niece were managing to live with her without speaking to her. Family members are technically allowed to speak to disfellow-shipped family members if they live together. Culturally, though, the woman was viewed as diseased. The more you talk to her, the more disease rubs off on you. Though her children were completely innocent in the situation, they were viewed as tainted or diseased as a result of her actions. They had no choice but to speak to her, which meant it rubbed off on them, even if it was inadvertent.

She came to every meeting after that for six months, being shunned the entire time. Nobody looked at her. She sat in the back of the Kingdom Hall entirely alone. Nobody, not even her own family, would sit within six feet of her. That's part of the shunning process. The family isn't required to sit in another row of chairs. Still, they do it anyway to show their loyalty to the religion and decrease the blow to their own social status. After six months, which is unusually fast for a reinstatement, she had to write a letter describing her repentance and how badly she wanted to be a part of the organization again. She was reinstated shortly after that.

Reinstatement usually requires a year of attending every meeting, studying every magazine, and actively being shunned by everybody. There's one exception: the disfellowshipped person can communicate with a single elder—your handler—but only about the reinstatement process or repentance. The elder is typically one member of your judicial committee, if available.

My brother was disfellowshipped when I was about ten for having a relationship with a woman outside of the religion. He eventually tried to get reinstated when I was in my teens, but it just didn't happen for him. When I was young, I was told he wrote 11 letters. That probably isn't accurate. It's usually one letter every six months. Either way, they never reinstated him. He gave up after two years.

The process is different for markings. Marking is an uncommon practice in my experience. I've never seen a marking take place. Officially, markings are done for behavior that doesn't quite meet the level of disfellowshipping. In practice, they're done for the exact same reasons as reproof. If you watch an R-rated movie (without nudity), if you use words that might not be outright swears but are still vulgar, it could get you marked. When I was young, having a beard could also get you marked.

Some other reasons for marking are as follows: laziness, being critical, dirty, meddling, taking advantage of people, dating somebody when you aren't "scripturally" free to remarry, or dating a non-member of the religion. There's a difference between dating and sleeping with somebody. Sleeping with somebody outside of a scripturally free marriage will lead to disfellowshipping rather than marking. I imagine people have also probably been marked for having close friends who were not part of the religion. It's probably on a congregation-to-congregation basis if they choose reproval or marking. Unfortunately, marking is arguably far worse than being reproved. Disfellowshipping can be reversed with reinstatement, but there's no reversing a marking.

Different congregations have different cultural rules. Pokémon was okay to play in my congregation but not in others. Football or chess were okay in mine, but not in others. The reason is that they both started as military strategy games. Anything political or military-related is banned. It doesn't quite reach disfellowshipping territory since it's not direct military or political involvement. Doing any of those things could be worthy of a marking, though, if you find yourself in front of the wrong judicial committee. Additionally, you could be considered worthy of a marking or disfellowshipping if you were molested, raped, or otherwise sexually assaulted, and the judicial committee suspects (or can't decide if) you liked it or you didn't fight back hard enough.

Marking works similarly to reproof. It involves delivering a local needs talk on the specific problem at hand. In the case of sexual abuse, the talk would likely focus on modesty and premarital sex. No individual is named in the marking talk. The issue is simply discussed and flatly condemned, even though the things I listed aren't disfellowshipping offenses. Those aware of the wrongdoing should avoid associating with the person but can speak to them at the meetings.[1]

Marking is particularly sadistic because members aren't allowed to have friends outside the religion, which risks being marked. When a member is marked, their entire friend group no longer exists. Society effectively completely isolates a member except for at meetings. Presumably, the goal here is to force people to attend meetings to have some social interaction, any social interaction at all.

Disassociation isn't technically a punishment but deserves an explanation. It is the process of publicly announcing to the organization that you no longer want to be associated with Jehovah's Witnesses. This is typically done by handing a letter to local elders or mailing it to the headquarters. You are effectively disfellowshipping yourself. The punishment didn't always include shunning, but the Governing Body eventually added it.

HOW TO ESCAPE WITHOUT FACING CONSEQUENCES

Elders can't disfellowship based on conjecture or allegations. They must get proof, a confession, or solid evidence that something nefarious occurred. Disfellowshipping is much less likely if you don't talk to the elders.

However, they will absolutely follow you around for a while to see if they can catch you doing something questionable. If they see you smoking a cigarette or entering an establishment alone with somebody of the opposite sex, it's over. They have what they need to disfellowship you.

The "pastoral care" they offer rises to the level of harassment pretty quickly. If you're trying to escape the religion, here's my advice:

1. Transfer to another congregation.
2. Make up an excuse—tell them you're moving or something.

3. Ask them to transfer the publisher's card to the new Kingdom Hall.

4. Show your face at the new Kingdom Hall once, and never again. Just long enough for them to see you're a real person who really is in the area, but not long enough for them to memorize your face to recognize it if they see you around.

5. If elders try to contact you, don't answer. Ever.

The process I just described is called fading. It can sometimes allow you to preserve relationships with family members still in the religion. However, even though you haven't been disfellow-shipped, people in the congregation will absolutely start pre-shunning you if anyone notices what you're doing. Therefore, it's better to start building a friend group outside the religion sooner rather than later.

IS SHUNNING BIBLICAL?

Shunning is not Biblical. So, what's the basis for the Society's claim that the Bible supports shunning? A single, cherry-picked Bible verse:

I wrote to you in my letter not to associate with sexually immoral persons—not at all meaning the immoral of this world, or the greedy and robbers, or idolaters, since you would then need to go out of the world. 11 But now I am writing to you not to associate with anyone who bears the name of brother or sister who is sexually immoral or greedy, or is an idolater, reviler, drunkard, or robber. Do not even eat with such a one. For what have I to do with judging those outside? Is it not those who are inside that you are to judge? God will judge those outside. "Drive out the wicked person from among you."

This is the verse they use to justify their shunning policy. It seems clear at first glance. "Do not even dine with such a man." So, what's the context behind the verse? Knowing how Jehovah's Witnesses have manipulated historical context to suit their interests, it seems wise to look deeper.

When 1 Corinthians was written, Jesus had been dead for a while. The Christian church was slowly but surely growing. A man named Paul came along about three years after Jesus' death. He knew nothing about Jesus other than the few stories other people had told him. All he had to do was follow the culture of Christianity at the time. He posthumously named himself an apostle and started several Christian churches in the area throughout his life. He's also responsible for writing about seven New Testament books, though he's credited with writing 13.

The Corinthian congregation—that is to say, the Christian congregation in the city of Corinth—already existed before Paul came along. He caught wind that people in the Corinth congregation were openly discussing sleeping with prostitutes in church. One man also bragged about sleeping with his stepmother.[2] Paul worried that it would reflect poorly on Christianity at a critical moment in its formation, so he tried to stop it. He wrote a letter to the Corinthians and gave them a list of "wrongdoings" to root out the sin in the congregation. The Corinthians did just that—they followed Paul's instructions in 1 Corinthians 5:9–13. It didn't go well.

It's hard to shun somebody. Human beings are social creatures. We aren't supposed to cut connections like that. It hurt the people in the Corinthian congregation terribly. It was a miserable experience to cut off one of their closest friends and family members. The Corinthian congregation wrote a response letter to Paul and told him that they did what he instructed, but it was ugly and wrong. Nobody should have to do something like that. It brought people to the breaking point. Shunning was not helping the reputation of the early church.

In response, Paul sent another letter to the Corinthians and responded to their pleas to walk back the policy. In the second chapter of his next letter to the congregation, Paul said the following:

This punishment by the majority is enough for such a person; so now instead you should forgive and console him, so that he may not be overwhelmed by excessive sorrow. So I urge you to reaffirm your love for him. I wrote for this reason: to test you and to know whether you are obedient in everything. Anyone whom you forgive, I also forgive. What I have forgiven, if I have forgiven anything, has been for your sake in the presence of Christ. 11 And we do this so that we may not be outwitted by Satan; for we are not ignorant of his designs.

2 CORINTHIANS 2:6–10

Paul seemed to say, "That's it. It's too much, and I understand that. It's wrong to shun people. Reaffirm your love for him. This isn't a behavior we want to push. Disconnecting people from their family and friends isn't easy, natural, or right."

Additionally, Jesus never endorsed shunning. He didn't say a single word about it. If the Watchtower Society fancies themselves Christians, they should follow Christ's example. Jesus famously spoke to shunned people in the story of the Samaritan woman in John, Chapter 4.

Jehovah's Witnesses opposed shunning up to at least 1947. Their stance started to change in the early 1950s. The organization released an issue of one of their magazines, the Awake!, using

Hebrews 10:26–31 to condemn shunning. And—you guessed it—it's now considered apostate literature. Jehovah's Witnesses have been ordered to burn it if they find a copy. Thanks to the impeccable record-keepers among ex-members, we have a copy in digital form.[3] Let's look at a couple of lines in the Awake! magazine from 1947.

> If you are one of the 138,000,000 people in the world that were born and raised as "Protestants", then you are already excommunicated by the Roman Catholic Hierarchy. This means that you are looked upon with the blackest contempt by the Vatican, being cursed and damned with the Devil and his angels.
>
> JEHOVAH'S WITNESSES. *AWAKE!* JANUARY 8, 1947. P. 27

I couldn't have said it better myself. It's almost like they used Catholic excommunication as a model to institute within their own ranks. Keep reading.

> Where, then, did this practice originate? The Encyclopedia Britannica says that papal excommunication is not without pagan influence, and its variations cannot be adequately explained unless account be taken of several non-Christian analogues of excommunication.

I agree with their assessment in this 1947 article—shunning is wrong. The Bible simply does not endorse it. But even back then, Jehovah's Witnesses' fundamentalist, black-and-white view of everything led them to believe the right things for the wrong reasons.

Thereafter, as the pretensions of the Hierarchy increased, the weapon of excommunication became the instrument by which the clergy attained a combination of ecclesiastical power and secular tyranny that finds no parallel in history. Princes and potentates that opposed the dictates of the Vatican were speedily impales on the tines of ex-communication and hung over persecution fires.

Jehovah's Witnesses seem to recognize the sick power shunning has to ruin people's lives. Also, their interpretation of the word "pagan" appears to be extremely broad, once again.

SHUNNING OFFENSES

Let's talk about just a few of the reasons people are disfellow-shipped. This list is by no means comprehensive. The list also changes slightly from edition to edition of the elder's handbook. We'll discuss the most glaring and important ones here. Even if an item is removed from the list, it continues to warrant cultural shunning. Obscene speech was technically removed in the 2019 edition. Still, other Jehovah's Witnesses absolutely will not talk to you if you swear. A more comprehensive list can be found on jwfacts.com.

- Abortion
- Anal or oral sex (within or outside of marriage)
- Apostasy (being critical of the religion to any degree)
- Taking part in or encouraging prohibited celebrations (birthdays, Christmas, etc.)
- Receiving a blood transfusion
- Reviling—insulting speech/heaping abuse on somebody
- Obscene speech—swearing (removed in 2019)
- Extortion
- Adamant refusal to provide for one's family, physically or spiritually

- Fits of anger or violence
  - Boxing falls under the violence category and is specifically mentioned. No boxing under any circumstances. Even for fun.
- Blood guilt—ending a life, intentionally or otherwise; also includes blood transfusions.
- Violation of secular law—this only applies if there's a "flagrant attitude"—that's the description Jehovah's Witnesses use. However, violation in defense of the Watchtower Society is acceptable. Not your own defense, but for the Watchtower Society specifically.
- "Brazen conduct," or "loose conduct," which includes…
  - Associating with disfellowshipped person (with limited exceptions)
  - Criticizing a disfellowshipping decision
  - Child sexual abuse
  - Dating while not "legally or scripturally free to marry."
    - If you get legally divorced, you haven't been divorced in Jehovah's eyes. You will be disfellowshipped for bigamy if you remarry; not bigamy in a legal sense, but religious bigamy. This can also mean people who get married when they're only "spiritually separated" from their spouse for physical abuse, willful physical non-support, or spiritual non-support.
- Cybersex, phone sex, or sexting
- Fraud
- Porneia—the Greek word for a type of love. It roughly translates to "lust." This includes a lot, but a basic, rough, simplistic definition is looking at porn.
- Misuse of addictive drugs—prescribed medicine wasn't always okay, but now it is.

- Gambling—this includes working at a store where you sell lottery tickets. You can't participate in the gambling process in any way, even selling tickets as a store clerk.
- Greed
- Gluttony
- Homosexual activity—that could include the victim of a rape if the elders suspect or can't decide if the victim enjoyed it. Elders ask detailed questions to make that determination.
- Interfaith activity—that includes attending the funeral, wedding, or church service of a non-Jehovah's Witness. Even if it's your grandmother's funeral.
- Political activities: These include attending demonstrations or rallies of any sort and expressing an opinion not explicitly expressed by the Watchtower Society.
  - Subversive, antigovernment activity
  - Voting in political elections
  - Joining the military—no matter what, even if it's mandatory in your country.
- Spiritism—includes going to a tarot card reader, psychic, Reiki healer, or other forms of "false worship." It also includes certain types of psychology. Dream interpretation, for example, is absolutely forbidden. That's reserved for prophets of God, even in a psychological context.
- Theft
- The use of tobacco—that includes selling tobacco at a cash register, just like gambling

There are a few other disfellowshipping offenses that didn't make the cut. For example, disobeying the elders is forbidden under any circumstances. They are your leaders, and you must follow their instructions without asking questions. If they tell you to jump, you ask how high. If you refuse, it's a disfellowshipping offense because you're not respecting "the arrangement." "Rebellious attitudes" are a disfellowshipping offense.

Unlike Mormons, Jehovah's Witnesses tend to drink—a lot. Drunkenness is banned, but drinking alcohol is not. That line between tipsy and drunk gets a little blurry sometimes, especially after ten beers. Getting drunk will lead to disfellowshipping if it's discovered.

Jehovah's Witnesses commonly hold regular yearly events, such as talent shows and costume parties. On occasion, one family in my congregation hosted bonfires. When I was about 15 and already baptized, I remember sitting in front of the fire with a Jehovah's Witness who was completely drunk and unable to stand. He was the nephew of the family who hosted many of the events, though, so the incident was covered up and forgotten pretty quickly.

Abortion is banned even for life-saving treatment, even if it's the product of a rape, even if the entire head is missing, and even if it's an ectopic pregnancy. No excuses. These people are strictly anti-abortion at any cost. However, they don't have objections to birth control. Jehovah's Witnesses aren't necessarily encouraged to have children. I knew deeply devout Jehovah's Witnesses who believed the end was coming any five minutes, and they didn't want to bring a child into this sick world.

Jehovah's Witnesses have a section on their website which addresses birth control and family planning.

Jesus did not command his followers to have or not to have children. Neither did any of Jesus' disciples issue any such directive. Nowhere does the Bible explicitly condemn birth control. In this matter, the principle outlined at Romans 14:12 applies: "Each of us will render an account for himself to God."

Married couples, therefore, are free to decide for themselves whether they will raise a family or not. They may also decide how many children they will have and when they will have them. If a husband and wife choose to use a nonabortive[sic] form of contraception to avoid pregnancy, that is their personal decision and responsibility. No one should judge them. (Romans 14:4, 10–13)[4]

The word "non abortive" is doing some heavy lifting there. They were probably referring to Plan B birth control, which is not abortive. Most people think it is. It works by preventing an egg from attaching to the uterine wall. If the egg has already attached, it's too late. Plan B won't work. Either way, at least birth control is allowed. I do find it amusing that they're using the fact that Jesus didn't mention it as the basis for allowing birth control. They don't apply that same standard to blood transfusions, shunning, Birthday celebrations, Christmas, or any other banned practices.

Regarding forbidden sex positions, I once asked an older ex-Jehovah's Witness when and how this was communicated to young couples. Do they pull people aside before marriage and explain it to them? The answer is no; they don't pull you aside and explain it. However, as with everything, Jehovah's Witnesses want to know the limitations in any given situation. When couples get married, they go in search of the answers.

The answer to which positions are banned is basically all, except for regular old missionary. By and large, though, they seem to have a "don't ask, don't tell" policy. Don't ever talk about your sex life with anybody under any circumstances. That's day one, even if you have nothing to hide. Discussing it at all could "cause somebody to stumble" to have lust in their heart, which is a sin.

Since discussion of such a subject is so heavily regulated, Jehovah's Witnesses don't typically find themselves in a position to receive criticism or punishment for breaking a "sexual positions" rule. However, other sexual "sins" are commonly discussed and adjudicated, like homosexuality. Somebody can be gay, but sex outside of marriage is forbidden, and same-sex marriage is forbidden. Breaking one of those rules is a disfellowshipping offense.

Jehovah's Witnesses of the opposite sex and roughly similar ages are never permitted to be alone before marriage under any circumstances. If a Jehovah's Witness couple wants to go on a date, which is permissible only if you're seriously considering marriage, you must bring a chaperone. Generally, if a member is in the dating phase, the engagement phase is only a couple of months away. Being celibate through your late teens and early twenties is hard. Most people will look for the first opportunity to rectify the situation, even if that means marrying somebody you don't really know.

Kissing quickly on the lips in front of your chaperone is permissible if you're already engaged to be married. If a Jehovah's Witness couple is found to have crossed a line before they're married, the consequences range from bad to dire.

My family lived in Connecticut until I was about eight. When I was five, my sister, who was much older than me, started dating a Jehovah's Witness she met on the internet. He was from Texas. He visited Connecticut a few times to visit her, and they were married soon after. Their dating-to-marriage period might have lasted four months.

The wedding was scheduled to take place in Connecticut, and I was the ring bearer. For the week leading up to the wedding, my parents allowed her future husband, Tom, to stay in the finished basement of our house. Everybody found out they did questionable and unspeakable acts before the wedding. I have yet to learn what they did, but the elders decided they weren't allowed to have the wedding in the Kingdom Hall. They weren't disfellowshipped. It's not entirely unheard of, but it's extremely rare for somebody to decide of their own free will to have their wedding somewhere other than a Kingdom Hall. Everybody knows what will happen if you don't.

Some "sins" are considered more minor than others. For example, lying must be repeated and habitual to be worthy of shunning. It will likely be dealt with through a marking talk or reproof. The same standard applies to the broad category of "violence." It can lead to disfellowshipping if it's habitual and doesn't improve.

Some congregations have rules that aren't precisely disfellow-shipping offenses, but they're enough to be culturally shunned. For example, some congregations view Pokémon as spiritism. My congregation was mostly okay with Pokémon, but we didn't discuss it at the Kingdom Hall.

Spiritism also included reading the Harry Potter books in most congregations. Anything that contains magic, like Harry Potter or the card game Magic the Gathering, will warrant a marking, at minimum. Dungeons and Dragons is another banned game, even though a Jehovah's Witness created it. The degree of extremism within the congregation largely determines those examples.[5]

Even a child who commits one of these "sins"—even attending a parent or grandparent's funeral—will be shunned. If the child is shunned, regardless of the age, there are some expectations on the parents for how they're supposed to treat the child. If the disfellow-shipped person is an adult, which means over the age of 18, they will no longer be allowed to stay in the house.

Family communication is allowed in serious medical emergencies, though families usually choose not to inform shunned family members. If a family member is shunned, the person dealing with a medical emergency won't want to see or speak to them, even if they're on their deathbed.

There is only one unforgivable sin for Jehovah's Witnesses. They call it "grieving the Holy Spirit." It basically amounts to being an apostate after being baptized. If you were baptized, you know Jeho-vah's Witnesses are correct. You're only rejecting it because you want to make people as miserable as you are. It can be forgiven if the person rejoins the religion after being an apostate. It's only unforgivable when the person doesn't want forgiveness.

Some religious groups believe that suicide is an unforgivable sin. Not because it's any worse than adultery, for example, but because it's a form of murder. Murder can be forgiven, but suicide can't because repentance can't be shown after you're dead. Many denominations hold this belief—not just Catholics. To their credit, though, Jehovah's Witnesses tend to view suicide as the result of a mental condition.

In the eyes of the Watchtower Society, Jehovah will judge people's heart conditions when they die. If they weren't grieving the Holy Spirit, they would be forgiven. Families who lose somebody to suicide don't factor it into whether they'll see them again in paradise. They assume they'll see them again if they believe the person genuinely did their best.

POSITIONS ON LGBT ISSUES

Homosexuality has become culturally acceptable within the United States relatively recently. Jehovah's Witnesses began in the 19th century. Throughout the 20th century, sodomy laws have gradually been repealed within the United States, the home of the Watchtower Society. I assume Jehovah's Witnesses didn't feel the need to focus on it in their early years because it wasn't a primary focus in U.S. culture until the mid-20th and 21st centuries.

A video released by the Watchtower Society in May 2018 shows a woman shopping at what appears to be a clothing store. Standing in line holding a blanket, she glances around and notices that most people in the store are wearing rainbow wristbands. As she approaches the counter, the cashier holds out a rainbow wristband and says, "Should I put it in a bag, or do you want to wear it now?"

The situation as portrayed is already farfetched. The video showed support for the LGBT community as expected and mandatory. If they don't comply, there will be consequences. In reality, that's not how it works. Support for gay marriage has fluctuated over the years, but in 2022, U.S. support was at 71 percent overall.[6] By no stretch of the imagination has the gay community taken over or earned the respect and acceptance of society. This is one more example of a fabricated persecution complex at work.

After being offered the wristband, she responds, "No, thank you."

A simple response that everybody would have respected. Jehovah's Witnesses have to take it a step further, though. The scene continues as Woman 2, frustrated, glances over to the Jehovah's Witness (Woman 1), who just rejected the wristband.

Woman 2: "What's wrong, honey? You got something against them?"

Woman 1 looks around hesitantly, and after a few seconds, she responds: "Well, no, I—I don't have anything against them personally—"

The conversation would have ended here if it even got that far. Jehovah's Witnesses are desperate to make their members feel like they're under constant attack over their beliefs. In reality, nobody cares. If they keep to themselves and do their thing, nobody pays any attention to whether they're wearing an LGBT wristband.

Woman 2: "So, what's the problem?"

After a long pause, Woman 1 responds: "I respect that they have a right to choose their lifestyle, but as a Bible reader, I choose—"

She's cut off as Woman 2 explodes. "Excuse me," she says with violent undertones, "I'm a Bible reader, too. I go to church. And our church is one of the biggest supporters for this marathon. So what are you trying to say?"

The frame freezes as the camera zooms in on the victimized

Jehovah's Witness. She must decide whether to stand up for Jehovah or pretend she's uninvolved. As discussed previously, Jehovah's Witnesses are expected to tell the truth—no matter what. If she "rejected Jehovah" by avoiding a public confrontation in this case, there would be consequences. That is one of the gravest sins one can commit.

Members can omit information, twist the truth, or outright lie to protect the Watchtower Society. However, if they face danger personally, they must tell the truth, no matter the cost. This double standard costs people their lives without purpose.

Woman 1 sees other people walking by, staring at her. As the camera pans around her, an ethereal voice appears, as if she's looking in from the outside. She thinks, "Displaying courage now will help me display courage in the future..."

The camera unfreezes, and she says to Woman 2, "Well, I'm one of Jehovah's Witnesses, and we believe the Bible teaches sex is for a man and a woman who are married."

Woman 2 looks disgusted at her and responds, "Intolerant people."

Woman 1 takes her bag and leaves. The scene fades to elders sitting around a table discussing the incident. One elder says to another, "Wow. That sure took courage."

Jehovah's Witnesses claim that they don't have a problem with gay people. They just aren't gay themselves. Roughly 7 percent of any given population is part of the LGBT community.[7] They might be hiding it for fear of retribution, but there are definitely gay Jehovah's Witnesses.

"Homosexuality" is listed as a disfellowshipping offense within the religion. If somebody comes out as gay, they will try desperately to "deprogram" them from being gay in a process they call "putting on the new personality." The same process is used on transgender people. It's a poorly disguised conversion "therapy." There isn't much Jehovah's Witness literature on being trans, but the little bit of literature that does address the subject says that you were born in a specific body, and that body represents the gender with which you identify. Either live as the sex at your birth, or you'll be disfellowshipped.

"Putting on the new personality"[8] means you're taking on the Jehovah's Witness persona, which all Jehovah's Witnesses share. They're almost like clones of each other. They even talk similarly. Any ex-Jehovah's Witness will immediately recognize the cadence used from the stage.

When Jehovah's Witnesses are inevitably unsuccessful in their gay conversion technique of cramming their beliefs down people's throats, the person will eventually be disfellowshipped—if that wasn't the first step. That means losing everything: their family, their friends, and even their job in many cases. Jehovah's Witnesses do their best to integrate the religion into every part of your life.

I was disfellowshipped for trying a cigarette. Jehovah's Witnesses pulled the rug out from under me when I was disfellowshipped. They wanted to ensure the people at the Kingdom Hall, my fellow Jehovah's Witnesses, saw it happen. They took everything from me and hoped I'd have no option but to come crawling back at any cost.

Cooperating with the Scriptural arrangement to disfellowship and shun unrepentant wrongdoers is beneficial. It preserves the cleanness of the congregation and distinguishes us as upholders of the Bible's high moral standards. (1 Pet. 1:14–16) It protects us from corrupting influences. (Gal. 5:7–9) It also affords the wrongdoer an opportunity to benefit fully from the discipline received, which can help him to produce "peaceable fruit, namely, righteousness."

JEHOVAH'S WITNESSES. *KINGDOM MINISTRY.* AUGUST 2002. P. 3

Jehovah's Witnesses frame shunning as a benefit to the practice's victim. People lose everything and everybody that means something to them because the Governing Body members seem to want people to suffer to prevent others from leaving the religion. Talking to a disfellowshipped person is a disfellowshipping offense. "If you don't want to lose everything like he did, don't talk to him, or you'll be in the same boat."

Now tell me again, who is persecuting whom? Jehovah's Witnesses are free to live their lives the way they please. They aren't harassed or bothered by society in any way until they conflict with society's laws. If they want to isolate themselves, that's their right. Nobody will twist their arm and force them if they don't want to go to a restaurant with coworkers after work. It's important to note that there's a difference between criticism and persecution. This book is not an attempt at mockery or persecution. It is criticism, plain and simple.

Jehovah's Witnesses, on the other hand, absolutely will twist people's arms and force them to behave exactly as they expect. The consequences for not doing so are dire and permanent. Jehovah's Witnesses' methods of forcing compliance cause lasting mental damage and lead to suicide entirely too often, including but not limited to Governing Body member Stephen Lett's own nephew.

Stephen Lett's nephew came out as gay and was shunned by friends and family, as was expected. The boy committed suicide because of what he lost. There was no apology for what they'd done. Stephen Lett didn't even appear to show sorrow over the situation—not publicly, at least. This is what the Watchtower Society does to people. They do it intentionally as a lesson to those around them. It's unacceptable and must be condemned.

ANTI-GAY LITERATURE

The article on the Jehovah's Witnesses website titled "I'm Attracted to the Same Sex—Does That Mean I'm Gay?" Gives some fascinating insight into the mindset of the Watchtower Society. Here's how the article opens:

> I'm Attracted to the Same Sex—Does That Mean I'm Gay?
>
> Not at all!
>
> Fact: In many cases, same-sex attraction is nothing more than a passing phase.
>
> That's what Lisette, 16, who was at one time attracted to a girl, found.[9]

I must say, I can't help but laugh at the absurdity. The last paragraph of the article clearly lays out the position.

> The Bible's stand is not unreasonable. It simply directs those with homosexual urges to do the same thing that is required of those with an opposite-sex attraction—to "flee from fornication." The fact is that millions of heterosexuals who wish to conform to the Bible's standards employ self-control despite any temptations they might face. Those with homosexual inclinations can do the same if they truly want to please God.

The Watchtower Society has produced a weirdly large amount of material on the subject. Jehovah's Witnesses have a book series titled "Young People Ask: Answers That Work." In the 1990s, they tried to make a video about it, but it felt like an anti-drug PSA. I reviewed the series on my "Owen Unfiltered" YouTube channel in 2023.

Young Jehovah's Witnesses are commonly withheld from sex education classes. The religion doesn't want children learning their sex education from the world. They have an alternative to sex education: the Young People Ask book, or the YPA book for short. The predecessor to the YPA book was red, titled "Your Youth: Getting the Best Out of It." The Youth book was from the 1970s and contained deeply bizarre doctrine. Take a look at this quote from the Youth book:[10]

In fact, masturbation can lead to homosexuality. In such instances the person, not satisfied with his lonely sexual activity, seeks a partner for mutual sex play. This happens much more frequently than you may realize. Contrary to what many people think, homosexuals are not born that way, but their homosexual behavior is learned. And often a person gets started when very young by playing with another's sexual parts, and then engaging in homosexual acts.

JEHOVAH'S WITNESSES. *YOUR YOUTH: GETTING THE BEST OUT OF IT.* 1976. P. 39

According to this book, touching yourself can turn you gay. Of course, that's complete nonsense. People don't learn to be gay. If learning to be gay was an option, then anybody could do it.

They published an article about the subject in their 1995 *Awake!* Magazine. It seems to contradict their stance on the issue from 1976.

A youth who desires to please God must therefore conform to His moral standards and shun immoral behavior, though doing so may be agonizingly difficult. True, some individuals may very well be prone to homosexuality, just as some individuals are, according to the Bible, "prone to wrath." (Titus 1:7) But the Bible still condemns displays of unrighteous anger. (Ephesians 4:31) Similarly, a Christian cannot excuse immoral behavior by saying he was "born that way." Child molesters invoke the same pathetic excuse when they say their craving for children is "innate." But can anyone deny that their sexual appetite is perverted? So is the desire for someone of the same sex.

> JEHOVAH'S WITNESSES. "WHY DO I HAVE
> THESE FEELINGS?" *AWAKE!* FEBRUARY 8,
> 1995. P. 16

Apparently, some people *are* born gay. It's irrelevant, though, because it's like being a child molester in Jehovah's Witnesses' eyes. Child molestation does real psychological damage to somebody incapable of offering consent with a complete understanding of the consequences. Being gay doesn't affect anybody negatively in any way.

The last article should make their position clear. They view the LGBT community the same way they view child molesters. At best, they pity them for having a damaged brain. At worst, they view them as mentally diseased, borderline inhuman monsters who God will take out in the end. Jehovah's Witnesses dodge criticism for their position on the LGBT community by saying that they "love everybody." They just want everybody to make it through Armageddon. Paragraphs like these can be scattered throughout their literature, even today.

This next article is from 2023. I doubt every "personal story" they tell in their books because they tend to look for statistical anomalies to back up an already-existing belief—if the story is even real.

Some even try to bully our young ones into breaking their loyalty to Jehovah. Note, for example, what happened to a young man named Graeme, who lives in Australia. He faced a challenging situation when he attended high school. The teacher asked the class how they would react if a friend confided in them about being a homosexual. The teacher said that all in the class who would support a friend in pursuing such a lifestyle must stand on one side of the room; those who would not, on the other side. Graeme says, "The entire class stood on the side that supported that lifestyle except for me and another Witness." What happened next was a real test of Graeme's loyalty to Jehovah. "For the rest of the hour-long class," he says, "the other students and even the teacher taunted and insulted us. I did my best to defend my faith in a calm and reasonable way, but they didn't listen to a word I said." What effect did this test of loyalty have on Graeme? He says, "I did not like being the target of such verbal attacks, but I felt incredibly happy that I was able to defend my beliefs without compromise."

JEHOVAH'S WITNESSES. THE WATCHTOWER. AUGUST, 2023. P. 6

Jehovah's Witnesses are, by no stretch of the imagination, the only religious group that has it out for the LGBT community. This perfectly represents the Jehovah's Witness mindset on this and many other subjects. Persecute other people, and when you're criticized for it, pretend that you're the one being persecuted. It's a template that they've applied to countless other issues.

Does it seem like Jesus hated gay people? If he didn't say a word about being gay, then why does a denomination of *Christianity* like Jehovah's Witnesses drive gay kids to commit suicide, as it did to Stephen Lett's nephew? Is that doing right by "the least of [Jesus'] family?" (Matthew 25:40) Disturbingly, Jehovah's Witnesses even shun children. You read that correctly—they shun children. Let's talk about the logistics.

HOW TO SHUN A CHILD

Jehovah's Witnesses mandate that their members shun people who have been disfellowshipped. Age is not a function of this rule. If a person swore allegiance to the organization and backed out of that agreement, even at 12 years old, they should be shunned. If a child is shunned, regardless of age, there are some expectations on the parents for how they're supposed to treat the child.

First, the parents are not permitted to eat dinner with the child. The child will eat dinner in another room. That rule refers to the first letter to the Corinthian congregation about "not even eating with such a man." Second, they will not discuss anything considered critical of the religion. They'll keep general communication to a minimum.

In my experience, the parents will attempt to get rid of the kid. If they're lucky, a non-Jehovah's Witness aunt or uncle will take them in. This isn't mandated, but I'm sure I've already made it clear that the culture reigns supreme in this religion. If the disfellowshipped person is an adult, which means over the age of 18, they will no longer be allowed to stay in the house. That's a mandate from the Watchtower Society.3 Disobeying the mandate will get the parents disfellowshipped. Elders will be checking in to make sure instructions are followed. Sometimes, they'll even show up randomly to see if the kid is there.

Many churches have special programs for children. When I left Jehovah's Witnesses and found a new family who took me in, I went to their Methodist church with them. Some Methodist churches can be extreme, but this church wasn't. During services, adults would sit upstairs in the pews. Children would go to the basement area and play church-related games with a couple of church leaders. That got children excited about church. Jehovah's Witnesses have no such program.

Children sit in the main hall with everybody else. Babies, five-year-olds, teenagers, and everybody in between are expected to sit perfectly silent for two hours. I didn't understand a word that was said until I was about 12. It isn't dumbed down to be understandable by children—the talks are designed for adults. This religion simply isn't designed for children. When they get fidgety or difficult, the children are blamed. Falling asleep is deeply frowned upon, even for young children. My dad drew mustaches on our faces when we fell asleep once. We thought it was funny until the elders threatened him with punishment.

Not only are the services not designed for children, but nothing else is, either. The religion sets up a pseudo-government that hinges on something called the Two Witness Rule. The rule relies on everybody within the religion to be competent, obedient, and agree with everything happening. If they disagree, they shouldn't be a part of the religion. As a result of this fundamentally flawed perspective, children have been terribly mistreated in the organization. The Two Witness rule has led to countless lawsuits against the Watchtower Society for gross incompetence. The following chapter will cover the Two Witness rule in more detail.

SHUNNING ADULTS

The anti-outsider doctrine even manifests in the jobs chosen by members. The Watchtower Society heavily discourages college education, so Jehovah's Witnesses commonly get into trade jobs like carpentry or plumbing. Oddly, Jehovah's Witnesses regularly become window cleaners.

It's common for a single person in a congregation to own a window cleaning or plumbing company and employ most of the congregation. In my congregation, it was computer repair. My family had been involved in the industry since before I was born, independent of Jehovah's Witnesses.

My dad was a computer repairman throughout the 1990s. The

computer repair shop shut down after he got in a car accident, and we moved to West Virginia when I was eight. My interest in computers, however, did not. I learned every programming language I could from ages nine to eighteen. It was my passion. I bought large, thousand-page books about C, C++, Java, PHP, and other languages. The point is that I was qualified to work in the industry. Even at a young age, I might have been more knowledgeable than anybody in my congregation.

A family in my congregation installed just about every cash register and POS system within a 15-mile radius. They employed many Jehovah's Witnesses. If I hadn't been disfellowshipped, they certainly would have hired me.

It's probably illegal for them to reject my application for religious reasons, but who will challenge that? It would be miserable to work with people who absolutely detest you. On top of that, most people who leave the religion, like me, feel like they deserve that treatment.

A big part of the punishment when Jehovah's Witnesses leave the religion isn't just losing friends and family—it's losing your job, too. It's often the only marketable skill a person has. Jehovah's Witnesses commonly dominate a niche industry in the area. Good luck breaking into the plumbing, computer repair, carpentry, or window cleaning business after being disfellowshipped. The degree to which the religion ruins members' lives after they exit cannot be overstated.

RUSSIA BAN: THE REASONING

Shunning is a mandate. They must shun ex-members and apostates. If they don't, they'll also be disfellowshipped. That hardline stance has led to problems around the world. Jehovah's Witnesses were banned as an extremist organization in Russia, and they had their status as a religion removed in Norway.

In April 2017, Jehovah's Witnesses were banned from Russia. The move was denounced by the United Nations and a variety of human rights organizations, raising Jehovah's Witnesses' public profile in the process. It's a controversial subject among ex-Jehovah's Witnesses, but generally, I disagree with banning a religion outright in that way.

A case moved through Russian courts that was set to determine whether Jehovah's Witnesses are an extremist organization. During the court case, quotes directly from the Watchtower Society were presented, including an excerpt from a 2011 issue of Watchtower. The word "apostate" literally means runaway slave. The Watchtower Society is using it, though, to refer to anybody critical of the religion—anybody, and to any degree.

The Bible says that apostates are *mentally diseased* and that they use their teachings to make others think like them. (1 Timothy 6:3, 4) Jehovah is like that good doctor. He clearly tells us to stay away from false teachers. We must always be determined to follow his warning.

What must we do to avoid false teachers? We do not speak to them or invite them into our houses. We also do not read their books, watch them on television, read what they write on the Internet, or add our own comments about what they write on the Internet. Why are we so determined to avoid them? First of all, it is because we love "the God of truth." So we do not want to listen to false teachings that go against the truth in God's Word.

JEHOVAH'S WITNESSES. *THE WATCHTOWER 2011, STUDY ED. (SIMPLIFIED).* JULY 15, 2022.
P. 11

This Watchtower can still be found on their website. The quote perfectly outlines how they feel about apostates. They view people critical of the religion as mentally diseased. That means me, and that means you. Having read this book, you are now considered mentally diseased.

Ex-Jehovah's Witnesses already know how Jehovah's Witnesses view outsiders and apostates. It was culturally built into us from a young age. Even outsiders who are not apostates are viewed as dirty and disgusting. I wouldn't even want to hug an outsider, fearing something would grow on me. The Watchtower Society didn't have to tell me to feel that way; it was programmed into me by my family when I was young. Seeing it in print, though, gives the rest of the world a glimpse into the mindset.

Russia's court decided to ban Jehovah's Witnesses for quotes like that. They labeled them an extremist organization. They're allowed to believe it, but they can't meet at a Kingdom Hall and pass their literature around to each other.

I don't agree with the ban, but I agree with the reasoning. Just as we wouldn't accept it if the Catholic church started strapping people to tables and cutting their hearts out as a sacrifice to god, other religions must also respect laws and rights. Jehovah's Witnesses mandating their members to avoid speaking to ex-Jehovah's Witnesses is a violation of human rights and a blight on society. It's simply unacceptable.

In my opinion, the solution is to fine the organization until everything it owns belongs to the government and continue fining it for each violation. In my ideal scenario, the company won't exist within the country anymore—not because it's been banned, but because it's gone bankrupt from all the human rights abuses. Let the company crumble each time it disfellowships and shuns somebody. If Jehovah's Witnesses want to meet in each other's homes to discuss their beliefs, be my guest.

The government should exist to protect people's rights. Everybody should be equal. In my opinion, religions shouldn't receive benefits unless they respect people's UN-recognized human rights —namely, Articles 18 and 20.

> Everyone has the right to freedom of thought, conscience and religion; this right includes freedom to change his religion or belief, and freedom, either alone or in community with others and in public or private, to manifest his religion or belief in teaching, practice, worship and observance.
>
> *UN DECLARATION OF HUMAN RIGHTS.*
> ARTICLE 18.

> Everyone has the right to freedom of peaceful assembly and association.
>
> No one may be compelled to belong to an association.
>
> *UN DECLARATION OF HUMAN RIGHTS.*
> ARTICLE 20.

No one may be compelled to belong to an association. By shunning anyone who criticizes the group to any degree, the group punishes anyone who leaves the religion, compelling them to belong to the association.

RUSSIA BAN: THE FALLOUT

When Russia banned Jehovah's Witnesses, there was a full-blown effort to suppress them. They were treated like an international drug network trying to smuggle drugs rather than copies of the *Watchtower*. Suffice it to say Russia genuinely persecuted Jehovah's Witnesses. They now have martyrs to plaster all over their monthly TV program, JW Broadcasting.

There's a famous image of a Russian elder being arrested for spreading extremist material. He assisted in the distribution of *The Watchtower*. As he was arrested, he had a gigantic grin on his face. He knew what it meant. It meant Jehovah's Witnesses were right all along. They really were on their way to persecution, and that means the end is closer than ever before.

In 2016, Jehovah's Witnesses dramatized what the Great Tribulation would be like. It's commonly called "the Bunker Video." The video portrays characters sitting around a table in an unfinished basement—on the floor, beanbag chairs, anywhere they could fit—telling stories about being Jehovah's Witnesses.

A woman says, "When I think how far we are now into the—" Just then, somebody outside knocks slowly three times. One of the people inside the basement stands up and approaches the door. He looks to the oldest person around the table for confirmation, and the man nods his approval. The man slowly knocks twice in response to the set of three knocks. The person on the outside finally gives one singular knock, and the door opens. A Jehovah's Witness family with young children walks in.

They're asked by one of the other young men, "How is it out there?"

The father, who just walked in with his children, replies, "Not good. It won't be long—maybe an hour." The young man says, "Is —is Kevin with you?" The father replies, "He said he's not coming." He looks grim. A look of fear and sorrow flashes across his face. "...that he doesn't want to have anything to do with us anymore."

Everybody in the basement, particularly the young man who asked about him, is filled with deep sorrow. The young man closes his eyes for a moment in disbelief. Despite the deep shock and pain he feels at having lost Kevin, he stands resolute, more determined now than ever to continue on the path that destiny—or Jehovah— has laid for him.

As the young man looks to the side, knowing he will likely never see Kevin again, another older man replies, "How sad—now —this far into the Great Tribulation."

A look of trepidation passes each person's face. The worry lines clearly show on every face in the room—even the youngest among them. The looks on the faces of the young children send a clear message: Somebody has explained to them exactly what's about to happen. They're going to be arrested or killed.

That's a rough approximation of the events portrayed in a video colloquially known as "the Bunker Video." The Watchtower Society hasn't come out and said the Great Tribulation has begun, but every time there's some serious persecution, real or otherwise, the news spreads like wildfire.

Everything portrayed in the bunker video was or is happening in Russia. Jehovah's Witnesses are desperate for the end—they'll take any sign they can get. Russia helped further that persecution complex. The video acted as fear porn for the members. It gets them amped up and ready to do anything—literally anything—that the Governing Body asks of them. Russia's ban made it that much harder for ex-Jehovah's Witnesses like myself to call it what it is. It's simply propaganda designed to get people into a heightened state of perpetual fear and, therefore, perpetual subservience to the religion's leaders.

THE NORWAY BAN

Norway's conflict with the Watchtower Society was similar to Russia's, but Norway handled it much more satisfactorily. Their complaint was the same: They violated human rights by forcing members not to speak to ex-members.

Jehovah's Witnesses were disqualified as a religion in Norway. The country gives a government subsidy to groups that qualify as religions. The amount they get is proportional to the number of members they have. They didn't ban Jehovah's Witnesses from practicing their faith in the country. They simply disbanded their status as a religion. The company was allowed to continue running as it was before. There is no difference except now that they aren't considered a religion; they don't get government subsidies and must have another official perform their wedding ceremonies.

This is a win-win solution. If I were Norway, though, I would take it one step further. I'm glad they've disbanded the company's status as a religion, but I want to see the company fall to pieces. Again, if individuals want to meet in their homes, they're free to do so. Until the religion complies and stops violating people's rights, they should slowly lose absolutely every asset they own.

Jehovah's Witnesses argued that shunning is not part of their official doctrine in court. If their members individually choose to shun their friends and family, then it's because they want to. That is, of course, a blatant lie. One look at their elder's handbook reveals that socializing with disfellowshipped people or apostates is strictly forbidden and is a disfellowshipping offense. Not to mention all the material they release to the public. Videos, magazines, and public talks regularly address relationships with disfellowshipped people.

Such a glaring, blatant lie is hard to overlook. It's deeply disturbing that an organization can convince its members to lie to defend The Watchtower Society as their lawyers did in open court, but not in the members' own defense. How does the Governing Body justify lying so glaringly? They do it with the doctrine of theocratic warfare.

LYING FOR JESUS

Theocratic warfare is a concept not often openly discussed among Jehovah's Witnesses. The idea behind the doctrine is that anything is justified in service of Jehovah. The leadership is allowed to lie, cheat, or manipulate. As I'm sure you can guess, the line between Jehovah's desires and the Watchtower Society's desires gets a little blurry.

The Watchtower Society's desires don't coincide with God's desires, as they seem to believe. The situation is reversed. The Watchtower Society projects their desires and interests onto God. I haven't done my job if I haven't proven that up to this point.

Here's a quote regarding theocratic warfare from a 2004 issue of the *Watchtower:*

> The faithful witness does not commit perjury when testifying. His testimony is not tainted with lies. However, this does not mean that he is under obligation to give full information to those who may want to bring harm to Jehovah's people in some way. The patriarchs Abraham and Isaac withheld facts from some who did not worship Jehovah.
>
> JEHOVAH'S WITNESSES. *THE WATCHTOWER.*
> NOVEMBER 15, 2004. P. 28

The philosopher Kant famously believed there was no good reason to lie under any circumstances. He believed that even a lie to protect somebody's life could have unforeseen results, so the only correct choice is not to lie at all. Obviously, a rigid, black-and-white view such as this is not reasonable or logical.

There are some situations in which people should lie. For example, if Nazi soldiers come to your door and demand you turn over the names of any Jews you know, the moral thing would be to tell them you don't know any Jews. Protecting lives is a perfectly reasonable justification for a lie.

Jehovah's Witnesses are held to a very high "moral" standard—if one could call it moral. Within their moral framework, you can rely on a Jehovah's Witness to be completely honest and trustworthy. You could leave your wallet on a counter before them, and it's very unlikely they'd take anything from it. They're mandated to follow their moral system and will not break from it no matter what —even unto death.

That being said, a deep hypocrisy runs through this entire subject. The deeper you dig, the clearer it becomes that the Watchtower Society expects Jehovah's Witnesses to lie to protect the Watchtower Society—not themselves. In fact, protecting themselves with a lie is a disfellowshipping offense—even a lie of omission.

I've had to deal with theocratic warfare personally. My mother and I don't speak anymore since I'm an apostate. My mother was in my life exactly long enough to spend time with her grandchild. She drew a line beyond that. I allowed it because I thought it was good for a grandchild to know their grandmother. I set only one rule: don't discuss Jehovah's Witnesses with them.

My mother couldn't handle the simple task of keeping her religion to herself. However, she lied to me and claimed she didn't bring it up. I knew that was patently false when my kid came home talking about getting baptized as a Jehovah's Witness.

Lying is a mandate if it means following the instructions of the Watchtower Society. If Jehovah's Witnesses are willing to blatantly lie for something as simple as attempting to brainwash kids in their care, what else are they willing to lie about? The answer is likely absolutely anything if the Watchtower Society instructed them to.

Theocratic warfare uniquely applies to apostates. Jehovah's Witnesses assume that apostates are going to twist anything they say to hurt Jehovah, or more accurately, to hurt the Society. For that reason, they're barred from speaking to them at all. No exceptions.

Governments around the world have complaints about Jehovah's Witnesses, not just Norway and Russia. Australia launched an investigation against the group, the Australian Royal Commission, to determine their degree of culpability in child sexual abuse cases. To nobody's surprise, he lied when Governing Body member

Geoffrey Jackson sat in front of the ARC to testify. He lied blatantly. He lied through his teeth. He didn't just twist the truth a little bit; he fabricated information and pretended it was real. It was all justified under the banner of theocratic warfare.

Chillingly, he was lying to protect the organization from being forced to make changes to protect children from sexual abuse. The root of the problem lies with the Two Witness Rule. It's a rule that exists as a means of creating a pseudo-government that can step in and maintain civil order when the world governments inevitably crumble. Unfortunately, it doesn't work in practice.

The Two Witness Rule has led to countless loopholes being exploited. The religion has had to pay massive amounts of money to people who were wronged by its handling of their situation.

CHAPTER 7

THE TWO WITNESS RULE

JEHOVAH'S WITNESSES' "PASTORAL CARE"

t's difficult to pinpoint when the Two Witness Rule officially started. In the 1960s, under Nathan Knorr's leadership, the Watchtower Society began pushing people to report crimes to the elders rather than the police.[1] That wasn't the start of the Two Witness Rule, but it was the prerequisite for a terrible, deadly loophole. As of the 1960s, countless people have been turned away or ignored after being abused because of this set of doctrines.

It was deeply frowned upon to bring secular authorities into what Jehovah's Witnesses viewed as their business. They feared it would "bring reproach on Jehovah's name." That means it would make the organization look bad to have child abusers reported to the police. I guess they'd rather give the abuser a free license to continue abusing completely undeterred.

By 1991, the end of Fred Franz's presidency, the Two Witness Rule was in full effect. Not only were members discouraged from going to the police, but elders were also barred from going to the police in some cases. Jehovah's Witnesses had set up their own pseudo-government.

Jehovah's Witnesses are convinced they've got everything worked out to care for everybody independent of the U.S. government. However, the structure of their pseudo-government is honestly absurd. It would fall flat within a week if it were really tested.

From time to time, elders might set up a shepherding call. A shepherding call happens when they notice that a family isn't attending as many meetings as they should be—which is all of them—or they aren't going in service as regularly as expected. The elders might also do a shepherding call if they suspect something questionable is happening in the household. That could be any number of things or nothing at all, and it's entirely up to the elders on an as-needed basis. Two elders perform shepherding calls. If they learn something damning on their visit, there are two witnesses there to attest to what they heard. The Two Witness Rule is the cornerstone of their pseudo-government.

Some reasons for shepherding calls might include a suspicion that the person or people in the household are communicating with disfellowshipped family members—that's a disfellowshipping offense. Maybe they suspect the person is going to see R-rated movies, or they think the person drinks too much alcohol. Two elders—NOT a judicial committee of three elders—will show up to the house and knock. The person is not obligated to let the elders in or to say anything to them. If they turn the elders away without saying a word or they don't answer at all, the elders will have no choice but to ... go home and do nothing about it. No consequences will be enacted against the person unless the elders can prove wrongdoing, typically in the form of a confession given to at least two witnesses. If no proof is forthcoming, an accusation, up to and including an allegation of child sexual abuse, is ignored.

The same goes for judicial committees. A judicial committee is a group of three elders who convene to discuss whether a member should be disfellowshipped, reproved, or marked. However, the committee is required to talk to the member before disfellowshipping happens. In some extreme cases where somebody's guilt is apparent, they can be disfellowshipped without establishing communication.

As nominal pastors, congregational elders act as police, therapists, judges, and more. That's intentional. The elders in each congregation should be capable of acting as a full-blown stand-in government when the actual government falls to pieces or outside forces shatter the Jehovah's Witness hierarchy during the Great Tribulation, which is the period directly before Armageddon.

The problem with Jehovah's Witnesses' stand-in government is that elders aren't therapists, police, investigators, or judges. They're plumbers and window cleaners. They aren't paid for this position. It's entirely on a volunteer basis. So when a six-year-old girl comes to her mother to tell her that somebody in the congregation is sexually abusing her, the first step Jehovah's Witnesses are supposed to take is to call…the elders. Not the police, the elders. Why? Because the internal culture of the religion is one where there's an autonomous government in place, every problem somebody has should go through the elders.

After finding out about an accusation of sexual abuse, the elders' next step is to call…the Service Department. The Service Department is in control of appointing or deleting elders, managing inter-congregation issues, and handling legal problems. The Service Department will let the elders in the congregation know if they should call the police, but the form they have to fill out has questions about the reputability and age of the accuser. Does the elder believe the accuser is telling the truth? Has there been an opportunity or a reason to think this took place? As you can see, they fancy themselves little investigators.

Are the parents barred from calling the police? No. Are the

elders barred from calling the police? That one is complicated. Technically, they were, until speaking to the Service Department at a minimum. For the sake of argument, let's assume nobody is barred from calling the police under any circumstances. It doesn't matter because the internal culture forces them to handle things internally. Elders will even investigate wrongdoing, driving around in their cars and spying on people. Joe, the plumber, finishes replacing a pipe fitting, gets in his car, and goes down to John's house to watch and see if Joe's girlfriend shows up to be alone with John. That alone is grounds for shunning. Not the act of having sex with somebody else but being in a room alone when you could have feasibly had sex with them. The reason? The elder who sat at John's house isn't personally in the house and doesn't know what they did. The assumption is that he did something he shouldn't have done. As you'll see, the same standard is not applied to certain "sins" like child abuse. The accused's guilt is assumed if they're in a room alone with an adult. If they're alone in a room with a child and an accusation arises, innocence is presumed until proven other-wise. Until then, it's swept under the rug.

The point is that the leadership rarely says anything outright. They don't have to. They guide culture in the right direction, and the membership does it without them having to say a word.

Unfortunately, in most cases and with few exceptions, Jehovah's Witnesses apply the Two Witness Rule. The rule derives from bible verses about how the ancient world should handle legal matters—between 2,000 and 5,000 years ago. You know, before DNA tests, cameras, or rape kits existed, during a time when the ability to read and write was limited to about ten percent of the world's population.

> No single witness may convict another for any error or any sin that he may commit. On the testimony of two witnesses or on the testi-mony of three witnesses the matter should be established.

DEUTERONOMY 19:15

Moreover, if your brother commits a sin, go lay bare his fault between you and him alone. If he listens to you, you have gained your brother. But if he does not listen, take along with you one or two more, in order that at the mouth of two or three witnesses every matter may be established.

MATTHEW 18:15–16

On the testimony of two or three witnesses every matter must be established.

CORINTHIANS 13:1

When these verses were written, religion and law were inextricably linked. The Old Testament law dictated how these people were supposed to live, and it was harshly enforced, though it was never intended to apply to serious crimes.

If you make a deal with somebody and agree to buy a donkey from them, you go to two scribes and ask them to witness the transaction. If there aren't two people to witness the transaction, it's like it never happened. The reasoning here is that 90 percent of the ancient world, even around the time of the New Testament, were illiterate; they didn't know how to read OR write—the two were not as ubiquitous as they are today. Many people didn't even know how to write their own names, let alone an entire contract.

Scribes were like ancient librarians. They reviewed agreements, read the law, and made copies of books—remember, they didn't have a printing press yet. If a copy of something existed, somebody meticulously copied it by hand, word by word.

The Bible is pretty clear about the difference between civil and criminal matters. Deuteronomy clearly states that the two-witness rule should not be used for serious crimes.

> If, however, the man happened to meet the engaged girl in the field and the man overpowered her and lay down with her, the man who lay down with her is to die by himself, and you must do nothing to the girl. The girl has not committed a sin deserving of death. This case is the same as when a man attacks his fellow man and murders him. For he happened to meet her in the field, and the engaged girl screamed, but there was no one to rescue her.
>
> *DEUTERONOMY 22:25–27*

The Bible says criminal matters should not be adjudicated using the Two Witness Rule. Despite that fact, Jehovah's Witnesses insist on using the Two Witness Rule for sexual assault, rape, child sexual abuse cases, and a variety of other serious crimes.

Elders were instructed to report every single accusation of child sexual abuse to the Society. They're supposed to describe the situation to the Service Department by phone. If there's an accusation, the Service Department will look up the accused's history in their database and tell the elders what they need to know about the situation. That means there's a list floating around. The loophole was being exploited so much that the religion has faced an endless barrage of lawsuits and lost many of them. They've paid out hundreds of millions of dollars in lawsuits for the way they mishandled these cases.

On March 14, 1997, the Watchtower Society sent a letter to the elders of each congregation. Here's what it said on page 2:[2]

> If, after contacting the Society, it is determined that the elders should report a matter such as child abuse to the authorities, it would not be a breach of confidentiality to make such a report.

Elders should always contact the Society before providing any information on confidential matters to secular authorities.

JEHOVAH'S WITNESSES. *LETTER TO ELDERS.*

MARCH 14, 1997. P. 2

Not only was it part of the culture to avoid contacting authorities, but the Watchtower Society also specifically mandated it. Do *not* contact the police unless we tell you otherwise.

Much of this information was given to the public by Barbara Anderson, the head researcher in Bethel, in the 1990s. She saw the effects of the Two Witness Rule and was disturbed. When she started to push back against the rule, the Watchtower Society disfellowshipped her and her husband. She was disfellowshipped for slandering the organization, and he was disfellowshipped for being unable to control his wife.[3] She paid a high price for the information she provided. She lost contact with her son after being disfellowshipped. In exchange for her suffering, though, there's no telling how many lives she saved.

After a litany of lost lawsuits and public outrage from multiple governments, the Watchtower Society finally released an update to its *Elder's Manual* in 2010. Unfortunately, the updated version of the book's section on child sexual abuse is nearly indistinguishable from its previous version. I guess they decided it wasn't worth addressing despite the lawsuits. The following are quotes from the 2010 edition of the *Elder's Manual*.

There must be two or three eyewitnesses, not just people repeating hearsay; no action can taken if there only one witness.

...

If the accused denies the accusation, the investigating elders should try to arrange a meeting with him and the accuser together. (Note: If the accusation involves child sexual abuse and the victim is currently a minor, the elders should contact the branch office before arranging a meeting with the child and the alleged abuser.) If the accuser or the accused is unwilling to meet with the elders or if the accused continues to deny the accusation of a single witness and the wrongdoing is not established, the elders will leave matters in Jehovah's hands. (Deut.19:15–17; 1 Tim 5:19, 24, 25; w95 11/1 pp. 28–29) The investigating elders should compose a record, sign it, put it in a sealed envelope, and place it in the congregations confidential file. Additional evidence may later come to light to establish matters.

JEHOVAH' WITNESES. SHEPHERD THE
FLOCK OF GOD. 2010. PP. 71–72

That line about leaving it in Jehovah's hands means you do nothing. Let God handle it. And, of course, that's led to an endless stream of abuse cases being ignored and swept under the rug because Jehovah will handle them once they're under the rug.

Additionally, the suggestion that an abuse survivor should confront the accuser is horrific. At that time, when that edition of the *Elder's Manual* was written, the criticisms had definitely reached the ears of the governing body—at least in the form of lawsuits.

The issue wasn't even addressed in the 2012 update to the *Elder's Manual*. They finally added the following line in the 2019 edition:

A victim of rape or of child sexual abuse is never required to confront the accused.

JEHOVAH' WITNESES. SHEPHERD THE
FLOCK OF GOD. 2019. CHAPTER 12, POINT 41

At least they don't have to face the accused. Next, I'd like to see a line instructing elders to call the police. Don't investigate. Don't send a plumber moonlighting as a private investigator to sit outside their house. Don't force the survivor to describe the situation vividly to an older man. Don't leave it to untrained volunteers with no background in early childhood development or psychology. And *certainly* don't allow the abuser to walk back into the Kingdom Hall as if nothing happened or leave him in a position of authority because there isn't a second victim speaking out—yet.

Additionally, Jehovah's Witnesses are sending pedophiles to people's doors to talk about Jesus. It's not a safe situation. And it's not a *necessary* situation, either. **CALL THE POLICE.** Let them sort out the person's guilt or innocence. There's no shame in putting a situation in capable hands. It seems so obvious to outsiders, but when you realize how deeply totalitarian this organization is, you start to understand why even the parents of the child refuse to call the police. Elders don't have access to DNA tests, subpoenas, search warrants, or databases of offenders.

> When circumstances limit the extent of the assistance the elders can provide on a particular occasion, elders should still seek to share words of encouragement, assuring a victim of Jehovah's love, reading an appropriate scripture, and offering a prayer. This will confirm the elders' interest and willingness to help to the extent possible.
>
> JEHOVAH' WITNESES. *SHEPHERD THE FLOCK OF GOD.* 2021. CHAPTER 14, PARAGRAPH 16

It doesn't seem like an autonomous government if elders can't provide the support the membership needs when they've been subjected to a heinous crime. Either they're autonomous, or they aren't. It sure seems like the Governing Body wants to have it both ways.

Despite that fact, members are scared into compliance. They do Armageddon drills at the Kingdom Hall and their homes. One ex-Jehovah's Witness told me of a time when his parents said to him that "it" was happening—the end was here. Really here. Earthquakes, fires, and tsunamis are everywhere. People are dying left and right. It's real.

The family kept go-bags, as all Jehovah's Witness families are instructed to do. The go-bags contain IDs, passports, money, medicine, and anything else they might need when the world falls to pieces around them. When this ex-Jehovah's Witness was told by his family that it was happening, a surge of fear started at his feet, moved up his legs, stuck in his chest, and continued up his face until he was feeling pins and needles. He was about to lose everything. His classmates were probably already dead.

…And then his parents hit the stopwatch button as he walked down the stairs with his go-bag. That's the culture they program into people from the moment they're born. Society is about to break apart. Any minute now. If you have a problem with a brother or a sister, work it out with them or tell the elders. You do NOT rely on the secular authorities. If the secular authorities have your name on a list, your address will be the first one they visit when the tribulation starts in full force and they start hunting Jehovah's Witnesses.

By the way, we're in the 2019 edition of the *Shepherd the Flock of God Elder's Manual,* and they still haven't instructed people to call the police. At least the child doesn't have to face the abuser now. We've been fighting these absolutely terrible policies from the 1960s clear through to 2019. Finally, in 2019, they still have to describe the attack in vivid detail to a moonlighting plumber, but that doesn't seem quite as bad as facing the abuser again.

As of the writing of this book, the most recent edition of the *Elder's Manual* explicitly states that the elders will neither instruct the victim or their family to contact the police nor to avoid contacting them.

> Child abuse is a crime. Never suggest to anyone that they should not report an allegation of child abuse to the police or other authorities. If you are asked, make it clear that whether to report the matter to the authorities or not is a personal decision for each individual to make and that there are no congregation sanctions for either decision. Elders will not criticize anyone who reports such an allegation to the authorities. If the victim wishes to make a report, it is his or her absolute right to do so.
>
> JEHOVAH'S WITNESSES. *SHEPHERD THE FLOCK OF GOD.* CHAPTER 12, "CHILD ABUSE," SECTION 18–21. PP. 131–133

That means the family will not get in trouble if they choose to involve secular authorities. That's a dramatic change from the 1960s era of not bringing "reproach on Jehovah's name." Unfortunately, that's simply not enough. We're in the 2019 handbook edition, and they still haven't instructed the elders to tell the parents to call the police or even call themselves. I know the Governing Body doesn't like child sexual abuse, but it sure looks like they do.

The real kicker to this story is the fact that the Governing Body wants to lean on secular authorities when their pseudo-government falls apart, but when it's necessary, they attempt to handle things internally—with terrible results. This is from the section of the elder's handbook regarding Kingdom Hall security and safety in the event of a burglary, fire, or other emergencies:

Communication with Local Law Enforcement: The elders should have up-to-date phone numbers for the police. Two elders (or a capable ministerial servant along with one elder) should be designated to visit the police station to promote good relations, expressing appreciation for their assistance if called upon. It may be advisable to ask the local authorities for security suggestions. Where several congregations are in the vicinity of the same police station, there should be good coordination as to how this contact with the police will be maintained.

JEHOVAH'S WITNESSES. *ADDENDUM TO SHEPHERD THE FLOCK OF GOD ELDER'S HANDBOOK (2021)*. 2022. P. 11. PARA. 26

Two elders are instructed to connect with the police in case their assistance is required, but if the elders are aware of a case of child sexual abuse, they aren't instructed to inform the police. In some cases, elders have been instructed not to call the police.

A Jehovah's Witness can be disfellowshipped for simply entering a private place like a house or car alone with somebody of the opposite sex. A judicial committee will convene and discuss the matter with the accused. They'll lean on Jehovah's guidance and determine if they should permanently shun this person based on the accusation that they entered an establishment alone or even took a ride in a car with somebody of the opposite sex. To be clear, Jehovah's Witnesses treat accusations of child sexual abuse in the same way they would treat the accusation that somebody was caught smoking a cigarette.

Child sexual abuse is a problem that exists in every demographic of people, unfortunately. You can do very little to stop it except report it when it appears so the person can be held accountable and society can be protected. I don't have a problem with Jehovah's Witnesses because they have pedophiles in their ranks. I have a problem with the fact that their policy and culture are protecting pedophiles from accountability and allowing them to continue to offend without consequence or protection for the most vulnerable among us.

The Australian Royal Commission is a legal entity assembled to investigate cases of child sexual abuse by the highest members of religion and government. The prime minister of Australia at the time had a close childhood friend who had fallen down a QAnon rabbit hole. He was convinced that religious and government leaders were taking part in rampant and systemic child sexual abuse.

QAnon's claims about rampant sexual abuse are overstated and misinformed. Still, the fear campaign to which the prime minister was subjected by his QAnon friend encouraged him to point the Australian Royal Commission at major religions inside Australia.

The Governing Body was forced to testify publicly about their policies and acknowledge their own words that they tried to erase from history. Jehovah's Witnesses aren't even supposed to know about the elder's handbook, Shepherd the Flock of God, let alone outsiders. The Australian Royal Commission prosecutor held up the handbook before the governing body member Geoffrey Jackson and quoted from it. Geoffrey Jackson looked at the prosecutor and lied to his face multiple times.

Outsiders probably didn't fully understand the context then, but Jehovah's Witnesses knew what they had just seen. Ex-Jehovah's Witnesses spread clips of Geoffrey Jackson flat-out lying to people's faces far and wide. The governing body members believe they're hand-picked by Jesus himself, so if it's beneficial to Jehovah, then it's beneficial to the Governing Body members, and vice versa. Not only have they granted themselves the complete, infallible authority to speak on God's behalf, but they have also created an excuse for members to do anything for them, no matter what.

The numerous lawsuits brought about by their incompetence have seriously strained the organization's finances. Although they take donations from members, their primary revenue generation method is more complex. When the lawsuits started coming in, they started a plan they called the "Master Plan."

THE MASTER PLAN

The Society famously released a video in 2018 portraying a young woman looking at a bulletin board at the back of a Kingdom Hall. The woman seems dismayed as she approaches another member of the congregation.

Woman 1, later identified as Kim, says to Woman 2, "Did you see? They have us going to the south congregation, and everybody else from our group is going to the North."

Woman 2: "Yeah, I saw that. My aunt and cousins will be going there, too."

Kim: "Well that doesn't make any sense. They should keep you together."

Woman 2 looks away, obviously uncomfortable.

Kim: "Well, at least the brothers said that the list was just a recommendation."

Woman 2: "Well, they didn't say it exactly like that. They said *if* we have extenuating circumstances."

Kim: "So you don't have to go if you don't want to go?"

Woman 2 again looks very uncomfortable. She responds, "But Kim, don't you think if everybody did that—"

Just then, an older woman identified as Sister Taylor approaches, and Kim interrupts Woman 2 to say, "Oh, hello, Sister Taylor."

Sister Taylor: "Oh, hello, girls," with a smile and a happy countenance.

Kim: "I saw your name on the list for the south congregation, but your grandkids and your families—they're going to North. So, what are you going to do?"

Sister Taylor: "What do you mean?"

Kim: "Well, are you going to North or are you going to South?"

Sister Taylor: "Now, sweetie, didn't you say you saw my name listed under the south congregation?"

Kim: "Yeah, but—"

Sister Taylor interrupts, saying, "So, I'll be going to the south congregation."

An elder, clearly listening in on the conversation from a few feet away, smiles as Sister Taylor sets Kim straight on the notion that this list was simply a recommendation.

Kim: "Well, don't you think it would make more sense if you were in the same congregation as your grandkids and their families?"

Sister Taylor takes a deep breath and says, "Does it make more sense…Well, that's a whole different question. The brothers outlined an arrangement. They said they hoped we could support that arrangement unless we have extenuating circumstances and I don't have any right now, so, for me, it's simple. Whether I know all of their reasons or not, I'm going to support that arrangement."

Sister Taylor glances in another direction and, with a smile and an excited tone in her voice, says, "Oh look, girls—I've got to go. Oh, and by the way, I hope to see you *both* in the south congregation."

The elder, still listening in on the conversation, smiles as the scene fades.

This type of messaging was rampant at the time. Not only did it reinforce the "obey, or else" mindset they've been pushing since the early days of the religion, but it also betrayed a degree of desperation from the Watchtower Society. They were clearly preparing for pushback against what they called the Master Plan.

Jehovah's Witnesses had just lost several legal cases relating to child sexual abuse and were ordered to pay millions of dollars collectively. Most organizations of their size don't just have millions of dollars sitting around in bank accounts. It's usually tied up in assets, like stocks or physical properties. The Society had to liquidate assets quickly to compensate the victims in those lawsuits.

The Master Plan involved combining congregations, selling off extra Kingdom Halls, and even having other congregations build new Kingdom Halls. It felt like they were getting something new—but the old Kingdom Hall was perfectly fine.

When the Watchtower Society orders a new Kingdom Hall, Jehovah's Witnesses participate in a "quick-build." Congregation members commonly supply property and building materials, but if not, the Watchtower Society provides the necessary land and materials. The building process starts on Friday. The complete structure is constructed over the weekend, and the wallpaper is put up the following Monday.

The most expensive part of constructing a building is the labor. Materials might cost $30,000, but paying workers to construct it could cost an additional $300,000. By the end of the process, the building might sell for $500,000. In recent years, the quick-build process has been a source of revenue for the organization. The Society retains ownership of all Kingdom Halls and uses the assets as leverage to receive loans.

The Society has also merged congregations and drawn up staggered meeting schedules—one congregation uses the kingdom hall from 9:00 AM to 2:00 PM, the next congregation uses the kingdom hall from 4:00 PM to 7:00 PM, and so on.

The quick build effort didn't stop at their Kingdom Halls. They also sold off their original headquarters (owned since 1909) and their newer, much larger headquarters (purchased in 1969) in Brooklyn, New York. A follower gifted their original headquarters.

Part of the Jehovah's Witnesses Master Plan was to sell off their main Brooklyn headquarters for an estimated $1.3 billion and build a new headquarters in a more remote location where it would be easier to go off the grid and be entirely autonomous when the United Nations comes for the leadership right before Armageddon starts.

They exchanged their headquarters in the heart of Brooklyn, New York, for a more remote headquarters in Warwick, New York, significantly reducing their expenses.

After implementing their Master Plan to dig themselves out of their financial hole, they had what they needed to pay off the victims of their stubborn incompetence. Logical leadership would have changed their doctrine and rules to prevent future lawsuits, but not Jehovah's Witnesses. This should serve as a clear indication that the organization's leadership is not hearing the voice of God and that the organization is not God's chosen organization.

If the Governing Body really did hear the voice of God, he would undoubtedly tell them to report every crime to the secular authorities—no questions asked, no suggestion that "you shouldn't push them in one direction or another" or "it's up to them." Call the police.

HOW TO TREAT DISFELLOWSHIPPED FAMILY

My brother Jeff was disfellowshipped when I was ten, and the standard treatment applied to him from then on. I was too young to understand what was happening, but to my knowledge, he was disfellowshipped because he had an outsider girlfriend. I assume he slept with her, which is what got him kicked out. As aforementioned, I was ten and living with my parents when he was kicked out of the religion.

I shunned him because I believed it was the right thing to do at ten years old. It's been a challenge to accept what I did to him, though he told me he doesn't believe I'm to blame. I was ten. That doesn't remove the guilt, but it helps a little.

When I was nine, my brother Lance and I would sit in the basement and learn programming languages. At nine years old, I learned my first language, C. I learned various other languages, including but not limited to C++, Java, PHP, and JavaScript. He and I were very skilled in software engineering, which is how I eventually managed to bust into the field—a difficult feat unless you have a degree, which I never had.

Lance knew I had the know-how and ability to do anything a company could ask of me when I was about nineteen—a year after I had been disfellowshipped. He worked at Google as a system administrator, which was an extremely stable job. I called him and asked if he could help me get into Google.

On that phone call, he effectively told me that he knew I could do the job, but he didn't think he could trust me "not to chase after the first piece of tail I come across." At the time, I had been in a long-term, monogamous relationship. I've always been a monogamist. I had even recently found out my wife was pregnant. There was no reason for him to view me that way, except he was still a Jehovah's Witness, and I was disfellowshipped.

As of the time of the writing of this book, every single family member who was involved in Jehovah's Witnesses to any degree is now out—except my mom. She's still going strong and will likely die in the religion. She gets a military pension from before she was in the religion, and I've been told it's a lot—100 percent disability.

My brother got in a bind in 2023 and needed $3,000 to get himself out of it. My mom didn't have $3,000 even though she lived in a tiny one-person house in the middle of nowhere, Connecticut. Where's all that money going? I'd be surprised if it isn't all going to the Watchtower Society. When she dies, there will be as much to inherit as there was with my dad—only this time, it won't be because he was dirt poor; it'll be because she sent it all to the Governing Body.

The last time I spoke to my mother, she told me I was repulsive to her. The bridge completely burned after that. I told her I didn't want to see her again until she was in a coffin. She lit my life on fire for years because she wanted to—not because she had to. She tried to do the same to my daughter. She hasn't shown remorse, and I'm certain she never will.

There are many more problems ingrained in this situation than the ones Jehovah's Witnesses might have created. However, religion amplified every problem in my life. My mom couldn't just leave my dad and start a new life—even after all the kids had left the house—because she wasn't scripturally free. The congregation specifically did not assist me when I needed it the most.

As an adult, I can't get restitution for their contribution to the living hell I experienced—but others can and have. Victims of Watchtower Society's incompetence have taken so much from the Society through child sexual abuse lawsuits that they have had to sell properties and build new headquarters. That's worth something.

CHAPTER 8
EVEN MORE FALSE PROPHECY

FRED FRANZ—THE FOURTH PRESIDENT

red Franz was president of the Watchtower Society after Nathan Knorr—the fourth to control the Watchtower Society. Fred Franz was president from 1977 to his death in 1992. He's hugely influential even today because Jehovah's Witnesses believe he has a special role in an active end-time prediction called "Second Generation teaching."

If there were a single word to sum up Franz's era, it would be "vindictive." He was responsible for the blood transfusion ban and countless end-times predictions. Fred's presidency might have been just as crazy as Rutherford's.

Fred had a nephew named Ray Franz, who was a member of the Governing Body from 1971 to 1980. He eventually realized precisely what I came to realize—the Watchtower Society is rife with corruption and no more good or "pure" than any other Christian denomination. The leadership is made up of people who engage in hypocrisy regularly. That's right—a Governing Body member defected from the organization.

After leaving Jehovah's Witnesses, Ray Franz wrote a book titled *Crisis of Conscience*. The book revealed several significant revelations. As an ex-Governing Body member, he provided previously unknown and extremely valuable insight into the organization's inner workings. He was disfellowshipped shortly after leaving the organization during his uncle's presidency.

Ray revealed the inner workings of the Watchtower Society in great detail—information kept private until he exposed it. In fact, Governing Body members weren't even considered public figures until the early 2010s. The information could be obtained, but they hadn't shown themselves yet.

When Ray Franz left the organization, he was employed by a disassociated Jehovah's Witness. At that time, if someone had disassociated rather than been disfellowshipped, shunning was not required.

In September 1981, about six months after Ray's employer submitted his letter of disassociation, the Watchtower Society announced a change in its disassociation policy. If somebody disassociated, it was effectively the same as being disfellowshipped. Shunning rules apply. If a member associates with an ex-member, whether disfellowshipped or disassociated, they will also be disfellowshipped. Ray Franz was disfellowshipped in 1982 for continuing to associate with a known ex-Jehovah's Witness.

Jehovah's Witnesses had no reason to disfellowship Ray Franz. Up to that point, he had declined media interviews and hadn't said a negative word about the organization, but they found a reason to disfellowship him anyway, even changing policy to do so. Remember, this took place under his uncle's presidency. That doesn't seem like something a God worth worshiping would condone—it sounds like the actions of vindictive, angry humans.

Sadly, Ray Franz died on June 2, 2010, and the book went out of print. The Watchtower Society attempted to purchase the copyright, but luckily, a close acquaintance of Ray's acquired it and put it back in print.

NO BLOOD - ORGANS ARE OKAY (FOR NOW)

Jehovah's Witnesses are possibly most famous for the belief that taking blood from transfusions is evil. The blood ban was instituted around 1945 under the leadership of Nathan Knorr, but it was heavily pushed by his vice president, Fred Franz.

> After the Judge's death, as World War II was ending and persecution against the Witnesses began declining, along with the attendant drop in news-media publicity, Hayden C. Covington told the author [of THE FOUR PRESIDENTS] that Fred Franz saw the prohibition against blood transfusions as a way to accomplish two things: to continue to publicize the religion, and to create an uproar in the community. This reaction would convince the membership they were being "persecuted" and "suffering for righteousness sake," a sure sign they were "in the truth."
>
> JERRY BERGMAN. *BLOOD TRANSFUSIONS: A HISTORY AND EVALUATION OF THE RELIGIOUS, BIBLICAL, AND MEDICAL OBJECTIONS.* 1994. P. 5

It's hard to say exactly what was going on in these people's minds when they banned blood, but one thing is for sure: The blood doctrine is false and indefensible. They base their position on one specific verse in the Old Testament: Leviticus, which is part of the Old Law that Christians are not required to follow.

And anyone of the people of Israel, or of the aliens who reside among them, who hunts down an animal or bird that may be eaten shall pour out its blood and cover it with earth.

For the life of every creature—its blood is its life; therefore, I have said to the people of Israel: You shall not eat the blood of any creature, for the life of every creature is its blood; whoever eats it shall be cut off.

LEVITICUS 17:13–14

Setting aside the fact that Jehovah's Witnesses believe the old law was fulfilled and no longer necessary when Jesus came to earth, the keyword in those verses is "eat."

I thought "eat" was odd, so I looked deeper. The Hebrew word looks like this: אֹכְלָיו. It's pronounced 'ō·ḵə·lāw.

The word means explicitly to eat—to devour through your mouth and into your stomach. It doesn't relate to using blood in a lifesaving medical procedure. At no point did God ever demand regular human sacrifice. The life of his people came before all else, even in the Old Testament, with only a couple of notable exceptions, such as the great flood.

The concept of a blood transfusion didn't exist when the Book of Leviticus was written. However, God is all-knowing and all-wise. If he wanted us to avoid blood transfusions, he could have had Jesus condemn the use of blood in medical procedures. That would have been clear.

When I was young, I carried around a "no blood" medical directive. If I had gotten in a car accident when I was young, I could have died. I carried that card with me everywhere. We have no way of knowing how many children did get into that car accident—not just children, but how many people required serious surgery for one reason or another and simply died because they refused to take a blood transfusion?

We'll never know exactly how many people died for refusing a blood transfusion, but the Watchtower Society used to publish articles about young kids who gave their lives for Jehovah by refusing blood. They realized how... well, tacky isn't the right word. Morbid? Grotesque? Either way, they realized how bad it looked and stopped running the articles. They kept telling the kids to sacrifice their lives; they just stopped telling people about it happening. One would think they were ashamed of something.

They're so serious about not taking blood that they expect you to lean forward when you have a bloody nose (which is actually good advice anyway) or spit blood out if you get a cut in your mouth. That's not a doctrinal thing technically; it's a cultural thing. But it should show how serious Jehovah's Witnesses are about not consuming blood in any way.

This is absolutely a matter of life and death for Jehovah's Witnesses. My dad was on his deathbed when I was about 14. I was studying to get baptized at the time. I sat on the hospital chair reading the Jehovah's Witness book while my dad was in the hospital bed dying because he needed a quadruple bypass, and no doctor would perform the surgery without a blood transfusion.

The Hospital Liaison Committee is a group of Jehovah's Witness elders who visit Jehovah's Witnesses in the hospital and threaten the hospital with legal action if they attempt to give a blood transfusion to the patient. They act as a looming threat to the patient and the hospital staff.

The staff will separate the patient from the liaison committee and ask them, but the committee will make sure the patient is aware of the consequences if they get the transfusion, even if it's just through their presence. It's effectively the same punishment as if you murdered somebody—blood guilt. You have somebody else's blood on your hands because you took a part of their soul from them. That's how it's viewed.

In my dad's case, a doctor came from several states to help him. He said he could put in stents without the need for a blood transfusion. He got the stents, but eventually, he needed the bypass. There was no other option. They delayed the procedure by a few years.

The doctors finally decided that he was going to die if they didn't do it. It was a risk assessment: his chances of surviving without the surgery were 0. His chances of surviving the surgery without blood was about 20 percent. They decided to go ahead with the surgery after thoroughly explaining the risks. He agreed and said he understood.

They performed the surgery, and he "miraculously survived." Jehovah carried him through. The kid who got in a car accident, on the other hand—it was his time. Or maybe Jehovah was too focused on my dad.

God only ever demanded human sacrifice three times. The first was Jesus, which is arguably not even a human sacrifice. The second was Abraham and Isaac, which he called off at the last moment. The third was Jephthah.

Jephthah offered God "whatever came out of his door" when he returned home from war as a burnt offering. All God had to do was help Jephthah win the war. Jephthah might have won the battle with or without God's help, but he made the promise. His daughter excitedly ran out to greet him when he returned, making her the first thing to come out of his door. The Bible says, "he did to her as was vowed," but there is debate over the meaning of this. Some scholars believe he "sacrificed" her to a tabernacle to live as a maid since she was mourning her inability to marry leading up to the sacrifice instead of mourning her own death. This is argued because God explicitly says he abhors child sacrifice. If refusing a life-saving blood transfusion isn't a human sacrifice, I don't know what is. God didn't demand human sacrifice back then, and I have no reason to believe he expects it today.

Organ transplants also have a fascinating history within the religion. The December 22, 1949 *Awake!* mentions organ transplants explicitly. Here's what it said:

Have your teeth or hair fallen out? Has arthritis frozen your joints? Have a hole in your skull that needs plugging up? Need a new roof in your mouth? Or do you need a replacement for your lungs, kidneys or heart? If so, you will be interested to know that there are many shops around the country that are now in the business of supplying "spare parts" for the human body, both natural and artificial.

JEHOVAH'S WITNESES. *AWAKE!.* DECEMBER 22, 1949.

I'm not exactly sure what point they were trying to make, but there it is: one of the first mentions of organ transplants…or something. The subject was next mentioned in the August 1, 1961, *Watchtower*. The following is a question from a reader.

Is there anything in the Bible against giving one's eyes (after death) to be transplanted to some living person?-L. C., United States. The question of placing one's body or parts of one's body at the disposal of men of science or doctors at one's death for purposes of scientific experimentation or replacement in others is frowned upon by certain religious bodies. However, it does not seem that any Scriptural principle or law is involved. It therefore is something that each individual must decide for himself.

JEHOVAH'S WITNESSES. "QUESTIONS FROM READERS." *THE WATCHTOWER.* AUGUST 1, 1961.

As of 1961, it wasn't officially banned but frowned upon. At this point in their history, Nathan Knorr led the organization as president, and Fred Franz was vice president.

The next mention was 1967.

Sustaining one's life by means of the body or part of the body of another human...would be cannibalism, a practice abhorrent to all civilized people...It is not our place to decide whether such operations are advisable from a scientific or medical standpoint...Christians who have been enlightened by God's Word do not need to make these decisions based simply on the basis of personal whim or emotion. They can consider the divine principles and use these in making personal decisions as they look to God for direction, trusting him and putting their confidence in the future that he has in store for those who love him.

JEHOVAH'S WITNESSES. *THE WATCHTOWER.* NOVEMBER 15, 1967. PP. 702–704

I have to wonder how many people died between 1961 and 1967 because they were hesitant about getting an organ transplant out of fear they might upset God. The most fascinating part of their 1967 belief, in my opinion, is that they viewed it as cannibalism to get a kidney transplant. That is absolutely bizarre.

The next mention was in the *Watchtower* from September 1, 1975.

A peculiar factor sometimes noted is a so-called "personality transplant." That is, the recipient in some cases has seemed to adopt certain personality factors of the person from whom the organ came.

JEHOVAH'S WITNESSES. *WATCHTOWER.* SEPTEMBER 1, 1975. P. 519

It's a personality transplant. That one is even stranger than the cannibalism belief. They literally thought that people who received organ transplants would adopt part of the personality of the organ donor.

When this article was published, Fred Franz was about to replace Nathan Knorr as the president.

The final mention is from a 1980 *Watchtower*.

There is no Biblical command pointedly forbidding the taking in of other human tissue. It is a matter for personal decision.

JEHOVAH'S WITNESSES. THE WATCHTOWER.
MARCH 15, 1980. P. 31

And just like that, organ transplants are acceptable again. That surprises me because organs often contain a little bit of blood from the original donor when being transplanted. You can't have any. Remember what I said about having a cut in your mouth? Regardless, organ transplants are now 100 percent acceptable.

Nowadays, Jehovah's Witnesses have been told that blood transfusions are outright banned, but medicines that are made using blood fractions, like plasma or red blood cells, are a "conscience matter." That means they don't know if it'll lead to your death in Armageddon, so you're doing it at your own risk. You'd be surprised how valuable blood has been in creating new medicines.

When Jehovah's Witnesses change their beliefs like that, they call it "new light." Their explanation for the fumbles is as absurd as the screw-ups themselves. The idea behind new light goes like this: Jehovah sheds more light on his expectations as we get closer to the end. Why wouldn't he just shed all the light on them right now? Why would he specifically tell you one thing and then tell you the exact opposite later? How is that considered "seeing a clearer picture?" Your guess is as good as mine. The Governing Body claims ultimate authority. How could they possibly flip-flop like that and claim, with a straight face, that they hear the voice of God? It is, of course, an unjustifiable position.

Regarding other types of medical treatment, Jehovah's Witnesses are perfectly fine with taking any medicines as prescribed (except blood transfusions, of course). Jehovah's Witnesses have a reputation for abusing anxiety and depression medicines, as well as alcohol, because of the life they live. It's not an easy life. You're expected to give every free moment to the Watchtower Society in one way or another.

Whether you're going through your Watchtower and under-lining the answers to the question-and-answer segment or prac-ticing presentations for service, there's always something to do. Attending the meetings and going in service suck up enough time on their own, let alone studying and preparing for them.

MENTAL HEALTH AND THERAPY

The last official note from the Watchtower Society about therapy was a message discouraging it in the September 1, 1990 Watchtow-er. The society believes that people should turn to the Bible to deal with their mental health, not the outside world. You'll always be happy if you just come to meetings and go in service. Problem solved.

The sister then told her how a knowledge of Bible truth had helped her. She had lost an 18-year-old daughter in death and had gone into a state of deep depression for eight years. Neither psychiatrists nor costly medications helped her to overcome this depression…

Then, she told the lady, one day Jehovah's Witnesses called and left her some Bible literature. That sparked her interest in God's Word, and she began to read the Bible all the way through. Some-thing started to change within her. She began to get up in the morning and take an interest in her household. She finally decided to take care of the house by herself and found she was able to do so. It was as though she had never been sick! This made her feel very happy.

She did not return to the psychiatrist. Her will to live was stimulated by her knowledge of God's Word, which proved to be the best medicine.

JEHOVAH'S WITNESSES. THE WATCHTOWER.
SEPTEMBER 1, 1990. P.15

A woman loses her 18-year-old daughter. She falls into a deep depression. Therapists couldn't help. She came to the meetings, and that resolved it.

That was a fascinating little addition at the end of the article: "Her will to live was stimulated by her knowledge of God's Word, and this proved to be the best medicine." I guess that means people don't need *actual* medicine.

That's still the Watchtower Society's official stance on medicine and therapy. You shouldn't go to a therapist. That runs the risk of being deprogrammed. Hypnosis is also considered spiritism and is strictly banned. Hypnotism is fake, but you'll be disfellowshipped for spiritism anyway.

Both my mom and my dad had intense mental conditions growing up. When I was too young to fully understand what was going on, between the ages of two and eight, my mom was dealing with a severe mental health crisis. This was in the 1990s when medicine was heavily discouraged, doctrinally and culturally. Even outside of Jehovah's Witness culture, mental health was not taken seriously by most.

To deal with her mental health crisis, she worked with a Jehovah's Witness named Sandy. Sandy tried to "uncover" hidden memories in my mom's mind. For the record, actual, licensed therapists never do this. It's impossible to tell the difference between false and hidden memories.

As expected, Sandy pulled a bunch of false memories to the surface—deeply horrific stuff.

My mom was always very close to her parents, neither of whom was a Jehovah's Witness. When Sandy started pulling false memories out, she began to believe that my grandfather had done horrific things to people. She thought he murdered people and buried them in his backyard, where he and his wife had lived for 50 years. She believed he sexually assaulted her, and there were other victims.

My mom was so confident these memories were real that she worked with the police, something that's seldom done in Jehovah's Witness circles.

He was innocent. The man was a Korean War veteran with seven children and a wife. When he was young, he and his father built a house on some property, and he has lived there ever since.

It ruined my family's relationship with my grandparents. We didn't speak to them for years. Not out of frustration or anger—my grandparents forgave my mom almost immediately after taking classes at a local college about how false memories work. The relationship was ruined during the time my mom was dealing with a mental health crisis and had a Jehovah's Witness helping her through it.

That was how it was in the 1990s, and it's largely done now. If you needed help, you turned to your fellow Jehovah's Witnesses. Their position on medicine doesn't appear to be as intense as it used to be, but therapy is still frowned upon.

STAY ALIVE TO '75

In the years before Fred Franz officially took office, the Watchtower Society started pushing a new prophecy: Stay Alive to '75. It came and went two years before Fred Franz took over as president. He was still vice president, but as we know from the blood ban, he was extremely influential—even as a vice president.

When I was young, my mom told me about some Jehovah's Witnesses who mistakenly believed that the end would come in 1975. It wasn't the Watchtower Society's fault—it was eager Jehovah's Witnesses reading into things that weren't there. That should have served as a clue that I should be suspicious of the story. She attempted to poison the well, which had worked for a long time.

Jehovah's Witnesses famously made a very specific prediction in 1975. They believed the end would come that year because, according to their calculations, it had been 6,000 years since the creation of Earth. The leadership's inner numerologists appeared, creating a catchphrase: "Stay alive to '75." If people could make it "one more day, one more week, one more month"—they may never have to die at all. As with other end-times predictions, Jehovah's Witnesses didn't think this could easily be explained, so they attempted to erase it from their history instead.

The Dutch branch overseer—a very influential position—told members they should be pioneering for at least 50 hours per month (this number has changed over time) as the year 1975 approached:

Many of us have suffered misery, sickness and death. You don't have to experience that any more. The new order is near [...] Sell your house, sell everything you own and say, oh boy, how long can I carry on with my private means. That long? Get rid of things! Pioneer! Plan to shower people with magazines during these last few months of this dying system of things!

TAPE-RECORDING OF "DIVINE PURPOSE"
DISTRICT CONVENTION, UTRECHT, THE
NETHERLANDS, AUGUST 1974, QUOTED BY
SINGELENBERG, 1989.

Audio recordings of statements like this are all over the place. Jehovah's Witnesses couldn't erase their history, and it is now a perpetual embarrassment. It should serve as evidence to everybody that the leadership of this organization has no idea what they're talking about. They never have.

THE Y2K PROPHECY

Jehovah's Witnesses also believed the end would come at the end of the millennium. As they did with other end-time predictions, like 1975, they stopped saying "the end is near" in their literature and began saying "the end is *here.*" They got increasingly urgent and gave the membership reason to believe something big was about to happen.

They seemed to have learned their lesson from their end-time prediction in 1975 because they became more cautious about naming specific dates after that prediction fell flat. They did, however, get specific in the January 1, 1989, *Watchtower* by saying the following:

How thrilling that must have been for Paul and Barnabas—sailing to their first foreign assignment! The apostle Paul was spearheading the Christian missionary activity. *He was also laying a foundation for a work that would be completed in our 20th century.*

JEHOVAH'S WITNESSES. *THE WATCHTOWER.*
JANUARY 1, 1989. P. 12

That *Watchtower* was printed under Fred Franz's presidency. Fred was baptized and anointed around 1914, so he saw the failed predictions of 1914, 1918, 1919, 1925, and 1975. For some reason, he chose to make another end-times prophecy. As always, the Watchtower Society had to pretend they never said it.

Jehovah's Witnesses used to release bound volumes every year. It was a large book that contained every *Watchtower* for the entire year. When the *Awake!* existed, they had a bound volume for that, too. The bound volume containing the 1989 Watchtowers had that section changed. Jehovah's Witnesses leadership has ordered members to burn all old literature at different times. Hence, an intact copy of this magazine is extremely difficult to find. Still, Lloyd Evans, on his self-titled YouTube channel, displays the original, unedited text featured prominently in the original magazine sent to him by a viewer. On the Watchtower Online Library and in the bound volume released later that year, the text was changed to say the following:

> ... He was also laying a foundation for a work that would be completed in our day.

At various points in its long history, the Watchtower Society has made predictions of this type. They erase them when possible. When they can't be erased, they try to claim the date really was significant—it just wasn't significant in the way they thought.

THE SECOND GENERATION TEACHING

The Watchtower Society claims that the generation alive to see the events of 1914 would not die out—but there's one problem: people died. We're in the 21st century now—a time the Watchtower Society never expected to reach. So, the Watchtower Society used Fred Franz as a generational gauge. They claimed that Fred Franz was baptized and anointed on November 30, 1913.

He was baptized on November 30, 1913, and the following year he left the university and entered the colporteur (pioneer) work.

JEHOVAH'S WITNESSES. *THE WATCHTOWER.*
MARCH 15, 1993. PP. 31–32

By Fred's own account, though, he was baptized on April 5, 1914.

On April 5, 1914, in Chicago, Illinois, I symbolized my consecration —as we used to call dedication—by water baptism.

JEHOVAH'S WITNESSES. "LOOKING BACK
OVER 93 YEARS OF LIVING." *THE
WATCHTOWER.* MAY 1, 1987. PP. 22–30

Despite contradicting each other and breaking prophecies, both articles are still available on the Jehovah's Witness website.

That means he wasn't part of "Jehovah's Organization" before 1914. That blows a hole in their whole prophecy, but let's ignore that momentarily. Pretending Fred was baptized and anointed in 1913, or more importantly, before 1914, that means Fred is part of the generation who will never die.

…except Fred died in 1992 at the age of 99. Fred fit the "first generation" better than anybody Jehovah's Witnesses have found. Now that the first generation was officially and absolutely dead, the Governing Body put their heads together to figure out how they would extend their false prophecy even further. They came up with what they call the "second generation" teaching. Here's how it goes…

Anyone baptized and anointed during the lifetime of anybody baptized and anointed in 1914 is still part of the first generation.

That means anybody baptized and anointed before 1992, when Fred died, still counts as the first generation.

However, the prophecy wasn't "anybody alive to see anybody alive to see 1914 might not die," it was millions now living will never die. Either way, they've put themselves in something of a pickle. They have a current, active prophecy that's going to fail.

The youngest I've ever heard of somebody being anointed was 30 years old. Let's be extra generous and assume the youngest they could be is 20. If they were baptized at ten years old in 1991, one year before Fred Franz died, they were born in 1981. The median lifespan in the United States, where the governing body lives, is just under 78.

Somebody born in 1981 will be 78 years old in 2060. That means Jehovah's Witnesses have until 2060 at the latest until they have yet another false prophecy on their hands. That's being extremely generous. Realistically, the prophecy should fail sometime around 2040. The prophecy already failed because millions living in 1914 are now dead. However, even if they are extra charitable and accept all their workarounds, they still face another failure.

Governing Body members discussed the possibility that the beginning of COVID might have been the start of the Great Tribulation, but after some time, decided that it couldn't have been the beginning of the end...of the end, because world peace hadn't been declared by the Great Beast—the UN. That's a prerequisite of the end of the end. After world peace is declared, the UN bans all religions worldwide, recognizing them as the source of humanity's problems. While all this is happening, pestilence, war, pain, and suffering will run rampant. We'll cover their eschatology in more detail in an upcoming chapter.

I'm sure you can imagine the look of surprise on the Governing Body's collective faces when the Watchtower Society was exposed for being members of the United Nations from February 1992 to

2001. Fred Franz left the presidency in 1992, but they applied for NGO status with the Great Beast in 1991.

Fred was the president when the Watchtower Society applied for NGO status. That makes it Fred's responsibility. Either way, something as scandalous as this would absolutely have to at least pass by the president for approval first. Let's talk about why they believe the Great Beast is the UN and the firestorm that rained down on the Watchtower Society when they were exposed.

TONY MORRIS'S EFFECT ON PROPHECY

Anthony Morris III joined the Governing Body of Jehovah's Witnesses on September 1, 2005. On February 22, 2023, to everybody's surprise, he was fired from the Governing Body. I didn't know that could happen. To my knowledge, that's never happened before—a Governing Body member can't simply be fired. Tony Morris dramatically affected prophecy and doctrine within the Jehovah's Witness religion, including an effect on the Second Generation teaching. Let's talk about what happened.

Tony Morris was a combat medic in Vietnam. Jehovah's Witnesses aren't allowed to be involved in politics to any degree, including being a part of the military. He joined Jehovah's Witnesses after serving. Both my mom and my dad are also Vietnam War veterans. That made Tony Morris my mom's favorite governing body member. Yes, Jehovah's Witnesses have favorites. Seems a little idolatrous to me.

Tony Morris was harsh and blunt. He seemed to shoot from the hip more often than not. Human beings are not supposed to see or do some things the military makes you see and do. As a result, Tony Morris was graphic when describing what he expected the tribulation to be like.

In his talk at the 2009/2010 Special Day assembly, he gave a talk that was nothing short of chilling. He uses the term "the truth" in the video. That's how Jehovah's Witnesses refer to their religion. Here's what he said:

> Nearly 40 years have gone by since I'm in the truth. It doesn't seem like that long because I've been so busy. Every year. And that urgency thankfully has never left, because—erm, really, that's not much time. And now it's just very very concerning for me. You see I was in Vietnam, a medic in that war. Uh…I've seen what happens to humans when they're mangled… And you see it on TV and some of that, well…until you smell human flesh burning from a helicopter crash, People that look like, er, humans…like a hot dog on a grill, blackened and splitting open…I know what's coming at Armageddon. A lot of dead people…A lot of dead people. So it's absolutely urgent for us to get our minds off ourselves…and let's get out there and help as many as we can. Because when it comes, it's going to be numbing for you. You think seeing a deer mangled on the side of the road from the truck that hit it is upsetting? You see humans like that. So, it's going to be numbing."
>
> MORRIS, TONY. SPECIAL DAY ASSEMBLY
> TALK. 2009-2010.

I have to wonder how many children listened to that talk. That type of controversial talk from Tony Morris happened regularly. He was the focus of negative attention from the outside world and even for some on the inside. He seemed to have a massive problem with tight pants, too, strangely. He gave a talk in 2015 that was just as odd as the last, though not quite as haunting. Here's what he said:

> It's not that you don't dress nice to fit your physique. That's fine. That's what Max and I do. What's wrong is these extremely tight pants. It's not appropriate for a Christian. And I want you

brothers to think about this. You'll remember that many, many, many homosexuals are in the clothing industry and doing the designing. Don't you know they love it when you wear tight pants? Oh yeah… you chuckle. I don't think it's funny. I think it's disgusting.

MORRIS, TONY. PUBLIC TALK. 2015.

I can see a religious figure having an unhealthy obsession with women being modest and not wearing tight pants out of the house, but that's not what he's talking about. He's talking about men wearing tight pants. I didn't know that was a problem—or even a trend, for that matter. His bizarre obsessions would first come out in talks, then start appearing in the children's propaganda cartoons —Caleb and Sophia.

Let's talk about one more video from Tony Morris—higher education. Unfortunately, I don't have a date for this one. Tony Morris was giving another public talk, and in it, he said this:

Sometimes people say, 'Well, you know, Jehovah's Witnesses are against education!' Well, that's ridiculous! We're not against education. Ah, we are PRO-education. It's just that we are selective with who does the educating. We promote divine education. We believe it to be superior because it leads to everlasting life…

They start you off there, you, you'd be going for another thing, but you…you have Philosophy 1 and you have Philosophy 2. And then all of a sudden it gets in there and the intellectual gripping of the mind, er…very hard to recover from. I've seen this so many times, and we could tell you so many horror stories… And the parents are all distraught. Well, you put 'em there! I remember one mother; I talked to her son. He went to Harvard, and we were in New England. He became an evolutionist! Raised in the truth. Mom couldn't believe it. But I got him to tell me what he really thought.

She was devastated. Well, you let him go there! And this real bright professor got a hold of him.

MORRIS, TONY. PUBLIC TALK.

This one manifested in "Caleb and Sophia" videos, too. Technically, higher education isn't banned for Jehovah's Witnesses. You just don't do it. Culture and association have always been the enforcing hammer within the religion. They believe it's just a waste of time for Jehovah's Witnesses to pursue higher education. It doesn't accomplish anything. Who knows if this system of things will even last another four years? If it does, what are the chances it'll last long enough, past four years, for you to use your degree?

Jehovah's Witnesses consider it extremely valuable for members to know trades. The Governing Body says that when the new system sweeps in, learning carpentry or plumbing will be valuable so Jehovah's Witnesses can rebuild homes after Jehovah levels them.

I find it interesting, though, that they discourage people from pursuing higher education while the Governing Body starts new projects that will take four or more years to complete—like a 1.5 million-square-foot audiovisual production center in upstate New York, which they announced in 2019.

What's the point of starting a project like that if the new system is right around the corner? There is no point, of course. It's yet another hypocrisy within the religion.

The point is that Morris's obsessions manifested in doctrine. He gave a talk in Trinidad on January 13, 2018, where he said that people who don't knock on doors as much as they can are considered blood guilty—effectively guilty of murder. When Armageddon comes, Jehovah is going to judge you for your blood guilt. That wasn't the official doctrine. He said it anyway. I can't imagine that made the other Governing Body members happy.

When I was young, I remember my mother telling me that nobody knew who would be resurrected after Armageddon, but if you died in Armageddon, you were gone for good. I don't know if that was an official doctrine in the 1990s, but it was a cultural belief among most Jehovah's Witnesses. Jehovah will judge your heart condition to determine if you should make it to the new system.

The book of Romans talks about not judging your fellow man because you don't know what's in his heart. He is responsible to God and God alone. Jesus said that those who gave him water when he was thirsty, food when he was hungry, and a place to sleep when he had nowhere to go would make it through to the kingdom of God. In Jesus' parable, the people pointed out that they didn't do any of that stuff for Jesus. He said, "What you do for the least of my brothers and sisters, you do for me."

That's what's really required: simply being a good person in your heart and helping people who need it—no more, no less. Tony Morris claimed that knocking on doors was a precondition for making it through Armageddon. The Bible doesn't say that anywhere—it's not even implied.

After Tony Morris was fired, Stephen Lett announced on their hour-long monthly show, JW Broadcasting, that "nobody knows" who will make it to the other side. To my knowledge, as of this moment, just about everybody will be resurrected on the other side of Armageddon—a resurrection of the "righteous and the unrighteous," as Jehovah's Witnesses have always said. Tony Morris seemed to be shooting from the hip when he said going in service was a precondition of being resurrected, and after his tenure ended, that false doctrine, if it was indeed false doctrine, was corrected.

In mid-October 2020, he gave a talk about apostates. Look at what he said.

All of this growth and the advancements in this organization, the earthly part—it infuriates Satan the Devil. Just infuriates him.

Hence how we look forward to the end of Jehovah's *chief* enemy, as well as all of the other enemies that are under his influence.

MORRIS, TONY. PUBLIC TALK. OCTOBER, 2020.

When he says, "all of the other enemies," he's referring to apostates. He's saying that he can't wait to see the day when people critical of Jehovah's Witnesses are brutally murdered. He wishes death upon people who criticize or question him. That means me, and by reading this book, that now means you.

He continued to read a verse from the Book of Isaiah about people being thrown into Gehenna, "where the maggot does not die." He said, "What is this place called Gehenna?" He claimed to quote a Jewish scholar who described it as a fire that never goes out—used to burn carcasses.

The honest answer to that question is this: It was a killing field where battles took place, and people were sacrificed to other gods. It was a bloody, brutal location.[1] Here's a quote from the Encyclopedia Britannica:[2]

Named in the New Testament in Greek form (from the Hebrew Ge Hinnom, meaning "valley of Hinnom"), Gehenna originally was a valley west and south of Jerusalem where children were burned as sacrifices to the Ammonite god Moloch. This practice was carried out by the Israelites during the reigns of King Solomon in the 10th century BC and King Manasseh in the 7th century BC and continued until the Babylonian Exile in the 6th century BC. Gehenna later was made a garbage center to discourage a reintroduction of such sacrifices.

If you'll remember from Chapter 1, Jews weren't originally

monotheists. They believed that many Canaanite gods, including Moloch, were real.

Gehenna is commonly confused with Hell within modern Christianity. Tony Morris quotes some Jewish scholar who is apparently named "One Jewish Scholar." Wild name. It makes him very difficult to track down. Anyway, this "One Jewish Scholar" fellow said that whatever the fire didn't consume, the maggots would. In his public talk about apostates, Tony Morris goes on to say the following:

>...not a pleasant sight. But what a fitting picture of the final end of all of god's enemies. Sobering, yet something we look forward to. However, the apostates and the enemies of Jehovah would say, "Oh, that's gruesome. That's despicable. You teach your people these things?" No, *God* teaches *his* people these things. This is what he's foretelling. And frankly, for friends of Jehovah God, how reassuring that they're finally going to be gone—all these despicable enemies that have just reproached Jehovah's name—destroyed, never ever to live again. Now, it's not that we rejoice in someone's death, but when it comes to god's enemies... finally, they're out of the way. Especially these despicable apostates who, at one point, had dedicated their life to god and then... they joined forces with Satan the Devil, the chief apostate of all time.

Next, he quotes from a Bible verse saying,

>But the wicked will perish. The enemies of Jehovah will vanish like glorious pastures. Particularly, they will vanish like smoke. So... I thought this would be a nice memory aid [to help] this verse stay in the mind. Here's what Jehovah is promising.

He lights a match, holds it in front of him for a moment, and blows it out. He looks back up from the match and smiles as he chuckles. The crowd laughs.

He says, "That's Jehovah's enemies. They're going to vanish like smoke."

It's one of the most chilling videos I've ever seen from Tony Morris, and I've seen some deeply chilling videos from him. He clearly has a massive disdain for people who criticize him to any degree. He seems to have a particular disdain for people who were once baptized and left the religion behind, like me.

If this isn't proof that they're a hate group, I don't know what is. What else would you call it when the leaders in the religion are wishing death upon their critics? I have to wonder how much influence he had over the culture of Jehovah's Witnesses while he could influence them.

On January 18, about a month before Tony Morris was fired, the Governing Body brought in two new Governing Body members: Jeffrey Winder and Gage Fleegle. Tony Morris was fired within a month after the other two were added. The announcement was made at the headquarters and on the Jehovah's Witness website. It was a very quiet announcement, but it spread like wildfire.

Under the announcements section, a single line was posted for only a few days. The line read,

On Wednesday, February 22, 2023, it was announced at World Headquarters that Brother Anthony Morris III is no longer serving as a member of the Governing Body of Jehovah's Witnesses.

Something to note about the announcement—they called him "Brother Anthony Morris III." This is pure speculation, but it's educated speculation. I'd bet that means he wasn't disfellowshipped or disassociated. He's still part of the religion and presumably still believes he's Anointed. That means he's moving out of the headquarters and into his own house for the first time since at least

2005, when he was appointed as a Governing Body member, likely longer if he served as a Bethelite.

Here's another interesting wrinkle to the Tony Morris story: he claimed to be Anointed. That means he's expected to attend a congregation of Jehovah's Witnesses, have the bread and wine passed to him, and then eat and drink from them. He must take communion as an Anointed person. So, we had to wait until the Memorial to find out where he had gone. Surely, he would turn up by then.

…except that the Memorial came and went, and Tony Morris was nowhere to be found. As of the writing of this book, nobody in the ex-Jehovah's Witness community has any idea where he went. Nobody appears to have seen him at any Kingdom Halls or Bethel. There has been absolutely no word about him; dead silence. I thought for sure the 2023 Memorial would flush him out.

Is he taking communion? Has he decided he isn't Anointed anymore? Has he decided not to show his face to Jehovah's Witnesses ever again? I'd like to think those answers will be forthcoming one day. If there's one thing I know for sure, though, it's that Jehovah's Witnesses are terrible gossips. What else is there to do when everything fun is banned? Tattling on each other isn't just permitted; it's downright encouraged.

Bringing in the two new Governing Body members leading up to Tony Morris's firing (?) didn't make any sense doctrinally—it put a severe strain on a theology already stretched thin. The belief is that millions living during the events that unfolded in 1914 would never die. After being pushed against a wall, they changed the word "generation" to "contemporary." Anybody alive at the same time as somebody alive at the same time as Jesus came back in 1914 would never die. It was outrageous. It also didn't help the false prophecy. They only extended their time to around 2040.

The expectation among the active Governing Body members was that they were going to rule until the end. Nobody expected they'd need new Governing Body members. Yet here they are: Gage Fleegle and Jeffrey Winder, completely without explanation. A month later, Tony Morris was fired.

One of the most valuable pieces of information Ray Franz provided was how the Governing Body functioned. Every change was voted upon. Until 1975, every change had to be unanimous. After 1975, changes required a two-thirds majority. There was no word on how it functioned outside of Ray Franz's book until the 2023 annual meeting, released in early January 2024.

Jeffrey Winder illuminated the process. He said that the Governing Body orders a research crew to comb through everything the Watchtower Society has said about a subject since its founding in 1879. The research is presented to the Governing Body, and debate ensues. According to Winder, the decision must be unanimous. Either way, doctrinal change requires the input of other Governing Body members.

Leading up to his firing (or otherwise termination of his position), Tony Morris was the public face of absurdity within the religion. He came up with ridiculous, nonsensical rules. He also reversed historical doctrine seemingly at the drop of a dime. I'm dying with anticipation to see what he does next, if anything. I've never seen a Governing Body member fired. I can't imagine they ended on good terms after they parted ways and Tony disappeared.

WHO IS THE GREAT BEAST?

Revelation and Daniel had specific meanings to the people in that specific region and era. They don't make sense to us because we aren't members of that society. Historians have learned enough to piece together what the books of Revelation and Daniel were talking about. Let's discuss the actual, correct interpretation and the Jehovah's Witness interpretation.

Jehovah's Witnesses don't focus on the number 666 much

beyond believing that 666 and 6 alone are profoundly evil numbers. They think the number 666 represents imperfection, and when the Bible repeats something three times, it's for emphasis. Thus, 666 is imperfection to the highest degree. But what's imperfect? The Bible was clearly talking about a person or an entity. Jehovah's Witnesses believe the number 666 represents false worship. They believe everybody will be consumed by evil and false worship in the end. That's what they think Revelation means when it says people will take the mark of the beast.

Now that we know what Jehovah's Witnesses think, what did the number 666 actually mean? In ancient Jewish culture, there was a tradition called gematria.[3] The ancient Hebrew alphabet had 22 letters, all of them consonants. Vowels were inferred by context clues. Like the following example:

Sh slls s shlls t th sshr

It's hard to make sense of it, but if you squint, you can make out the phrase: "She sells sea shells at the seashore." Gematria was the practice of assigning a number to each letter, 1– 9. At the tenth letter, you would start counting in sets of ten. The eleventh number was worth 20; the twelfth number was worth 30, and so on. The letter N was worth 50. That'll be important in a minute.

To this day, gematria is used as a fun puzzle a Rabbi might put on the card of a bar mitzvah boy; it usually solves a moral statement of some sort. It was certainly never used to prophesy the future. Occasionally, it would be used to surreptitiously identify somebody in public writing without actually writing down their name.

Here's where the cultural context of the time was lost. When the book of Revelation was written, Christians were persecuted terribly by the Roman Empire under the rule of Nero, also known as Emperor Neron.

Revelation 13 talks about the number 666:

This calls for wisdom: let anyone with understanding calculate the number of the beast, for it is the number of a person. Its number is six hundred and sixty-six.

REVELATION 13:18

What's particularly interesting about this verse is that it appears in multiple manuscripts, including some that list the number of the beast as 616 rather than 666. Even more interesting is that the gematria for Emperor Nero is 616. When his full name is used, Neron, adding the "N" brings the number to 666 since N is worth 50 points.

The entire Book of Revelation is written this way. It uses cryptic, confusing language that makes absolutely no sense to anybody outside that place and time, but the people there understood what was being communicated.

Jehovah's Witnesses don't seem to correctly interpret basically any apocalyptic writing in the Bible. Their interpretation of the number 666 is wrong, but not as egregiously wrong as their interpretation of the scarlet-colored beast with seven heads and ten horns from Revelation 17.

Then one of the seven angels who had the seven bowls came and said to me, 'Come, I will show you the judgement of the great whore who is seated on many waters, with whom the kings of the earth have committed fornication, and with the wine of whose fornication the inhabitants of the earth have become drunk.' So he carried me away in the spirit into a wilderness, and I saw a woman sitting on a scarlet beast that was full of blasphemous names, and it had seven heads and ten horns.

REVELATION 17:1–3

So what did this mean? The beast with seven heads and ten horns is a dead giveaway. Rome was known as the city of seven hills since it was built on seven hills. Just as a whore sits on a beast with seven heads and drinking blood of saints, Rome sat on seven hills and persecuted God's people. The whore riding the beast represents Rome. If the angel didn't reveal the prophecies within the text itself, then it was assumed the reader would pick up on the context clues, like the gematria about Emperor Nero.

A few verses down, Revelation 17:11 says that another horn comes from the others.

> As for the beast that was and is not, it is an eighth but it belongs to the seven, and it goes to destruction.

REVELATION 17:11, NRSV

Jehovah's Witnesses translated it differently. The translation I used is the NRSV version. I think the acronyms are getting a little out of hand, but scholars prefer that translation. Here's the Jehovah's Witness translation:

> And the wild beast that was but is not, it is also an eighth king, but it springs from the seven, and it goes off into destruction.

REVELATION 17:11, NWT

The difference is slight, but it's there. The horn really represents a kingdom in the Roman Empire. The NRSV translation says the kingdom belongs to the "seven," as in the seven hills. It belongs to Rome. The Jehovah's Witness translation inaccurately says that it "springs from." It also portrays the other seven heads as separate kingdoms when it is obviously referring to the city on seven hills. In Jehovah's Witnesses' mind, the horn that "springs from" the seven represents the United Nations springing into existence from the other countries in the world.

Jehovah's Witnesses make a big, complex thing out of something that they completely misunderstood and even went so far as to translate it into their version of the Bible. If nothing else, this little translation "error" should be an example of why your translation matters. To my knowledge, no other translation has changed that phrase from "belongs to" to "springs from." This is by no means the only verse where they do this.

JOINING THE GREAT BEAST

On October 8, 2001, *The Guardian* released a story written by Stephen Bates, the religious affairs correspondent for the *Guardian*, revealing the Watchtower Society's status as an NGO, or non-government organization.

The United Nations is being asked to investigate why it has granted associate status to the Jehovah's Witnesses, the fundamentalist U.S.-based Christian sect, which regards it as the scarlet beast predicted in the Book of Revelation. Disaffected members of the 6m-strong group, which has 130,000 followers in the UK, have accused the Witnesses' elderly governing body of hypocrisy in secretly accepting links with an organisation that they continue to denounce in apocalyptic terms.

"JEHOVAH'S WITNESSES LINK TO UN QUERIED." *THE GUARDIAN.* OCTOBER 9, 2001.

The Watchtower Society withdrew membership from the United Nations a few days after the article was released. As usual, jwfacts.com wrote a full breakdown of the situation and included searchable PDF versions of every relevant document.[4]

Here's another excerpt from the original article:

The Watchtower Society has been denouncing the UN and its predecessor the League of Nations for 80 years, believing them to be a world empire of false religion, predicted in the Book of Revelation. A recent publication since the organisation [sic] obtained its recognition describes the UN as "a disgusting thing in the sight of God and his people". In an internal document, the WTBTS describes its policy as a "theocratic war strategy." It claims: "In a time of spiritual warfare, it is proper to misdirect the enemy by hiding the truth. It is done unselfishly; it does not harm anyone; on the contrary, it does much good."

The Watchtower Society is extremely cautious about discussing its theocratic warfare strategy. It's rarely discussed openly.

A former member said: "There is a glaring inconsistency which has emerged between the WTBTS's frequent portrayal of the UN as an evil organisation and its behind-the-scenes attempts to curry favour with that organisation [sic]. Were individual members to be aware of any formal link they would be devastated. "By no stretch of the imagination could the WTBTS be considered to share the ideals of the UN charter unless you suppose that destruction of the UN by God is consistent with that charter."

This one event should have been enough to destroy the religion entirely. Still, the Society is skilled at erasing history and covering things up. Hence, their people never have a chance to hear about it in the first place. Active Jehovah's Witnesses are banned from ever viewing apostate literature, which includes absolutely anything that runs the risk of being critical of the religion to any degree. It even consists of some of Jehovah's Witnesses' old literature.

Considering that they pulled out of the United Nations within days, I imagine they closely track articles about them. Either that or a flood of letters came in from outraged and confused Jehovah's Witnesses. Either way, it's a fascinating turn of events.

After what happened in Malawi—women being raped, men being killed for refusing to buy a card that registered them with the government—the Society's membership in the United Nations is simply a step too far. Joseph Rutherford's decision to write an endearing letter to Hitler was terrible, but that was 100 years ago. This was practically yesterday.

A UN official, Paul Hoeffel, released a public statement shortly after the Guardian revealed everything.

Recently the NGO section had been receiving numerous inquiries regarding the association of The Watchtower Bible and Tract Society of New York with the department of public information (DPI). This organization applied for association with DPI in 1991 and was granted association in 1992. By accepting association with DPI, the organization agreed to meet criteria for association, including support and respect of the principles of the Charter of the United Nations and commitment and means to conduct effective information programs with its constituents and to a broader audience about UN activities.

In October 2001, the Watchtower Bible and Tract Society of New York requested termination of its association with DPI. Following this request, the DPI has made a decision to disassociate the Watchtower Bible and Tract Society of New York as of 9 October 2001.

—October 9, 2001, Paul Hoeffel, Department of Public Information, United Nations

The fact that they were involved in a political organization is deeply hypocritical—especially after ordering countless Malawians to their deaths instead of allowing them to accept a political card with no relation to politics beyond the name. But to accept the charter and principles and be a part of an organization that they believe to be the Great Beast of the book of Revelation—it's just too much. This should be justification to leave the organization immediately for absolutely every Jehovah's Witness. The behavior of the Governing Body would be enough to get any other Jehovah's Witness disfellowshipped.

The Watchtower Society claimed that the application didn't require them to uphold the charter when they originally applied in 1991. They probably weren't expecting anybody to have the means to verify their claim. As it turns out, we have a copy of the application from 1991.

> Please note that the association of your Non-Governmental Organization)NGO) with the Department of Public Information (DPI) requires that you provide us with proof of your organization's non-profit status and with an annual report on its activities related to United Nations issues.
>
> UN APPLICATION FORM FOR NON-GOVERNMENTAL ORGANIZATIONS. 1991.

Every time the Watchtower Society offered an excuse, none of which should be acceptable by their own standards, the excuses were shot down by UN staff, the early internet, and researchers turning up irrefutable evidence to prove their claims false.

Shortly after being outed and exiting the UN, the Watchtower Society sent a letter to the *Guardian* and the congregations that said the following:

Dear Sir,

Stephen Bates' articles in The Guardian of October 8 and 15 substantially misrepresents the background to Jehovah's Witnesses registration with the United Nations and contains a number of factual errors.

ADDRESSED TO *THE GUARDIAN*—PAUL GILLIES, PRESS OFFICER FOR JEHOVAH'S WITNESSES IN BRITAIN, OCTOBER 22, 2001

Presumably, the following paragraph should contain a list of specific factual errors within the original article published by *The Guardian.* Let's keep reading.

In 1991, one of our legal corporations registered with the United Nations as an NGO (non-governmental organization) for the sole purpose of getting access to the extensive library of the United Nations. This enabled a writer who received an identification card, to enter their library for research purposes and to obtain information that has been used in writing articles in our Journals about the United Nations. There was nothing secret about it.

At the time of the initial application no signature was required on the form. Years later, unbeknown to the Governing Body of Jehovah's Witnesses, the United Nations published "Criteria for Association," stipulating that affiliated NGO's are required to support the goals of the United Nations.

After learning of the situation, our membership as NGO was withdrawn and the ID card of the writer was returned.

Sincerely, Paul Gillies

ADDRESSED TO *THE GUARDIAN*, PAUL GILLIES, PRESS OFFICER FOR JEHOVAH'S WITNESSES IN BRITAIN, OCTOBER 22, 2001

Absolutely no excuse is acceptable for being a part of the United Nations—none. The excuse given, though, was that the Watchtower Society's research and writing department required access to the UN library. I'm sorry—not the research and writing department. They said, "The writer's ID card was returned." That's singular—one writer. They could feasibly refer to the writing department, but that's not how the sentence should have been structured if that was the intended message. The message delivered, whether intentional or not, is that one person filled out the application, one person required access, and one person had an ID card.

Aside from the grammatical tricks the Watchtower Society attempts to pull, the claim that "the writer" needed a library card to access the UN library is simply false. Jehovah's Witnesses worldwide sent inquiries to the UN to uncover the truth and extent of the Watchtower Society's affiliation. The UN employees responded to inquiries in letter form.

> The procedure for a library pass is the following: the interested party needs to fill out an application form and supply a letter of recommendation in support of the research. If the needed material is not available in a UN depository library (the list of depository libraries is posted at: http://www.un.org/depts/dhl/deplib/coun tries/, the application is approved and sent to UN security, UN security checks the application and, if approval is granted, instructs the Pass Office to issue a library pass for the applicant.

> The issuance of a Library pass is independent of NGO status or any other status. There has been no change in the library pass policy in general; however, please be advised that, as a consequence of the September 11 attacks, no library passes are being issued for the time being while the security situation at the UN is being studied.

—Dana Loytved, Senior Reference Librarian, January 3, 2002

Jehovah's Witnesses claimed *"the* writer" needed access to the UN library for research purposes. The senior reference librarian shot that to pieces by pointing out the fact that all books and research materials are available without being registered as an NGO—all you need is a library card.

The entire situation is a massive embarrassment for the Watchtower Society. It should be all the evidence any Jehovah's Witness needs to conclude that the Watchtower Society, the Governing Body, the Anointed, the helpers (such as the president), the writing department, and every other member of the Watchtower Society don't have the mandate of heaven. They aren't speaking to God. They don't receive prophecy from Jesus. The organization is just as hypocritical, calculated, and cynical as any other church out there, if not more so.

Jehovah's Witnesses have held a series of end-times beliefs for a very long time. They get much of those end-times beliefs from the apocalyptic writing in Revelation, Daniel, Isaiah, and Ezekiel. Next, let's talk about Jehovah's Witnesses' interpretation of the apocalyptic writing found in the Bible and what the apocalyptic writing *meant.*

CHAPTER 9

JEHOVAH'S WITNESSES' BELIEFS ABOUT "THE END"

Many of Jehovah's Witnesses' most famous apocalyptic prophecies started from their Revelation book, *"Revelation: Its Grand Climax At Hand!"* The 1980s and 1990s were full of end-times prophecy. They published the Revelation book in 1988, the "Daniel's Prophecies" book in 1999, and a two-part series about the book of Isaiah released in 2000 and 2001, respectively. Since much of it came from the book of Daniel, let's talk about when Daniel was written and why Jehovah's Witnesses' interpretation is wrong.

WHEN WAS THE BOOK OF DANIEL WRITTEN?

The book of Daniel is one of the earliest examples of apocalyptic genre writing in the Bible.[1] It wasn't meant to be taken literally. It was intended to be read like science fiction or fantasy. It was, however, commonly intended to convey a point. People wrote in apocalyptic writing for a variety of reasons. Maybe they wanted to catch the reader's attention with vivid imagery or specifically warn against some persecutor without putting themselves in danger, or maybe they simply liked the style.

Unfortunately, modern Christians—including Jehovah's Witnesses—either don't realize or completely ignore the fact that the apocalyptic genre existed. The people reading the book of Daniel or Revelation when it was written understood exactly what was being communicated because the message was glaringly obvious in the societal context of the time.

The apocalyptic genre always follows a similar pattern: the writer experiences a bizarre vision, an angel appears to explain what the bizarre vision means, and the story ends with God's people being saved or vindicated in some way.

Jerusalem has been conquered by empire after empire over the millennia. Cultures from various empires permeated the area. Since different empires had different writing styles, languages, and cultures, writing from the area can be dated very accurately to within fifty years or so. As you'll see, cultural markers and even the language used give us an idea of when the Book of Daniel was written. If those factors aren't dead giveaways, then the fact that the Book of Daniel named kings from the Babylonian era who never even existed[2] should be the final nail in the coffin. It was not written in the time and place it claimed to have been written.

New Testament scholars can date Greek writing within 50 years based only on the writing style. In 500 years, archaeologists will likely be able to read writing sections from the 18th to the 21st centuries and date the works within 50 years. Fonts could also indicate when books were written, as in ancient Greek writings. More than anything, researchers could determine when books were written by the words and phrases used in them or in articles.

It's been a while since anybody used "bearcat" or "gongoozler" —two common insults in the 1920s. Common terms used in the 1970s include "diggin' it," "dingbat," "bogart," and "foxy mama." If those terms frequently appear in a text, scholars will know that the writing is from the 1960s but more likely from the 1970s. It couldn't be any earlier than when the terms were invented. It's possible and certainly worth considering that the writing might have attempted to imitate older texts. However, the writing absolutely wasn't trying to accurately replicate a writing style that won't exist for 400 more years—and succeeding.

If a shipwreck is discovered, dive teams might look for artifacts to date the wreck. Divers come across coins and find some dated to 1953. That means the shipwreck absolutely did not happen in 1950. It might have happened in 1975. It might have even happened in 2020, but it simply did not happen in 1950. This concept is called an anachronism.

Anachronisms demand an explanation. It's conceivable to think that maybe somebody dropped their change off the side of a boat in the mid-2000s. But the conclusion is simply unavoidable when you start finding coins between 2002 and 2010 inside every single suitcase onboard the shipwreck. It would be even more damning evidence to find the captain's diary dated to the mid-2000s. The shipwreck did not happen in 1992. The date needs to be adjusted.

Jehovah's Witnesses' dates for Daniel are between 617 BCE and 537 BCE. Scholars determined that the book was written between 167 BCE and 164 BCE[3], around the time of the Maccabean revolt—the event that created Hanukah. If we find anachronisms throughout the book, we know beyond a shadow of a doubt that the book was written later than it claimed. Jehovah's Witnesses claim that Daniel's anachronistic qualities result from prophecy. Daniel 8:20–22 talks about the empires that will conquer the area between 600 BCE and 164 BCE:

> As for the ram that you saw with the two horns, these are the kings
> of Media and Persia. The male goat is the king of Greece, and the
> great horn between its eyes is the first king. As for the horn that

was broken, in place of which four others arose, four kingdoms shall arise from his nation but not with his power.

DANIEL 8:20–22

If Jehovah's Witnesses' dates are correct, then this is an anachronism. The angel describes events that took place between 600 BCE and 164 BCE, and it purports to have been written around 600 BCE. For the sake of argument, though, let's pretend it's a prophecy rather than an anachronism. Maybe Daniel saw the future to determine which empires would take control of the region.

…except that prophecy isn't the only anachronism in the book. In his book titled The Hebrew of Daniel, W. J. Martin indicates that at least 30 Greek words are used in the book of Daniel.[4] If the book had been written when it claimed, the words used would have been written in Aramaic. In his scholarly paper, W. J. Martin indicates that the book of Daniel was written at least as early as 334 BCE when Alexander the Great conquered the area. It couldn't have been written any earlier than that. Textual critics have placed it at 164 BCE, but here's the point: it didn't happen in the 500s BCE.

Daniel 8:20–22 is not a prophecy. It's an example of a writer using apocalyptic writing to tell a story of their people and give them hope. The style of writing, the words, and even the language used all matched a period 400 years later. Why would the book of Daniel use a style of writing and language that simply doesn't match the period? Jehovah's Witnesses are the biggest skeptics on planet Earth when it's convenient. When it's inconvenient, that skepticism goes right out the window.

Imagine finding a book dated to the year the King James Bible was first released—1611. You'd expect to see the famous King James style language when you open the book. But instead, you see that it has language commonly used in the 1980s. Additionally, the book expresses outrage over the Vietnam War. It would be evident that the book was not written in 1611 and that mentions of the Vietnam War were not prophecy.

Furthermore, Daniel wasn't even written in the correct language for the 550s. There are entirely too many anachronisms. Daniel was written in the year 164 BCE, not 550 BCE. It just was.

In 1931, a Greek copy of Daniel, dated to the 200s CE, was found. It contained much more than the original Hebrew writing. Daniel's Greek manuscript contained three additional stories that weren't present in the Hebrew manuscripts. Protestant Bibles don't include the stories, but some Catholic and Orthodox Christian Bibles still do.

INTERPRETING THE BOOK OF DANIEL

William Miller interpreted the book of Daniel as prophesying what would happen 2500 years into the future. It wasn't about some far-off future event that the writer of Daniel hadn't yet experienced. Charles Taze Russell and Miller both plucked numbers from Daniel seemingly at random to use as variables in their math equations. We've already discussed the variables and how they were used in prophecy. Now, let's talk about the apocalypses and what they actually meant.

The Millerites, who later splintered into the Seventh-Day Adventists, used apocalyptic writing to calculate Jesus' original arrival on earth in the year 1 BCE by referencing 70 weeks in Daniel 9. This calculation needs to be corrected by 4-5 years. Reliable sources place Jesus' arrival closer to 3 CE or 4 CE. This incorrect starting point would be a significant issue for both the Millerites and Jehovah's Witnesses when trying to prophesy Jesus' return.

To gain context for Daniel 9, let me summarize Daniel 7: Four beasts rise up out of the sea. The first beast looks like a lion with an eagle's wings. The second looks like a bear. The third beast looks like a leopard. Finally, the fourth beast was the most fearsome and terrifying. It had iron teeth and ten horns.

The writer then says he watched as three horns were plucked from the beast to make room for a smaller horn with human eyes "and a mouth speaking arrogantly." The little horn described here was Antiochus IV Epiphanes, the king of the Seleucid Empire.[5] He persecuted the Jews terribly, so naturally, any apocalypse about him would portray him in a negative light.

The Seleucid Empire resulted from Alexander the Great's Greek Empire "shattering" into four pieces after he died in the 300s BCE. Each of the four new kingdoms was controlled by one of his four generals. The Seleucid Empire, under the reign of Antiochus IV Epiphanes, took Jerusalem in 167 BCE, just three short years before Daniel was written, in 164 BCE.

Daniel, Chapter 8, starts by discussing the third year of the reign of King Belshazzar—a king who never existed. This chapter describes Daniel watching as a ram appears and chases off the four beasts from the sea. Then, a male goat appears from the west.

A male goat appears from the west, coming across the face of the whole earth without touching the ground. The goat had a turn between its eyes. It came towards the ram with the two horns that I had seen standing beside the river, and it ran at it with savage force.

DANIEL 8:5

This verse is about the struggle between the Syrian King Antiochus IV Epiphanes and the Jewish people. Antiochus was doing everything he could to force the Jews to "Hellenize," which meant integrating more into Greek culture. Unbeknownst to Antiochus, a rebellion was brewing among the Maccabees, a local Jewish militant group.

The verses are much less mystifying and confusing once you realize that the book was actually written around the time of the Maccabean revolt. Understanding the context behind the verses makes it clear how absolutely ridiculous it was for Jehovah's Witnesses to take these verses and twist them into some bizarre prophecy that supposedly took place thousands of years after it was written. Jehovah's Witnesses admit that some verses of the book of Daniel, namely, the verses about the King of the North and the King of the South, were talking about literal powers to the north and south of Jerusalem. They also believe there will be a figurative King of the North and South. Contrary to their belief, as referenced a few chapters later, the King of the North was also Antiochus.[6]

> Then I heard a holy one speaking, and another holy one said to the one that spoke, "for how long is this vision concerning the regular burnt-offering, the transgression that makes desolate, and the giving over of the sanctuary and host to be trampled?" And he answered him, "for two thousand three hundred evenings and mornings; then the sanctuary shall be restored to its rightful state."

> *DANIEL 8:13*

The last verse, about 2,300 mornings and evenings, is the last variable we needed to calculate the 2,300-year prophecy. This is the equation that Seventh-Day Adventists originally held. One glaring problem with the variable is the verse they use specifically says that 2,300 mornings and evenings will pass. Not years, but mornings and evenings. I'm not sure why the Adventists felt entitled to ignore what the Bible said and change it to years, but here we are. The 2,300-year prophecy supposedly foretold that the rapture would be here without a doubt and absolutely in the year 1843.

The failure of the Millerite 2,300-year prophecy is the starting point for the founder of Jehovah's Witnesses. He and many

Seventh-Day Adventists believed this prophecy was simply missing a secret variable to make it accurate. From this misunderstanding of scripture comes the entire Jehovah's Witness religion.

As is common with apocalyptic writing, the writer is baffled and confused by this bizarre vision he just made up, so he brings an angel into the story to explain the vivid imagery. Remember that this book was written in 164, Which means it was written 170 years after Alexander the Great conquered the area, three years after Antiochus took Jerusalem in the name of the Seleucid Empire. It took place right in the middle of the Maccabean revolt to reclaim the city of Jerusalem for themselves. The book was also written the very year that Antiochus died—164 BCE. That last point will be relevant later.

The writer of Daniel had all of this information as he wrote the following few verses in Chapter 8. The immortal messenger of God is about to explain the vision to Daniel, who claims to be living through the exile period in Babylon around the year 585 BCE.

> As for the ram that you saw with the two horns, these are the kings of Media and Persia. The male goat is the king of Greece, and the great horn between its eyes is the first king. As for the horn that was broken, in place of which four others arose, four kingdoms shall arise from his nation, but not with his power.

DANIEL 8:20–22

As I said, the writer of Daniel absolutely wrote this down with the knowledge I just explained—and he nearly followed what I listed to a tee. Cyrus took over Babylon and released the Jews from captivity; Alexander the Great took over the area in the name of Greece, the Great Horn was broken (Alexander died), and his four generals rose up in his place, but not with his power. It was very obvious what was happening at that moment in time. Jehovah's

Witnesses believe it had to mean something more, even though the book did not indicate additional meaning.

I want to take a brief aside to discuss one of the stranger doctrines of Jehovah's Witnesses. You could probably follow the rest of the explanation of their Daniel-based teachings without it, but it's too interesting for me to skip it.

MICHAEL THE ARCHANGEL

Modern Jehovah's Witnesses believe that Jesus is Michael the archangel. The doctrine is also believed by Lutheran denominations and Jehovah's Witnesses' cousin religion, the Seventh Day Adventists. Jehovah's Witnesses also believe that God created Jesus, and Jesus went on to create everything else.

Regarding the belief that Jesus is the archangel, the first argument Jehovah's Witnesses present is this: people are sometimes known by multiple names. For example, Jacob is known as Israel, and Peter is known as Simon.

They also note that the word archangel means "chief angel. " Therefore, Michael might not be an angel himself, but he is the chief of the angels. This would be a fair argument, except that's not what the word archangel means. It literally translates to "chief messenger"—the primary messenger for God.

The book of Jude refers to Michael as *the* archangel. In the Watchtower Society's mind, the word "the" used in the verse implies there is only one. This doesn't mean there isn't a class of primary messengers, a leadership class, like "the Governing Body"—a single group of nine individuals. Although the word "the" can be used to refer to a single item, obviously, it can also refer to a group of things.

The second part of the argument also uses 1 Thessalonians 4:16 as evidence.

For the Lord himself, with a cry of command, with the archangel's call and with the sound of God's trumpet, will descend from heaven, and the dead in Christ will rise first.

1 THESSALONIANS 4:16

Amusingly, this is the verse commonly used in Protestant Christianity to justify the rapture. Jehovah's Witnesses claim that Jesus will return to earth with the archangel's call. Strangely, the verse says he will have a cry of command. How many cries of command are there? Suppose Jehovah's Witnesses' logic is to be believed. In that case, there are a variety of cries of command since the article "a" is used instead of "the." There is, however, only one archangel call. Not one archangel, but one archangel call. The verse doesn't refer to an archangel. It refers to the call of an archangel. I'm relieved to find that God only has one trumpet, though.

I'm being facetious, but I hope I've adequately demonstrated why it's absurd to get hung up on a single word here or there. The letters to the Thessalonica congregation were written in Koine Greek—a different language than modern Greek, though likely recognizable by modern Greek speakers—and translated into English. The oldest copy of 1 Thessalonians is from 200 years after the original was written. Who knows which parts were modified or which words countless scribes decided to keep or toss? We probably have a rough approximation of the original—close enough to get the general gist of what Paul was trying to communicate. Playing word games, zeroing in on tenses, or using "the" rather than "a" is absurd, illogical, and will get you nowhere. Translate this sentence into a few languages, then back to the original, and my point will become clear.

The last argument offered goes like this: the Bible refers to Michael as having an army of angels. It also mentions that Jesus has an army of angels. The verse used to claim Jesus has an army of angels is cited as Matthew 13:41.

> The Son of Man will send his angels, and they will collect out of his kingdom all causes of sin and all evildoers...
>
> *MATTHEW 13:41*

The Son of Man was a role that an anointed man of God was expected to fulfill one day. He would take political leadership of the kingdom of Israel. The kingdom would be called The Kingdom of God, and it would stand until the end of time. Jesus never took political leadership of Israel. He never created the Kingdom of God. He's supposed to do that when he returns. That's why Jesus must return to earth in the first place. Aside from all of that, Jesus' apostles probably thought he was the Son of Man, but he likely did not. For the sake of argument, though, let's assume Jesus believed he was and, in actuality, was the Son of Man.

The verse used to justify the claim that Michael has an army of angels is Revelation 12:7:

> And war broke out in heaven; Michael and his angels fought against the dragon. The dragon and his angels fought back, but they were defeated, and there was no longer any place for them in heaven.
>
> *REVELATION 12:7–8*

Revelation 12:7–8 obviously describes a war in heaven that ended with "the dragon and his angels" being kicked out of heaven.

Here's the final part of the argument from the Jehovah's Witnesses website:

Since God's word nowhere indicates that there are two armies of faithful angels in heaven—one headed by Michael and one headed by Jesus—it is logical to conclude that Michael is none other than Jesus Christ in his heavenly role.[7]

The Bible doesn't describe balloons, cars, art, or music in heaven. That doesn't mean those things don't exist. The Bible is sparse on details about heaven. It's worth noting that something not being mentioned is not justification to believe it doesn't exist at all. The Bible never says Jesus had a beard, but Jehovah's Witnesses still believe he did.

Another simple refutation of this argument is that the Bible could refer to one army. Jesus may have commanded the army of the faithful at one time, and Michael commanded that same army in the Dragon fight. These events weren't happening simultaneously—they weren't even happening on the same plane of existence. The commander could have easily changed.

The final knock-down argument to their claim that Michael is Jesus can be found in Hebrews 1:13.

But to which of the angels has he ever said, 'Sit at my right hand until I make your enemies a footstool for your feet'?

HEBREWS 1:13

The Bible says that Jesus will sit at God's right hand. Hebrews 1:13 states that God has never invited an angel to do so. The only way those two verses could work cohesively is to accept that Jesus isn't an angel—he's something else.

Let's put one more nail in the coffin with Daniel 10:13. Let's read it from the NRSV translation:

So Michael, one of the chief princes, came to help me, and I left him there with the prince of the kingdom of Persia.

DANIEL 10:13, NRSV

This verse blows a hole right through the idea that Michael is Jesus. Scholars prefer the NRSV translation to the Bible translation. It's about as accurate as you'll get without reading it in its original language. Daniel 10:13 says that Michael is "**one of** the chief princes." This verse in Daniel pretty clearly explains that "chief messenger" is a category or a class, not a specific title for a singular entity as Jehovah's Witnesses believe.

Jehovah's Witnesses removed what they believed to be errors by translating it differently and translated it to be more favorable to their existing beliefs. Even so, this verse from their own translation destroys the belief that Michael is Jesus. Their translation of Daniel 10:13 says the following:

But then Michael*, one of the foremost princes*, came to help me; and I remained there beside the kings of Persia.

DANIEL 10:13, NWT

The Jehovah's Witnesses' footnote after Michael* says, "Meaning 'Who Is Like God?.'" The footnote for princes* says, "Or 'a prince of the first rank.'" I haven't seen anything in any translations that omits the term "one of" from this verse. Even their translation seems to affirm that Michael is one of the chief angels, not the chief angel. They tried to save it with the footnote on princes, but there is no indication it was talking about a singular being. It was obviously talking about a class of beings—one of the chief angels (or archangels)—which means that there can be multiple chief messengers. From a theological perspective, Jesus is not Michael. They are different characters with different roles in the Bible.

Not only do Jehovah's Witnesses believe Michael the Archangel is Jesus, but they also think that God created Jesus, and then Jesus created everything else. So, really, Jehovah's Witnesses think Jesus is the ultimate, divine creator. Here's a quote from the Jehovah's Witness website:

God created Jesus before creating Adam. In fact, God created Jesus and then used him to make everything else, including the angels. That is why the Bible calls Jesus "the firstborn of all creation" by God. (Colossians 1:15, 16)[8]

Okay. Let's read Colossians, then.

He is the image of the invisible God, the firstborn of all creation; for in him all things in heaven and on earth were created, things visible and invisible, whether thrones or dominions or rulers or powers— all things have been created through him and for him.

COLOSSIANS 1:15, 16

According to the NRSVA translation, when it says, "for in him all things in heaven and on earth were created..." the word "in" can also mean by. This is another prime example of Jehovah's Witnesses picking a single word in a verse and building an entire theology around that idea.

Reading the verse naturally, it could read, "He [Jesus] is the image of the invisible God, the firstborn of all creation; for in [or by] him [Jesus or God?] all things in heaven and on earth were created ... through him and for him." The verse could just as easily refer to God when it uses the second instance of "he." The first half of the sentence refers to two subjects: Jesus and God.

Jehovah's Witnesses chose the strangest and most nonsensical reading of the verse based on English grammar rather than accepting the fact that English wasn't the language it was originally written in. They're trying to apply grammar rules for English, not Koine Greek. This is a quintessential example of Jehovah's Witnesses building theology from nothing. After over 100 years of writing doctrine in their *Watchtower* magazines and various books, not contradicting old doctrine with new doctrine has to be a nightmare for the Governing Body. But hey, they can always label their old doctrine as apostate material and completely ignore it.

Now that we've thoroughly covered the bizarre angel beliefs, let's return to our close look at Daniel. The statue prophecy has always been particularly meaningful to me and particularly damaging to the Watchtower Society.

NEBUCHADNEZZAR'S STATUE

When I started my YouTube channel and Patreon page, I set the support levels to "gold," "silver," "bronze," "iron," and finally, "iron and clay" to reference this supposed "prophecy" from the Watchtower Society.

In the story, Nebuchadnezzar is struggling with another dream. Daniel is called in to interpret. Nebuchadnezzar had a dream about a giant statue of himself. The head was gold, the chest was silver, the waist was bronze, the legs were iron, and the feet were iron and clay. Daniel says that the different metals represent different kingdoms. Nebuchadnezzar, leader of the Babylonian empire, is represented by the head of gold. That's where Daniel 2:38 starts.

...you are the head of gold. After you shall arise another kingdom inferior to yours, and yet a third kingdom of bronze, which shall rule over the whole earth. And there shall be a fourth kingdom, strong as iron; just as iron crushes and smashes everything, it shall crush and shatter all these. As you saw the feet and toes partly of potter's clay and partly of iron, it shall be a divided kingdom; but some of the strength of iron shall be in it, as you saw the iron mixed with the clay. As the toes of the feet were part iron and part clay, so the kingdom shall be partly strong and partly brittle. As you saw the iron mixed with clay, so will they mix with one another in marriage, but they will not hold together, just as iron does not mix with clay.

DANIEL 2:36–43

This "prophecy" is another prime example of the book of Daniel having the benefit of hindsight. Though Daniel doesn't specifically list the empires correlated to the statue, he does say that the head of gold represents Nebuchadnezzar. In other apocalyptic prophecies throughout the book, angels link the characters in every apocalyptic vision to a list of empires. If you recall, Daniel 7 and 8 portray another apocalyptic vision with "great beasts" coming from the sea. An angel explains that the beasts represent the Babylonian, Persian, and Greek empires. These three empires were the next to control the area surrounding Jerusalem. The angel describes "four kingdoms" arising from the third empire. It was clearly referring to the Seleucid Empire, the empire they were in when Daniel was written. The Seleucid Empire arose after the Greek Empire shattered into four separate nations.

That interpretation continues throughout the book of Daniel. Jehovah's Witnesses and the rest of the Christian world largely agree that Nebuchadnezzar's statue represents the same empires that are described in Daniel 8:20. Here's a breakdown of the empires that the statue actually represented:

- **Head** (gold)—Nebuchadnezzar of the Babylonian empire
- **Arms** (silver)—King Cyrus of the Persian Empire

- **Waist** (bronze)—Alexander the Great of the Greek empire
- **Legs** (iron)—Antiochus IV Epiphanes of the Seleucid Empire (current empire)
- **Feet** (iron and clay)—?

Daniel conspicuously never mentions the next empire in line after the Seleucid Empire—the Roman Empire. He claims that the Seleucid Empire will fall, which isn't surprising. Sixteen thousand different empires had conquered Judea up to that point. The Jewish people habitually adapted to life under the latest empire and resisted the cultural changes that came with it. The fact that Daniel never mentioned the Roman Empire, which was around the corner —about 100 years away—is a death blow to the idea that this is a prophecy.

Jehovah's Witnesses, though, see that Daniel didn't list the last empire and took that to mean they could fill in whatever they wanted. Here's how Jehovah's Witnesses view the "world powers" represented by the statue:[9]

- **Head** (gold)—Nebuchadnezzar of the Babylonian Empire.
- **Arms** (silver)—King Cyrus of the Persian Empire.
- **Waist** (bronze)—Alexander the Great of the Greek Empire.
- **Legs** (iron)—Roman Empire.
- **Feet** (iron and clay)—Anglo-American Empire.

I have to ask, is there a reason why they skipped right over the empire that existed when the Book of Daniel was written? They went straight from Greece to Rome and apparently completely forgot about the Seleucid Empire, which existed for about as long as the United States has existed as of the writing of this book. Even stranger, they went from Rome to Anglo-America, skipping right over the Ottoman Empire, which controlled the area for at least as long as the Roman Empire. I believe the Ottoman Empire has an even stronger claim to the feet of clay and iron than the Anglo-American Empire.

When Jehovah's Witnesses use the term Anglo-American, they're using the word Anglo to refer to the combined British and American empires. I'm not sure why Jehovah's Witnesses decided to link them. The two empires fought each other viciously. They are clearly two separate empires. I imagine they chose to link the two empires together because they needed two empires to account for the iron and clay in the feet of Nebuchadnezzar's statue. Again, the Ottoman Empire could fit the bill much more cleanly.

For that matter, when did America ever control modern-day Israel and Palestine? If control of Israel and Palestine isn't a qualifier for being the feet of iron and clay, then why didn't they choose the many Chinese empires that came and went throughout the intervening years? They could have included the Sui Dynasty, the Tang Dynasty, the Five Dynasties, the Liao Dynasty, the Western Zia Dynasty, or all of the above. Babylon, Persia, Greece, and Rome did not control the world—they only controlled the section that happened to include modern-day Israel and Palestine.

Jehovah's Witnesses have one more prophecy about the Book of Daniel: the King of the North prophecy. Daniel mentions the King of the North in Chapter 11. The Jehovah's Witnesses' website outlines the standard by which they judge qualifying empires.

> To understand the prophecy recorded in Daniel chapter 11, we need to keep in mind that it identifies only rulers and governments that have had a direct influence on God's people. And even though God's servants make up only a small portion of the world's population, they are often at the center of major world events.

JEHOVAH'S WITNESSES. "THE KING OF THE

NORTH'IN THE TIME OF THE END." *THE WATCHTOWER, STUDY EDITION.* MAY, 2020.

Jehovah's Witnesses have an answer for this, though. They claim that Britain was part of the Roman Empire. The Roman Empire eventually broke into a billion different pieces in the west, and the Eastern Roman Empire became the Byzantines. The main problem with this assessment is that the Roman Empire did not turn into Britain. It turned into Italy. Or, rather, it always was Italy. If we're playing by those rules, then the Seleucid Empire, the Greek Empire, and the Persian Empire were actually the Babylonian Empire. None of them should have their own slot on the statue. In fact, the British Empire and the Roman Empire are also part of the Babylonian Empire. Why not? Let's throw everybody in together. There's only ever been one empire since the dawn of time.

Surprisingly, their justification for the idea that Britain was part of the Roman Empire continues. They note that one of the beasts in Revelation grew extra horns, representing Britain, Spain/Holland, and France. In the apocalypse, only one horn became prominent. Jehovah's Witnesses point out that, eventually, one empire found itself on top, just like in the book of Revelation. The British Empire eventually conquered the seas with its navy.

I suppose Jehovah's Witnesses ignore that France was the dominant world power and Britain's main rival for a long time. The tide turned in the war between the two rivals when Napoleon lost the Battle of Waterloo, which took place in 1815. It was a humiliating defeat and a clear sign that Britain had become the dominant world power. Jehovah's Witnesses claim it came into power in 1763 and joined forces with the United States in 1776. They're not even stretching the timeline to make it fit. They're completely ignoring relevant details. Their whole timeline is wrong.

Britain was once a northwestern part of the Roman Empire. But by the year 1763, it had become the British Empire—the Britannia that ruled the seven seas. By 1776 its 13 American colonies had declared their independence in order to set up the United States of America. In later years, however, Britain and the United States became partners in both war and peace. Thus, the Anglo-American combination came into existence as the seventh world power of Bible prophecy.

JEHOVAH'S WITNESSES. *"PAY ATTENTION TO DANIEL'S PROPHECY."* 1999. P. 57, PARAGRAPH 24

Either Jehovah's Witnesses are wrong about the statue prophecy, or they apply principles unevenly. Not only is the Nebuchadnezzar statue prophecy logically absurd, but it's nowhere to be found in the Bible. It describes a statue representing world powers and names the next world powers. The Watchtower Society didn't find a prophecy about the Anglo-American Empire; they made it up. They fabricated it out of nothing. How do they know the Book of Daniel refers to the Anglo-American empire? They know it because God told them. How can we trust that God told them? Because they speak for God, and he told them they speak for Him.

God didn't bother putting it directly in the Bible. Apparently, he put it in code that had to be deciphered by the Watchtower Society, God's chosen organization, 2,500 years later. I think God would have put it in the Bible if he wanted people to believe it. He doesn't have to play games—he can simply transmit the information he wants humans to have.

Believe it or not, that's not the only prophecy they completely fabricated out of nothing. I've repeatedly mentioned Jehovah's Witnesses' King of the North prophecy. It's finally time to see how it factors into this whole equation. Let's talk about who the King of the North was, and then we'll talk about how Jehovah's Witnesses have misinterpreted the verses.

KING OF THE NORTH: THE FACTS

The King of the North apocalypse can be found in Daniel 11 and 12. As with other apocalypses, the writer sees some bizarre, nonsensical vision that means nothing to the writer or the reader. An angel conveniently comes in from nowhere to explain what the recipient of the vision just witnessed. The vision itself is a confusing train wreck, as usual. He describes standing on the Tigris River when suddenly he received this vision:

> I looked up and saw a man clothed in linen, with a belt of gold from Uphaz around his waist. His body was like beryl, his face like lightning, his eyes like flaming torches, his arms and legs like the gleam of burnished bronze, and the sound of his words like the roar of a multitude.
>
> *DANIEL 10:5–6*

There's more to the vision, but you get the idea. As aforementioned, the "vision" portion of the story is largely unimportant because an angel is about to interpret it for us. In my estimation, we have no right to offer our own theological interpretations when the interpretation has already been provided.

This next verse not only disproves Jehovah's Witnesses' idea that Michael is Jesus, but it also describes an angel appearing to Daniel to explain the apocalypse.

> So, Michael, **one of** the chief princes, came to help me, and I left him there with the prince of the kingdom of Persia.

DANIEL 10:13

The angel starts by listing the empires leading up to the one the writer is currently in—the Seleucid Empire—originally a part of the Greek Empire. In Daniel 11:4, the writer is pretty obviously talking about the Greek Empire shattering into four pieces:

> And while still rising in power, his kingdom shall be broken and divided towards the four winds of heaven.

DANIEL 11:4

This is the exact same "prophecy" described in the statue apocalypse. In both apocalyptic explanations, the angel listed the empires that would come: the Babylonian Empire, the Persian Empire, and the Greek Empire. Alexander the Great had conquered the area in the name of the Greek Empire around 150–200 years before Daniel was written. When Alexander the Great died, the Greek Empire shattered into "four winds," or four separate empires, which arose when Alexander died and his generals took control. The four empires were the Ptolemaic Empire (Egypt), the Seleucid Empire (controlled Jerusalem), Pergamon (Asia Minor), and the Macedonian Empire.

Around the time Daniel was written, the sixth Syrian war was taking place between Antiochus of the Seleucid Empire (to the north) and Ptolemy of Egypt (to the south). Jerusalem was caught in the middle. Rome, not an empire quite yet, was busy fighting the Macedonians.

The Seleucid Empire fought the Ptolemaic Empire in Egypt six times between 274 BCE and 168 BCE, during the years before Daniel's writing. The Sixth Syrian War lasted from 170 to 168 BCE.

Verse 15 indicates who the King of the North is. Once you

realize that Jerusalem was caught in the middle of the sixth Syrian war, the reason the writer was even talking about kings of the north and south becomes impossible to miss.

> Then the king of the north shall come and throw up siege-works and take a well-fortified city. And the forces of the south shall not stand, not even his picked troops, for there shall be no strength to resist.

DANIEL 11:15

Verse 21 is an even clearer indication that the entire vision is about the sixth Syrian war.

> In his place shall arise a contemptible person on whom royal majesty had not been conferred; he shall come in without warning and obtain the kingdom through intrigue.

DANIEL 11:21

Both Ptolemy (King of the South) and Antiochus (King of the North) sent emissaries to Rome. Rome was powerful but would not become a full empire for roughly 150 years. Rome could have tipped the battle on either side but was busy fighting the Third Macedonian War.

Even though the angel clearly explained what the apocalypse meant, Jehovah's Witnesses interpreted their own additional meaning from it. They believe the King of the North and South will be revealed over time. They think it's a prophecy intended to provide insight into what's happening today. Jehovah's Witnesses even have a running prophecy about it.

KING OF THE NORTH: THE BELIEFS

Around the year 2019, shortly after Jehovah's Witnesses were banned from operating inside of Russia, the Governing Body conveniently received a message from God that Russia was the King of the North.

The following quote from the May 2020 (Study Ed.) *Watchtower* outlines the belief:

> The titles "king of the north" and "king of the south" were initially given to political powers located north and south of the literal land of Israel. Why do we say that? Notice what the angel who delivered the message to Daniel said: "I have come to make you understand what will befall your people in the final part of the days."

> JEHOVAH'S WITNESSES. "THE KING OF THE NORTH". *THE WATCHTOWER, STUDY EDITION.* MAY, 2020. PARAGRAPH 4

As indicated in their *Watchtower*, Jehovah's Witnesses seem to know that the kings of the north and south were the Ptolemaic Empire of Egypt and Antiochus of the Seleucid Empire. They simply believe there's an additional prophecy on top of what the Bible clearly outlines. As is common practice with Jehovah's Witnesses, they base this prophecy on razor-thin logic.

> In the time of the end the king of the south will engage with him [the king of the north] in a pushing.

> *DANIEL 11:40*

"The end" doesn't mean the literal end of time. Talk of the end is a common trope in apocalyptic literature. It means Jews will ultimately be victorious over their enemies. It's just part of the writing genre.

Another reasoning they use to conclude that it must have an additional meaning that applies to the 21st century is that, in their minds, the Jews ceased being God's people in the year 33 CE. Jesus came and died, and now all prophecies transfer over to Gentiles, even though the prophecies were laid down and subsequently fulfilled before Jesus even came.

> The United States and Britain were welded into a powerful military alliance during the First World War. At that time, Britain and its former colony became the Anglo-American World Power. As Daniel foretold, this king had amassed "an exceedingly large and mighty army." (Dan. 11:25). Throughout the last days, the Anglo-American alliance has been the king of the south.
>
> JEHOVAH'S WITNESSES. "THE KING OF THE NORTH IN THE TIME OF THE END." *THE WATCHTOWER.* STUDY EDITION. MAY 2020, PARAGRAPH 8

Looks like Jehovah's Witnesses have once again fabricated answers to a prophecy that they created in the first place. They named the King of the South the British and American alliance. I wonder why they named the King of the North now instead of 50 years ago. The Soviet Union was a much more formidable adversary to their King of the South, the U.S. Additionally, not to nitpick, but the United States is 2,747 miles from the equator, and Israel is 2,176 miles from the equator, making both the United States and Russia north of Israel.

Here's my point: Jehovah's Witnesses don't believe the end is near; they think it's *here.* When they officially named the King of the North as Russia, it meant that we were in the last day of the last days—something they've been saying for over a century. So, what happens when the end arrives?

THE END

Jehovah's Witnesses believe we're in "the end" right now. World War I, which started in October 1914, marked the beginning of the last days. They never expected to see 1918. When they *did* see 1918, they explained it away. Then, they never expected to see 1925. Then 1975. Then 2000. The end is supposed to be here already. Still, we've yet to see the conditions necessary to qualify it as the official "last day of the last days"—the start of the Great Tribulation.

At some point in the very near future, governments will unite with each other to declare peace and security.[10] This will be accomplished through the United Nations, which they believe to be "the great beast" of Revelation.[11] They think false religion is the harlot riding the great beast and drinking the blood of innocents, as described in Revelation 13.[12] The UN will declare "peace and security," and then God will turn the UN against false religion.[13]

After false religion is gone, the world governments, through the United Nations, will attack Jehovah's Witnesses. Then, God will kill the world leaders and every other non-Jehovah's Witness himself in Armageddon.[14] That chain of events is called the Great Tribulation, and it will last for seven years. Jehovah's Witnesses will be horrifically tortured and exterminated in death camps similar to Auschwitz. If they deny God, denounce Jehovah's Witnesses, or pretend they're unaffiliated with the religion during the Great Tribulation, God will let them die and will not resurrect them to a paradise earth after Armageddon is over.

In 2016, Jehovah's Witnesses released a video drama depicting a SWAT team busting in on Jehovah's Witnesses hiding in a basement. Ex-Jehovah's Witnesses colloquially know the video as "the bunker video." By this point, Jehovah's Witness leadership will be broken and scattered. They intend to operate in de facto sleeper cells. The sleeper cells were previously called book study groups and are now called service groups.

When the United Nations eventually breaks the chain of command, the leader of the service group will be responsible for accounting for all the people under his care. Remember, it'll be a man because women can't have leadership roles. The Governing Body members have trained the helpers to run the entire system without their input since the power structure will be shattered.

After the tribulation, Jehovah will start Armageddon in full by killing everybody who doesn't meet Jehovah's standards to make it through the other side. Apparently, Jehovah's Witnesses tweaked the belief slightly since I was young. They no longer believe fireballs will rain from the sky. What will be Jehovah's chosen method of wanton slaughter? One can only guess. The May 1, 2015, *Watchtower* describes the "white horse" of the four horsemen coming to earth to bring an end to "this system of things." The paragraph ends with this line:

> Though much of the language here is symbolic, we can readily discern this much: God will send an army of angelic creatures to exterminate his enemies.
>
> JEHOVAH'S WITNESSES. "'THE END'—WHAT DOES IT MEAN?" *THE WATCHTOWER, STUDY EDITION.* MAY 1, 2015. PARAGRAPH 3

Since the Anointed 144,000 go to heaven the moment they die, they'll be the ones doing much of the slaughtering in Jehovah's Witness theology. Jehovah's Witnesses used to (and still might) believe that anybody who dies in Armageddon is dead forever. This is another point on which their theology changes from time to time. It's a bit of a vivid picture to draw for a five-year-old.

THE NEW SYSTEM

After the wanton slaughter comes to an end, all that will be left are Jehovah's Witnesses—God's chosen people. After that, there will be "a resurrection of the righteous and the unrighteous." This part changes from month to month, too, but this is their current belief as of the writing of this book. The Governing Body used to say you wouldn't make it through Armageddon unless you were a baptized, believing, door-knocking Jehovah's Witness. If you aren't knocking on doors, you are "blood guilty"—effectively guilty of murder, and God will punish you by snuffing out your flame forever. This changed recently when Anthony Morris III was fired from the Governing Body—an exceedingly rare event. Tony Morris pushed the idea that getting through Armageddon and being resurrected was an arduous task. After Tony Morris was fired, Stephen Lett, another Governing Body member, said they "don't know exactly what will happen or who will make it through."[15] They simply don't know peoples' heart conditions. I guess that means I'm in with a chance after all.

Either way, even if you're unrighteous, you can be resurrected in the end. Jehovah's Witnesses used to believe that Adam and Eve already had their chance at perfection, so they wouldn't be among those resurrected. Some people did things so egregious that they wouldn't make it through either, like Hitler or Judas Iscariot. Do they still believe that since the new light has been released? One can only speculate. They believe that, for the most part, there will be a resurrection of nearly everybody who has ever existed.

Judgment day isn't a single day in Jehovah's Witnesses' eyes—it's a 1,000-year span of time where Jesus and the 144,000 kings and priests judge each person individually. Why would it take an immortal being 1,000 years to judge somebody when they have unlimited knowledge?

After Armageddon is over, Jehovah's Witnesses will be in "the new system." It'll be Garden of Eden 2.0. Everything will be destroyed. Buildings will be torn down, and hospitals (now unnecessary) will be completely nonexistent. Birds will assist in cleaning up the dead bodies by eating the flesh. Jehovah's Witnesses will have the arduous task of cleaning up dead bodies and rebuilding the planet. They'll also be responsible for explaining what happened to the people who were resurrected.

Everybody will have "everlasting life," not to be confused with immortality. Angels are immortal. People on the other side of Armageddon will have everlasting life. That means they won't die of old age or illness, but Jehovah, Jesus, or any of the 144,000 can still kill them.

Since Jehovah's Witnesses will spend time rebuilding the planet after Jehovah destroys it, Jehovah's Witnesses discourage people from being involved in higher education. Doctors, for example, will be completely useless. Trade jobs, like carpentry, plumbing, or electrical work, will be extremely valuable in the new system, so everybody should learn trades instead of going to college. Higher education isn't officially banned, but it's heavily discouraged, and people attending college are frowned upon and viewed as questionable associations, if not outright "bad associations."

For over 100 years, Jehovah's Witnesses have believed that the end is coming any five minutes now. In recent years, their construction of new media centers and headquarters has been criticized. Why would they start a five-year project like building a brand-new media center headquarters if the end is coming any five minutes now? Jehovah's Witnesses explain that their people still need training to build large structures for when the new system arrives. It's a paper-thin excuse, but an excuse nonetheless.

In the end, humans will go through 1,000 more years of judgment and have an opportunity to impress Jehovah. After that, Satan and his demons will be released on earth to put people to the test one more time. At this immediate moment, in "the last days of the last days, shortly before the last day of the last days" (that quote is accurate), Satan and his demons are running around, causing problems for everybody. They're apparently even possessing Smurf dolls and bringing them to life if Jehovah's Witness urban legends are to be believed. At the end of the 1,000 years, Satan will be released to rove around trying to trick people one more time. After the final tranche of suckers falls for Satan's tricks, he'll be destroyed forever.

HOW TO BE SAVED

As mentioned previously, nobody expected Jesus to die—even Jesus himself. It didn't make sense. He was expected to take control of a real, literal kingdom in the Middle East: the Kingdom of God.[16] If he didn't fulfill that role, the theology was nonsensical. Paul started coming up with explanations for why Jesus died.

Many Christian doctrines aren't biblical. Several are there only to explain problems with the existing theology. As the theology becomes more complex, more holes form, and more doctrines must be adopted to fill them. The simpler, the better.

For example, why do Catholics have something so complex and absent from the Bible as purgatory? Jesus never said a word about it. He said the prerequisite to getting into God's kingdom was based on a straightforward principle. He communicated it through the sheep and the goats parable.

> ...for I was hungry and you gave me food, I was thirsty and you gave me something to drink, I was a stranger and you welcomed me, I was naked and you gave me clothing, I was sick and you took care of me, I was in prison and you visited me.

> *MATTHEW 25:35–36*

Jesus tells his disciples that people will be separated into two groups: the sheep and the goats. To the sheep, he will say that they fed him when he was hungry and gave him something to drink when he was thirsty. The sheep will respond with the following:

Lord, when was it that we saw you hungry and gave you food, or thirsty and gave you something to drink?

MATTHEW 25:37B

And Jesus will say to them…

…just as you did it to one of the least of these who are members of my family, you did it to me.

MATTHEW 25:40B

To enter the kingdom of God, you must feed the poor, give them something to drink, and provide them with a place to sleep. You must also be a good person and love your neighbor as yourself.

Erase what you know about the Bible from your head. Erase all of it. Erase the idea of hellfire. It isn't real. It's been created over centuries of misunderstandings and doctrinal errors leading to absurd, complex concepts to fix it—which only creates even more holes.

Paul came around years after Jesus was gone and tried to explain why he died. He said that Jesus had to die for your sins as a savior for all. To make it through to the kingdom of God, you have to accept him into your heart. Others came along and said, "Well, you have to do more than just accept him into your heart. You have to 'be a good person'—and we're the arbiter of what that is. We say being gay is on the bad list."

Even Jesus didn't believe that. Jesus didn't create this absurd list of behaviors worthy of shunning. He didn't condemn gay people; he didn't tell people to accept a Governing Body as his representative on earth at some undetermined point in the future. He gave straightforward instructions, which people have still managed to distort: feed the poor. Love people. Take care of them. What you've done for the least of my family, you've done for me.

The concept of purgatory grew out of the belief that you only had to accept Jesus to get to heaven.[17] The early church's older generation saw people doing things they didn't appreciate. They thought the new generation was weak and stupid. They saw them doing things they didn't do, like sleeping with people outside of wedlock. The solution they formulated was that members of the Christian church didn't just have to accept Jesus into their hearts to be saved; they also had to avoid committing adultery.

What happens to those people who accepted Jesus into their hearts but still commit adultery? Well, those people won't go to Hell like the other sinners. They'll have to go somewhere to purge their sins before continuing to heaven. We'll call it purge… purge-a-tory. No, purgatory.

The concept of purgatory didn't appear until 1274, long after Paul. But it was still an attempt to correct doctrinal nonsense created by people who wanted to put contradictory words on Jesus' lips. It was one ridiculous religious concept after another to fill the gaps they had created in the first place. Almost every doctrine outside of the sheep and goats parable was invented by church leaders centuries or even millennia after Jesus' death.

CHAPTER 10
IN HIDING

et's talk about my story. I'll do my best to tell the story of my life in the order that it happened, but life is messy. This story is primarily written chronologically, but much of life overlaps or connects to past experiences. That said, I hope this chapter gives you a clear picture of my life, and I'm sorry if the sections jump too far or too often. I wrote it in the only way that made sense to me.

The connecting theme in my life is Jehovah's Witnesses' effect on it. I've spent my life hiding from people, good and bad. I want to talk about my dad's role in my life in the section "Hiding from my Father." Then, I'll talk about how I finally mentally freed myself from the belief system. Finally, I want to discuss the most important part of my story. Surprisingly, it's probably the experience that affected my life the most: my experience after officially being shunned: Hiding from Sue.

I was saved by a family—Sue and Charlie—who didn't have to help me. They helped me because they wanted to. As Methodists, they acted the way Jesus expected his followers to act. That's a quality Jehovah's Witnesses seem to have completely forgotten or ignored. However, before we get to all that, let's start at the beginning. How did my family get involved with Jehovah's Witnesses in the first place?

JOINING JEHOVAH'S WITNESSES

In the early 1980s, my mother was in an emotionally vulnerable state after her divorce from my father. She got a knock on the door from the Jehovah's Witnesses. The family who called on my mother eventually went on to "study" with her. They were an older couple named Jennifer and Chuck.

Jennifer and Chuck had a son named Tom. Tom married a Jehovah's Witness named Lindsay, and they had four kids together—an older boy about my brother's age, a girl about my age, Jess, and twin girls about three years younger than me. They were close family friends for decades.

Jennifer and Chuck brought my mother into the religion. Around 1983, when my sister was six and my oldest brother was two, my mother started working to join Jehovah's Witnesses. As my mom progressed through the process of joining the religion, a process that takes between one and two years to complete, my dad had been begging her to come back to him. The words I'm about to tell came from her lips—not my dad's. She told me she finally came to my father and said, "I'll give you two options. Either join Jehovah's Witnesses with me, and we'll get remarried, or you'll never see the kids again."

Looking back, I suspect the reason she decided to remarry him was because she wasn't "scripturally free" to remarry—he hadn't cheated on her in many years, and she had forgiven him for it at the time. Jehovah's Witnesses consider cheating to be forgiven if the aggrieved party sleeps with their spouse after discovering the cheating. Since it had been "forgiven," even before joining the religion, she was no longer "scripturally" free to remarry in Jehovah's

Witnesses' eyes. He was, however, a terribly violent drunk. She thought Jehovah's Witnesses would straighten him up. To his credit, he did eventually stop drinking altogether.

Jehovah's Witnesses found my mom in an emotionally vulnerable state and exploited that, as is common with Jehovah's Witnesses. They look for an angle to exploit when they go door-knocking or social media witnessing. I know because I did it myself as I was trained to do.

My parents remarried around January 8. They celebrated their first anniversary together by going out to eat and exchanging gifts —a standard anniversary celebration for Jehovah's Witnesses. On January 8, each year when I was growing up, we would all sit around a table and give each other gifts—a kind of pseudo-Christmas.

Some years were better than others. I got glue one year and an original Gameboy the next. My mother took us to the dollar store and let us spend one dollar per person. We were poor, so if I got a large present from my parents, it was usually a console at least one generation behind. What I just described is not a common practice for most Jehovah's Witnesses. The genuinely devout will avoid gift-giving events entirely.

When I was about six, my mom convinced my Aunt Cathy to bring my two cousins, Rob and Tim, to a meeting with her. Aunt Cathy was a single mom. Everything was a struggle for her, and she sought a community to help her find her way. My cousin Tim was only a couple of years younger than me and had deep problems as a young boy.

My Aunt Cathy had her hands full. She worked to keep food on the table and bring the children to every meeting. Raising two kids on your own is hard. She did receive some degree of help from the congregation. Not much, just the occasional babysitter or a small community of friends to speak to when she was having problems.

Her story isn't mine, so I won't tell it except to say that she eventually got herself and her kids baptized. They suffered deep and terrible losses when they left the religion, as the system is set up to cause when any member leaves.

With time, both Rob *and* Tim turned out to be great people. I've had problems with them over the years, but I now love and respect them. Tim has grown into a wonderful person. Rob got a PhD in mathematics—the same field as my Aunt Cathy—and taught at a university after completing school. All three—Rob, Tim, and my Aunt Cathy—know of the criticisms I level against the Watchtower Society on my YouTube channel, and they've told me that they respect what I do. They've each individually told me they're proud of what I've accomplished and hope to see my work criticizing the Watchtower Society spread further to even more people.

Sadly, I was one of the first in my family to leave the religion, and every single person involved in the religion at that time shunned me when I left. I understand it wasn't really their fault—it was brainwashing. Regardless, it's hard not to blame them for what the family did to me when I left.

MONSTERS IN THE CLOSET

Jehovah's Witnesses believe that demons can inhabit physical objects. This belief is a cultural stronghold within the religion, whether or not it's part of its official doctrine. It seems like a simple and meaningless belief, but it leads to odd and irrational behavior in people already radical in every other area of life.

In my own life, this belief led to my mom being very selective about yard sales. She absolutely loved yard sales—who can blame her? They're amazing. However, a good Jehovah's Witness would be cautious about yard sales. Demons attach to objects. If a person is dealing with a demon and you purchase something from them, it could make the jump from them to you. Ideally, they'd only go to the yard sales of other Jehovah's Witnesses.

Contrary to many (but not all) mainstream Christian religions, Jehovah's Witnesses uniquely believe that humans and objects can both be possessed. When I was young, my mom told me that my dad practiced "black magic" before joining the religion. She even had a compelling story to go along with the claim.

I should preface the story my parents told me by saying that magic is not real. If it were consistently repeatable, it wouldn't be magic. It would be science. It would be a fact of the universe that could be harnessed. If it really were a fact of the universe that could be harnessed, the U.S. military would have started using it already. I imagine they'd have a whole Mage Battalion. The fact that militaries worldwide don't weaponize it should be all the evidence you need to reach the same conclusion: it's fake. Now, about the black magic story…

When I was young, my mom told me about my dad's journey into "black magic." She said he held his arms parallel to each other and created a "Jacob's ladder." She said electricity shot between his arms, from the bottom to the top. Of course, this was completely made up, but my dad backed her up. Again, it seems like electricians would have harnessed this power a long time ago if it were real.

A good Jehovah's Witness would never do something like that, as it could lead to demon possession. My dad dropped his whole black magic practice when he joined the religion roughly twelve years before I was born. When I asked my dad about his mysterious past abilities, he had another story.

My dad told me about one night when he was in bed at the top of a set of stairs. My mom was sitting on a couch at the bottom of the stairs. Suddenly, my dad woke up to find a face hovering over him and laughing. He said he was completely paralyzed. All he could do was stare at the face as it laughed and laughed. He finally mustered up enough strength to move his arm. He knocked a Zippo lighter off of the stand by his bed. The lighter fell down the wooden stairs, clattering all the way. Mysteriously, my mom didn't hear a thing, but he was finally freed from the prison created by Satan. He quit black magic soon after.

The experience is obviously (to me, at least) a case of sleep paralysis. I've experienced sleep paralysis, too. The cause isn't completely understood yet, but a leading hypothesis is that it's caused by overlapping and mismatched sleep stages. It can be an extremely disturbing experience. There are paintings from the Middle Ages that portray people experiencing sleep paralysis. One famous painting depicts a demon sitting on a person's chest. The images are fascinating to review. If you have the time, type "sleep paralysis paintings" into Google Image Search. Some of the paintings capture precisely what the experience is like.

People experiencing sleep paralysis also commonly describe a feeling of pure, unadulterated fear. Sometimes, it comes with a sensation of something sitting on your chest. Sometimes, people even physically see something in front of them. It's bizarre and haunting. It's not a demon, and it's not the result of black magic.

The story my dad told was an exact description of what a person experiences under sleep paralysis. The young Jehovah's Witness in me didn't know that, though. I had never even heard the term sleep paralysis. The story served to fortify and reinforce my belief in demons and Jehovah's Witnesses.

The story was told to all my siblings, not just me. They believed it deeply, and it left scars. Even after leaving the religion, my two brothers and sister seemed convinced that there were ghosts and spirits. They thought there was something beyond this world—ethereal or metaphysical. Even after leaving the religion, they couldn't be convinced otherwise.

As many children are, I was afraid of the dark when I was young. I was convinced there were monsters under my bed or in my closet. When I expressed my fears to my mother, she told me that there were, in fact, monsters in my bedroom. "Actually," she said, "they're demons. But if you say Jehovah's name over and over again, they won't be able to hurt you. They recoil at the name of God."

She also told us that Jehovah was always watching us. That little line was enough to convince my sister that she should change under the kitchen table at about twelve years old because she didn't want Jehovah to see her naked. When my brother was trying to rejoin the religion as an adult, he started having dreams about Satan and demons. He believed it was caused by Satan trying to turn him away from the religion. The belief made sense then—I used to think that way, too.

When we were little, my mom gave each of us a fishing tackle box containing a flashlight and a Bible. Any time we felt the presence of demons, we were supposed to pull the tackle box out and start reading the Bible. The light was entirely too bright for demons to handle. They would cower in fear when we started reading. The existential dread that comes along with the story my dad told, combined with the fear of the dark experienced by many young children, caused an obsession with demons to become so deeply rooted that it was nearly impossible to remove, even as an adult. Jehovah's Witness leadership might not have explicitly stated the beliefs. Still, leadership didn't discourage them, just like the Jehovah's Witness urban legend known as the Smurf story.

The Smurf story is a logical extension of the beliefs held regarding demon possession. Anybody alive during the 1980s, 1990s, and even into the 2000s has probably heard it. In the 1980s, the Watchtower Society targeted Smurfs with ire. There was a fear-mongering campaign about Smurfs from when the TV show started. They were banned—not officially, but culturally. If you watched the Smurfs, you didn't talk about it.

Here's how the Smurf story goes: a girl had a Smurf doll in her bag when she went to the Kingdom Hall one day. They were sitting in the chairs listening to the meeting when suddenly, the Smurf doll came to life. It climbed out of the bag and exited the Kingdom Hall while swearing on its way out. Jehovah's light was too bright for it. The demon inside needed to escape God's glory, so it climbed out and left.

The story changes from person to person. In one version, the girl had a Smurfs book, and the Smurf jumped off the page. It made sense to a young Jehovah's Witness who hasn't built defenses against supernatural fear-mongering. Nobody knows exactly how the story started, but the prevailing suspicion is that it started as a fear, and by the time it spread, it had transformed into a real event.

A Jehovah's Witness simply can't have a normal life. Not only did we not celebrate holidays like everybody else around us, but we believed demons possessed objects and people. Our parents were telling us there really were monsters in our rooms. Even if a child lives in a perfectly stable middle-class home, which is uncommon for Jehovah's Witnesses, their lives still won't be normal.

Not only did other children in school think I was odd for knocking on their door on Saturday mornings, but even the name was odd to many people. When you tell kids that you're a Jehovah's Witness, they separate into two groups. The first group comprises some particularly religious kids who consider it a challenge to their faith. "Are you saying I'm wrong in believing his name *isn't* Jehovah?" The second group is made up of kids who aren't religious and think you're odd because it's such an integral part of your identity. "You really believe in that stuff?" My parents made my childhood difficult, but Jehovah's Witnesses heavily amplified the bad parts in nearly every way.

HIDING FROM MY FATHER

As I mentioned before, I have two brothers and a sister. I'm the youngest of the four. When my last brother moved out, I was alone with my parents. I was about twelve years old. I had been told that my father was abusive to my siblings and my mom. Still, I was either too young to see it, or I didn't fully understand what I was witnessing when the worst of it happened. Most of the time, nobody else was around when he really laid into somebody.

To this day, certain things trigger my PTSD. I hear a floor banging or a violin being played very softly as the violin player is warming up; I can close my eyes and see shelves being pulled down, blood everywhere, and phone cords ripped from walls. I'm not listing random things—those are the specific things I flashback to. I didn't realize that trigger existed until I was in sixth grade. I tried taking a violin class because my mom liked playing the violin.

Both my mom and my dad had been diagnosed with bipolar disorder before I was born; my dad also had IED—Intermittent Explosive Disorder. It's a condition where he burns with pure, unadulterated fury seemingly out of nowhere. About halfway through seventh grade, my dad became completely out of control. We got into a one-sided fight, and I was so black and blue that I literally couldn't sit down. I had to lie on my stomach with my face turned sideways on the pillow. That day was the last day I went to school—my parents started homeschooling me. In reality, I wasn't homeschooled. I was simply… not going to school anymore. They technically enrolled me in a homeschooling program, but I never did any work. The day I started, homeschooling was the last day I would spend with another human being besides my parents for about four years. I was still taken to weekly Meetings at the Kingdom Hall, but there was little socializing at Meetings.

The elders knew what my dad was doing. My mother would leave him and take me with her to another house of a Jehovah's Witness. She was an older lady—a grandmother—a very calm and kind woman, which was a dramatic shift from what I experienced elsewhere in my life.

With some time, the elders would talk to my mother and tell her she had to return to my dad. He told them how sorry he was, and in the eyes of Jehovah, repentance exonerated his behavior. If it happened again, which it always did, well... they would cross that bridge when they came to it. For now, my mother was expected to live with her husband again, in Jehovah's Witnesses' culture.

That cycle probably happened fifteen times between the ages of twelve and seventeen. My dad would explode, leaving me with scars and bruises; my mom would leave with me; the elders would tell her to go back; I would end up in the same position I was in a week earlier.

Within the Jehovah's Witness religion, there is a single reason for divorce: adultery. There are three reasons for separation, but separation only means living in different houses. You are NOT free to remarry or have a significant other under any circumstances—even dating. If you do, it's considered adultery, and you'll be disfellowshipped. The three acceptable reasons for separation are as follows:

- **Willful physical non-support**—This simply means the spouse can hold a job but refuses to work.

- **Spiritual non-support**—Spiritual non-support means your spouse isn't interested in going to meetings or knocking on doors with you anymore. Those aren't technically disfellowshipping offenses or even offenses worthy of reproval, but you'll be socially shunned for it anyway.

- **Physical abuse**—The name says it all. What it doesn't say is that this is treated the least seriously of the three reasons, with spiritual non-support being the most serious offense.

My father was obviously committing the third of the three justifications for separation. Despite that, the elders kept telling my mom to return to him. She did so because she worried that she would be living outside of Jehovah's guidelines if she refused. There was no risk of disfellowshipping or shunning—she just didn't want to displease Jehovah or the elders.

At the time, I assumed it was because the elders didn't believe he was really doing it. For context, my dad was in a car accident when I was about six, and it legitimately did serious damage to his spine. The doctors eventually installed a morphine pump directly in his abdomen area. They opened his abdomen and his spine, inserted a reservoir, moved the pump's catheter around to my dad's back, and enabled the pump. I was around twelve when it was installed. After the accident, he was unable to walk. My mother even had to help him with the toilet and other basic hygiene tasks until he figured out how to do them independently. He was completely wheelchair-bound.

When I was about nineteen, already disfellowshipped, I was at my parent's house for my annual check on their well-being. I was sitting on the couch when my father walked into the living room and announced, "I've been lying to you guys and myself for eleven years. I can really walk." As it turned out, my father had Munchausen syndrome—a psychological syndrome where the person fakes serious illness to get sympathy.

The first question people ask when they find out about that is, "What did you feel in that moment? How did you take it?" The answer is the same for every shocking or painful event I've experienced. I felt nothing. In the case of my dad physically attacking me, I understood I had work to do to resolve the situation. I had to run to my room, move the shelf in front of my door, and sit in front of it. There was no room for anger, fear, sadness, or other emotions. I've come to find that truly shocking things, truly damaging to people's psyches, aren't usually recognized as the damaging events that they are until much later, at least in my experience.

Of course, when he said that to me at 19, I had already realized my dad had at least some mobility for years. I was home alone with him at about 14; while my mom was at work at a call center, he would stand up and attack me. I believed he was in intense chronic pain for most of his life. Still, even when other people were around, he would carefully move from the wheelchair to the toilet under his own power. It turned out that he wasn't living in chronic pain. In fact, he didn't have any pain at all after that pump was installed.

And that is why I believed the elders didn't believe he was attacking me. They could see the bruises on me when I showed up to meetings, but my dad had convinced them that he was entirely innocent; I did it to myself. He told me on many occasions that if I continued to contradict him when he claimed to be innocent—to elders *or* social workers—he would have me sent to the local juvenile facility for incorrigible kids. After all, who was going to believe that a small teenage boy was being attacked by a massive man who hadn't been able to walk for over a decade?

So, it's forgivable for Jehovah's Witnesses' elders, right? They thought he was innocent and couldn't see how he could be guilty.

…except for one thing. Many years ago, somebody from my old congregation contacted me after leaving the religion. They said they recognized me when they saw one of my videos on YouTube. They were outside of the religion, too, and were so glad to hear what I was doing.

At the end of the conversation, I brought up the fact that Stan and Ben, the elders in my congregation, didn't believe me when I said my dad attacked me.

He said, "Oh, they believed you."

I asked, "Why do you say that?"

Because my dad was disabled, he often called in to listen to the meeting through the phone system. The congregation had yet to figure out how to route the sound system correctly, so the disabled callers' microphones were accidentally routed through it. However, it usually didn't matter because the disabled listeners always mute their microphones at home.

This old friend, though, told me that the entire dead-silent Kingdom Hall listened to my dad attack me when he forgot to mute his mic one day. I can't be sure how old I was then, but I was kicked out on my 18th birthday, which means I was a minor. I wasn't told any of this until I was 30.

The elders knew. They knew from the first day. They believed me. That's something they failed to mention. The amount of good that would have done for my psychological health as a teenager would have been immeasurable—to know that I wasn't alone, that other people saw what was happening and knew.

Instead of telling me they knew, instead of agreeing that my mother should keep him away from me, they instructed her to go back to him repeatedly through my teen years because she was his wife, and there was no adultery or spiritual non-support.

Not only did the elders fail me, but an entire congregation of 115 people sat there and listened to my father attack me. Not one of them called the police. Not one. They heard the sounds at least once; they saw the bruises multiple times. Not one person out of 115 called the police. That should tell you something about the culture of the organization.

In retrospect, I don't fully blame the congregation members for not helping. For one thing, they were brainwashed. They believed they did the right thing by sitting silently and listening to somebody get beaten over their sound system. They'd let the elders handle it.

In all fairness, somebody tried to help. I can't know if it was someone from the congregation or elsewhere, but CPS kept coming to the house to ask me questions. By the time they showed up, my dad would have me convinced that he didn't mean to do it and it wouldn't happen again. That was his carrot. His stick was the looming threat that he might send me to the nearby juvenile facility if I said a word. And, of course, I was convinced no one would believe me anyway because no one ever had.

At sixteen, I was allowed to return to public school for the first time in many years. There was a steep learning curve in figuring out how people interacted with each other again. Formative years spent completely alone led me to watch live news coverage to feel connected with the outside world. I knew that what I was watching was happening somewhere in the world at that exact moment. It was as close as I came to human contact before returning to high school.

Leading up to my re-entry into society, I attended a home-bound/pregnancy program for kids who couldn't attend school full-time. That was my first real contact with the outside world in years. It was a Monday/Wednesday/Friday program, and I had to walk about two and a half miles to the public bus stop to reach the trade school each day. Adapting to life among other human beings was difficult but absolutely worth it. Having been separated from society affected my psyche and personality in ways that are hard to articulate. Still, I was one step closer to freeing myself—not only from my father but from Jehovah's Witnesses, too.

After I finished the homebound/pregnancy program, I had to be tested for placement before I could rejoin regular high school. After four years of doing no schoolwork or learning of any kind, I jumped from a seventh-grade education to a tenth-grade education. I was pretty proud of it at the time. Unfortunately, it didn't matter because I still had to get credits for ninth-grade classes. On top of having no social understanding, all of the kids with whom I had gone to elementary and middle school were now in eleventh grade. I was technically in tenth grade, my peers from childhood were in eleventh, and I was taking ninth-grade classes. I was finally starting to re-establish my life without being completely reliant on my parents or Jehovah's Witnesses. Still, the joyous moment didn't last long. Within a year, things took a turn for the worse.

I was seventeen—about a year after rejoining High School—the last time my dad ever took a swing at me. My dad was an extremely intimidating person. I would guess he was about 6'5" and 350 pounds. At one point, I was on the floor looking up and saw him approaching me. I watched my mom stand in front of him, even though she knew the possible consequences of doing so. He threw her aside like a rag doll. That moment was the last straw. I stood up and punched back for the first time in my life. He never hit me again.

About six months before that event, when I was still sixteen, I had found my first real girlfriend. Her family was on the periphery of the Jehovah's Witness religion. Her parents were devout Jehovah's Witnesses at one time, but they had slowly faded away. They still seemed to believe it deeply but didn't attend meetings or participate—an extremely rare type of family to find. Their association with the religion was *just* enough for me to be allowed to speak to them.

The night I hit back, I got in my car and drove to their house. I showed up with bruises all over me and a hand that was bleeding from the knuckles. I really should have gotten stitches, but I just wanted to lie down and cry. I eventually had the chance to do so, and it would be the last time I would cry over my father for the rest of my life—including after his death around 2021. I can't even remember the exact year.

As soon as I arrived at my girlfriend's house, her mother, Susan, took pictures of my hand and other scrapes and bruises. She was an RN at a local hospital. I stayed on my girlfriend's couch, and she slept in her bed, both in a little loft area. All I could think about was the altercation I had with my dad. I was told my mom showed up trying to convince me to come home because my dad was sorry, but I didn't even go outside. Susan talked to her for me.

The next day, Susan called CPS on my behalf. My CPS worker, the same one who had been investigating reports of abuse since I was about twelve, showed up and said to my mom, point blank—if you don't move out, we're putting your son in foster care. I was already seventeen, so it was too little and too late. Still, my mom did decide to move out with me. We moved into government housing. We received $500 per month from a form of Social Security Disability, which was sent to my parents on my behalf to help take care of me. When I moved with my mother, the SSD followed me and went into her hands. Our rent was the lowest it could get in section eight housing, based on our income—$50 per month.

My girlfriend broke up with me within a few months of moving to government housing. That was the last straw. I had just gone through all kinds of feelings I hadn't processed—feelings I wasn't even aware existed. I lost it.

I started leaving my mom behind at our little government housing unit and going to parties—hanging out with people from school, talking to friends, and dating a new girl—Katelyn. Any of those things was enough to get me shunned—and that's exactly what happened. A couple of months before I turned 18, I went to a high school party, drank alcohol, and smoked a cigarette. For the first time, I was experiencing the world around me. My previous girlfriend had broken up with me—not to mention everything I'd just experienced with both my mom and my dad—and I was looking for some way to burn myself to the ground. I found it.

Jehovah's Witnesses at the high school watched me and reported everything I was doing to the elders. The elders knew something was happening, so they called me to a judicial committee meeting. I showed up to the meeting, and sure enough, they decided to shun me.

The following week, from the stage at my congregation and all the surrounding ones, they announced, "Owen Morgan is no longer recognized as one of Jehovah's Witnesses." That was the end. I lost everything. I lost my family, my friends, all of it. My mother kicked me out of our little government housing unit. I had nowhere to go, so I called Katelyn.

I asked if I could spend the night at her house. She said I could, so I showed up. I had nothing but the shoes on my feet, the shirt on my back, and a big white van five minutes from breaking down at any given moment—the last thing my parents ever gave me.

My life took a nosedive after my disfellowshipping in 2007. I had been tied down for my entire life, and I was finally free. I tried out every drug I could find. I was in the opiate capital of the world: Huntington, West Virginia. So it didn't take long for me to become hooked on Oxycontin and eventually heroin, but that's jumping ahead.

HIDING FROM SUE

I was disfellowshipped by Jehovah's Witnesses when I was in eleventh grade. My mother immediately kicked me out of the government house we shared. I was technically eighteen, but I was still in high school and still *felt* like a kid. I called my future (and now ex) wife, Katelyn, someone I knew from school, and asked if I could stay with her. She said, "Of course." When I arrived, she said, "You can stay, but my grandparents don't know you're here, so you'll have to sneak in and out of my window." I had to park my van down the street and go out the window to get to my job at Burger King. I had worked there after school for the past couple of years.

People don't realize how difficult it is to live in a house without anybody else knowing. I had to plan when I'd use the bathroom—waiting for everybody to be in bed before I could sneak across the hall. When people were awake, I peed in Gatorade bottles. She would bring her food to the bedroom so we could both eat. I had nothing. And that was the point. Jehovah's Witnesses wanted that to happen to me. In their ideal world, I wouldn't have known that "worldly" person to help me. After weeks of living this way, a coworker offered me a room for $150 per month.

After taking the offer, I moved into my new roommate's house and stayed on a tiny bed. I had no idea there were mattress sizes below Twin. My feet hung off the end. But at least I was alive and had a roof over my head. Katelyn came with me to my newly rented bedroom, and I got her a job working with me at Burger King. We were never apart.

We eventually went on to get married, so I didn't feel like I was living in sin despite already being disfellowshipped. We also had a kid together—the same kid who has made public appearances on my YouTube channel.

We got married only a few months into our relationship and moved back into her grandparents' house together. This time, they knew I was staying there. It turned out Katelyn also had bipolar disorder, just like both of my parents and my brother, Lance. This would later explain why *she* was willing to get married despite the fact she wasn't religious at all. It's not easy living with an unmedicated bipolar person, but we made it work. When I enter a relationship, I fully commit.

At this point in my story, I'd like to recognize the woman who saved me from everything you've read. This next section doesn't further the timeline, though it does cover a relationship that lasted for many years. Katelyn's grandmother, Sue, came to consider me her son, and I considered her my mother. She showed me unconditional love for the first time in my life. I want to share some of her story and honor her for the wonderful impact she had on my life.

———

Katelyn's grandparents, Sue and Charlie, were wonderful people who did right by me. Everyone in my life who was supposed to care for me didn't. Sue was a deeply religious person, a Methodist, and didn't hate anybody for anything. She followed the *actual* message of Jesus: to love your neighbor as yourself.

I spent my first Christmas with them. Sue bought Christmas presents for everybody. Some of the presents she bought were addressed *from* people who she knew couldn't afford to buy gifts. She bought a gift for Katelyn from me and a gift for me from Katelyn. Even that small gesture was important to me because I didn't have a penny to my name. I couldn't afford to buy a gift for anybody. I couldn't even afford to buy new shoes. Sue knew that, so she gave me shoes. She didn't have to; I wasn't her responsibility.

My first Christmas was spent with an extra gift Sue had bought on Charlie's railroad pension of about $2,000 per month: a fleece blanket. She had it lying around in case somebody was short a gift. She often reminisced and laughed about me walking around with the blanket that day. It was the very first Christmas I had ever celebrated.

Sue died on September 21, 2022. She was the only person I knew who seemed to care just for the sake of caring. The last words she spoke to me were to tell me she loved me. I'm not sure I've ever heard those words from my parents. Certainly not very often, if at all. Sue saw me through addiction to oxycontin and complete destitute poverty. She provided for me when I had nothing. She did everything she could to support and care for me, at great expense to herself. She asked for nothing in return.

She simply wanted to ensure I had a place to live—not because I was married to her granddaughter. Even after Katelyn and I split up when I was still destitute, she allowed me to stay in her house. Her granddaughter lived with her new boyfriend, and Sue let me live with her anyway. Her love for me was not conditional upon anything—not even a connection to other family members.

Conditional love is something I've dealt with for my entire life. If I didn't meet certain expectations, I'd lose everything. I didn't know what unconditional love felt like until Sue and Charlie came into my life when I was about eighteen—shortly after being disfellowshipped and losing everything. Sometimes, you don't know you've missed something until you have it.

Sue knew I wasn't religious after leaving Jehovah's Witnesses. She didn't try to force her beliefs down my throat or tell me I was going to hell when I died. She invited me to church occasionally but loved me for who I was. She sometimes debated theological ideas with me for hours. The discussions never morphed into arguments or heated debates. Regardless of my religious beliefs, she believed I would be in heaven with her because I followed in Jesus' footsteps, even if I didn't know it: I strived to care about others the way Sue cared about me.

We discussed much more than just religion. We discussed her feelings on feminism, gay rights, Black rights., and many other political topics. Sue loved everybody and thought they should be equal, and she couldn't understand why others didn't agree. Despite growing up in a sundown town largely controlled by the Ku Klux Klan and not seeing a single Black person until she was in her early twenties, she and her husband Charlie both fought for the rights of the Black community throughout the 1950s and the 1960s when it wasn't a popular position to hold—especially in a sundown area in West Virginia.

Sue has a gay sister who brought her girlfriend over every Sunday to dinner with the family. She treated her sister's girlfriend like she treated me -- like part of the family. She cared about others regardless of where they were in life or how anybody else's backward interpretation of the Bible said to treat them—even drug addicts like me. Jesus said to love everybody, so that's what she did.

She told me about what it was like to be in school in 1950s West Virginia. Glenwood, the area she grew up in, didn't get electricity until she was older. She used to go to her grandmother's house and wash the globes on the oil lamps in a big tub in the yard. If you didn't clean the oil lamp's globe once per day, they got dim from soot.

She told me about going to her single-room schoolhouse, now displayed at Marshall University.[1] In seventh grade, she was asked what her name was. Since the government had limited records compared to today, she could tell them anything she wanted. So, she told them her name was Sue, which wasn't even close to her real name. A few weeks later, the government showed up at her school to pass out Social Security cards to all of the kids, and sure enough, hers read "Sue."

She told me about dating her first boyfriend, Frank, when she was thirteen. Kissing was scandalous, but she did it anyway. Frank broke up with her, but his eighteen-year-old brother Charlie asked to court Sue, who was then fourteen, and she agreed.

Charlie had already been smoking unfiltered cigarettes, drinking, and working on the railroad since he was about fourteen. Sue's father, whom she referred to as "daddy," was a violent drunk, so alcohol was a central sticking point for her. She never smoked a cigarette, got drunk, or took a drug more potent than acetaminophen a single time in her life. They eventually made a deal for him to cut back on his drinking, which made it more tolerable for her. They got married as soon as she was of legal age.

As a woman, Sue received unique training in high school. It focused on being a good wife to her husband. Charlie never took advantage of the society-assigned position as Sue's "superior." He believed he was her equal from the beginning. Sue, however, took her position as a wife very seriously. Part of her wifely training was learning to make shoes out of newspapers and learning to make a bed with somebody still sleeping in it in case her husband was permanently maimed in a war or had radiation poisoning from an atomic blast and was incapable of moving under his own power. Fears of nuclear warfare were at an all-time high at that moment in history.

She was also trained to read and understand newspapers discussing political events. Her high school told her she should read the paper every day—if she didn't, her husband might get bored of her. Keeping up with political events was considered part of a woman's wifely duties, alongside cooking and cleaning.

She always said the best thing a person could be doing when Jesus comes back is rocking a baby. She believed he was on his way —any five minutes now. Despite her left-leaning views, she believed the earth was literally 6,000 years old, that Noah's Ark was a real, literal story, and evolution was just a misunderstanding of how God had created the world. God created evolution to work to some degree, which is why scientists have come to their conclusions. However, it was ultimately a very slow process that didn't have enough time to build what we see in the world today. Evolution is one of the subjects that Sue and I debated many times. We also discussed the existence of hellfire. She was a fundamentalist in many ways, but she didn't hate anybody for anything. There was only ever love in her heart.

Another fundamental characteristic of Sue's personality was that she couldn't allow somebody to go hungry. Ever. She didn't care what it cost or what she had to spare. She didn't care how late it was or if she knew for a fact that a child was only trying to avoid going to bed. If somebody told her they were hungry, she got up, went to the kitchen, and found something to cook for them. She knew somebody might be taking advantage, but she would rather be taken advantage of than risk someone being hungry.

We talked about when she and Charlie lost their son, Billy, to suicide when he was about 23 years old. He shot himself in the head with a shotgun in her basement. She told me that losing a child is a pain that human beings simply weren't supposed to experience. In the months before Sue died, she also lost her daughter, Katelyn's mother, to pneumonia. When her daughter died, she called me and said to me, "Why are people like Donald Trump alive when my girl is gone? There are so many people on earth that deserve it more." She just didn't understand why bad people were allowed to live long lives and gain power when her baby girl died an early death in her mid-fifties.

Sue was very important to everybody in her life. We were important to her, too. I was her child in every way that mattered. Sue stepped in when my mom stepped out. To this day, my mother refuses to speak to me. There have been a few instances of forced conversation between my mom and myself over the years, but the relationship has been nonexistent since 2007, when I was eighteen. As of 2024, I still haven't had a real relationship with her, and I'm expecting her to go to the grave without speaking again. Not only have I come to terms with that in recent years, but I have no interest in talking to her anymore, either. I idolized my blood mother once. Seeing her stand in front of a 6'5", 350-pound man to protect you will do that. But it took me entirely too long to find out who she was, deep down.

Sue knew exactly how I felt about my mother; I never hid my religious questions from her. Despite being possibly the most devout believer I've ever met in my life, she never viewed me or my beliefs (or lack thereof) as "repulsive" the way my blood mother does.

My mother calling me and my ideas "repulsive" was the final straw for me. I had tried to have a relationship with her since I was eighteen years old, to no effect. I felt that she really did love me, under everything. After watching her stand in front of my dad the way she did when I was seventeen, I believed there was something under all the Jehovah's Witness programming that really did care. After decades of being hated and treated like I was repulsive and disgusting, the bad finally outweighed the good. I told my mother that I never wanted to hear from her again. The next time I want to see her is when she's in a coffin. I said that in 2023, after Sue's death. My *real* mother, Sue, died in 2022. Sue was the model I used to figure out what a good person is supposed to be, and she could never be replaced.

My mother knew what Sue meant to me. One of the few times we spoke, I told her how much Sue meant—I said she stepped in where my mother dropped the ball. Sue acted as a mother when I didn't have one. After that, my mother would visit Sue once or twice a year and try to convince her that I was the problem in the relationship rather than her. She called Sue to ask if she could visit her when she went to see old Jehovah's Witness friends in West Virginia. After finding out what their conversations were about, it became clear what my mom's motives were for the visits.

Sue, having her pure heart, said, "Of course. Come on over." She believed the best of everybody, no matter what. Sue knew my mother refused to speak to me but invited her in any way—because that's who she was. It would be extremely hypocritical for me to blame Sue for giving another person another chance. She wouldn't be who she was if she didn't give everybody she knew yet *another* chance. She certainly gave *this* ex-addict more chances than I deserved. I blame my mother for being a snake.

The very last time my mother showed up at Sue's house, around 2021, she spent hours trying to convince Sue that I had ended the relationship, not her—a common tactic among Jehovah's Witnesses when questioned about their shunning policy. When she said that, she meant that I had ended the relationship by having a girlfriend ten years earlier, when I was seventeen years old—*not* an ongoing situation, but that's irrelevant to Jehovah's Witnesses.

My mom told Sue she'd be willing to have a relationship with me again if I just reopened the connection. That meant she expected me to get reinstated as a Jehovah's Witness. I told both my mother and Sue that the connection *was* open. I knew what these things really meant, but Sue didn't. She was excited when she called to give me the news: Your mother says she loves you and wants to be a part of your life again! I knew it wasn't true, but I tried texting my mother regularly for a while anyway, hoping to start a relationship —she never responded. If Jehovah's Witnesses are experts at anything, it's propaganda and victim blaming.

Despite hearing all these terrible things about me, Sue never believed them. She continued to love and trust me through everything. After these visits from my mother, Sue concluded that my mother was "spiritually" lost—my mother believed Jehovah's Witnesses were correct, which they obviously aren't. Sue believed that deep down, there was a good person inside my mom, but that good person was being suppressed by false religion. She reached to find the good in everybody, even my mom. That's what made her who she was.

In addition to concluding that my mom was spiritually lost but ultimately good, Sue also concluded that I had done nothing wrong and was sorry my mother had done so much to hurt me. She still believed it wasn't my mother pulling the strings. She insisted that I forgive her for what she'd done because the religion was really to blame—not my mom. I moved on and tried to work with my mom again multiple times, but the attempts made it clear that I wasn't the one blocking the relationship. No matter what I did, outside of rejoining the Jehovah's Witness religion, my mom would not have a relationship with me ever again.

Sue was the most influential person in my life. She showed me how a family and a normal human being should act, and I've carried that philosophy on in her stead. Sue may be gone, but her goals, beliefs, thoughts, feelings, and ideals will carry on through me—and hopefully through you, the reader.

A famous saying goes like this: "You die twice. Once when you take your last breath, and once when your name is spoken for the last time." As long as I'm alive, I will perpetuate the qualities which Sue valued. Even when her name is lost to time, everybody with whom I interact and who interacts with them will benefit from what Sue had to offer. She gave everybody unconditional kindness, love, and good faith by default. She deserves to be remembered at least as much as, if not more, than anybody I know. Anybody.

My blood mother, on the other hand, has lost all of her children because of her religion. Maybe she honestly did care for us at some point, but she has likely forgotten about all of us in large part, and her line and influence will die with her. Any good qualities she might have had were not only heavily outweighed by the bad qualities but were far better displayed by Sue. My blood mother will never act as a role model for anybody, and neither will my dad.

So, this is goodbye to both. Time will forget you, Mom and Dad, but it will not forget Sue and Charlie.

BREAKING THE CHAINS

Katelyn and I got married in 2008; nine months (to the day) later, our daughter was born. During the pregnancy, we had both stopped using drugs for the safety of the baby. However, in the hospital, after she was born, the nurses offered Katelyn an opiate pain medication. During our drug addiction, we split every drug 50/50, and that time was no exception. We both relapsed.

To no one's surprise, the marriage of an eighteen-year-old and a sixteen-year-old did not last. We eventually separated in 2011, the same year we each stopped using drugs. My daughter was about two years old at this point, so thankfully, she has no memory of my drug days. I'm going to skip over a lot of this period because it includes someone else's story. Katelyn and I were never apart while married, so my story is also hers. I've included the essential parts, but if you feel I'm skipping a large chunk of my life—I am.

In 2010, about a year before I got clean, my sister and her husband, Tom, moved to West Virginia from Texas. They stayed in the basement at my parents' house. The basement was mostly finished and contained a bathroom and kitchen—an entire living space with its own egress and legal address.

Shortly after moving there, they also left the religion. While they were still active Jehovah's Witnesses, we had many discussions about the organization. During those discussions, my sister and her ex-husband helped me wake up and realize that the religion was just as fake and corrupt as every other sizeable religious group out there. I will be eternally grateful for that. They even allowed me to stay in their living room when needed—something my mom was extremely unhappy about.

During one of our discussions, I learned about Joseph Rutherford's mansion, Beth Sarim. This was the fact that finally pulled me out of the religion. My sister was out of the house, so it was just me and my then-brother-in-law. He turned to me and said, "Did you know that Joseph Rutherford had a mansion built and deeded it to Bible characters in the 1930s? He stayed in it to 'keep it warm' for them."

It was a little thing, but that's all it took for it to click into place for me—Jehovah's Witnesses aren't God's chosen organization. Since day one, they've been as cynical and calculated as every other religion out there. The leaders *are* looking for an opportunity to sap the membership for everything they have. They *don't* have the mandate of heaven. They *don't* hear God's voice. Their Bible math *has* been proven false over and over again.

Everybody in my family, apart from my parents, had already left the religion by the time I got clean in 2011, including my sister and her husband. They were the last ones to go, besides my dad. After about 20 years of sobriety, my dad decided to pick up drinking and smoking weed again. It was around the same time I quit drug use altogether. His alcoholism and drug use seemed to come out of absolutely nowhere. He dyed his hair and got a cream-colored PT Cruiser. Usually, people in a midlife crisis get *NICE* cars, but not my dad. He invited me over to his house to hang out occasionally. I wouldn't say he ever actively shunned me; he just didn't talk to me often.

When he started drinking again, *that* was the final straw for my mother. She was completely and totally done with everything. For about a week, she seemed to be teetering on the edge of leaving the religion or buckling in even harder. She chose to buckle in even harder.

She left my dad shortly after that for willful spiritual non-support, a justification for separation. You may recall that when I was young, the elders always encouraged her to return to the abuse we both faced, and she agreed every time. When she left this time, she never returned and, to my knowledge, was never encouraged by the elders to return. She moved back to Connecticut, where the rest of her family lived.

My dad knew it was over from that point on. As one parting blow, my mother told the local elders my dad was drinking and smoking weed. He admitted to it and was disfellowshipped. My sister and her husband moved back to Texas, and Katelyn, my daughter, and I moved in with Katelyn's grandmother, Sue, again. It was the same house I was in when I was kicked out in eleventh grade. For the first time in many years, my dad was deeply and truly… alone.

After some time, my mom moved out of my dad's house and back to Connecticut. My dad was alone. Rumors started to spread that my dad might have a girlfriend. I don't believe they were true. If he did, he almost certainly would not have consummated the relationship. My mom called him in retaliation for the rumors. She intentionally got under his skin, blaming him for things and putting him in a heightened emotional state.

After getting him fired up, she asked if he really did have a girl-friend. He said, "Yes, I do." She said, "Are you sleeping with her?" He said he was. My mom recorded the entire phone call. That's what she needed to move her scriptural separation to a scriptural divorce in Jehovah's Witnesses' eyes.

The divorce proceeding started, and by the end of the year, she was officially divorced and scripturally free to remarry. She never did remarry, but she was truly and completely free from my dad, and that's what she really wanted—and what was best for her, short of leaving Jehovah's Witnesses. I only wish it had happened sooner. Each of his children (aside from me) left the state at 18 and didn't talk to him for years at a time. It was my mom's turn to walk away from him—and this time, she was walking away for good.

To summarize my life up to this point: I was kicked out of the religion in 2007, got married to Katelyn in 2008—the same girl whose room I stayed in when I had nowhere else to go—and had a baby with her in early 2009. By 2011, Katelyn and I separated. I had nowhere else to go after we separated since Katelyn stayed at her grandmother's, so I moved into the basement at my dad's house. He was alone and had lots of extra space, and I agreed to live there and pay rent. I was single, and Katelyn was preoccupied with… well, having a boyfriend. So, the kid stayed with me.

My baby is colloquially known on my YouTube channel and among fans as Alpha Force Zero or Kylie, and until she's ready to reveal her name on her own terms as an adult, I'll keep it that way. As of the time of writing this book, she's fifteen and a firecracker. I love her more than I love myself. I always have, and I always will. She was my reason for living, and that remains true to this day.

By the time I was invited to stay in the basement at my dad's house, I was going to college for substance abuse counseling—a two-year degree. I dropped my kid off at Sue's house each day when I went to college. I got student loans to help me survive while I was in school, and I gave my dad the rent and phone bill three months in advance since that was how often I'd get money from student loans. I was making about $700 per month, including student loans.

I had finally gotten off hard drugs and was taking Suboxone, which is an opiate that only activates the receptors attached to withdrawal. It's used as a method of helping people get clean from heroin so they can deal with the emotional problems that lead a person down that road in the first place before dealing with the physical aspect of the situation—physical withdrawal. Though it has its downsides, Suboxone saved my life.

I was only in the basement at my dad's house for about a year before he was reinstated as a Jehovah's Witness. He went through the standard process that I've explained. One night, seemingly out of the blue, he called the police on me and told them I was living in his house without his permission.

The timeline for when this played out coincided with a rise in his explosive disorder. He would have hit me if he hadn't finally been afraid of being hit back. Instead, he called the police. I showed rent receipts to the officer, but it didn't matter. The police officer said he didn't care if I had a receipt. I had to leave if my dad wanted me out of the house. If I didn't go willingly, he'd arrest me. Having my baby with me, I couldn't do anything that would get me put in jail. It would have been a total violation of my civil liberties, but I couldn't risk it with a baby to take care of. I left that night and went to my daughter's great-grandmother's house. Thankfully, my ex had moved out by then, so there was space for me again. I stayed there for a while after that.

When I was young, my dad would tell me, "Sit down." I sat, and he'd say, "Stand up." I would stand, and he would say, "Sit down, boy." I would sit again. He did that over and over again. If I didn't do as he said, there would be consequences. That experience made me feel helpless, as if I had no way to defend myself. The best I could do when I was young was run to my room and push a shelf in front of the door.

The night he called the police on me, the police helped him put me in a place of weakness once again, like I was the 12-year-old cowering behind a shelf, gripping a cordless phone, and trying to dial my mom's work number to tell her what was happening. Oftentimes, people who experience genuinely traumatic, PTSD-inducing events don't understand the full effects or weight of what they just experienced until later.

In my experience, people who've gone through a genuinely traumatic experience will come out the other side just fine. When the event happens, they'll organize their thoughts and plan for their next steps from moment to moment. It's a survival mechanism. Eventually, though, when things calm down and they find themselves in a reasonably safe place, they discover the inflicted trauma —jumping at loud pops and hiding in your house, afraid to leave. A sense of impending doom or urgency, like something is about to happen, but you don't know what that is. Those are the results of trauma.

The night that my dad called the police on me was the last night I ever really spoke to him. He put me through PTSD-inducing trauma from the age of thirteen to eighteen. By the time he called the police, I was about twenty-three. That's when it hit me with full force. I knew something was wrong, but I didn't understand the depth of the problem until then. My dad's last Facebook message to me, ten years later, about six months before he died in 2021, read, "Why the fuck don't you talk to me?" I imagine he knew exactly why I hadn't talked to him in his last years, but maybe he was that oblivious.

In 2021, he died alone in a trailer in Butler, Pennsylvania. Nobody was around him except for his little dog, Edison—the dog he'd had with my mom before she left him years earlier. My brother and sister showed up to the trailer after he died and got what important things they could find—a mug, a stuffed animal, and a cheap Walmart guitar—and left everything else behind. They made sure Edison went to a safe home.

My dad didn't get a funeral. He didn't get a viewing or even a burial. He was cremated, his ashes sent to his next of kin. There was no money to inherit, so we settled for a few small items to remember the good things from his life. I got a broken Walmart guitar. It hangs on my wall today. It can't be played without putting a couple hundred dollars worth of work into fixing it, which is about double what it originally cost. My siblings took the other little things. My mom didn't want anything to remember him by.

TEN YEARS A WATCHTOWER SPY

To understand the next era in my life, you need to know that Jehovah's Witnesses try to manage and produce everything within their own factories. Absolutely everything. They have farms that grow the food eaten in their live-in compounds. Jehovah's Witnesses produce animated TV shows and monthly broadcasts for their members. All animation, recording, and script writing is done by active, believing, door-knocking Jehovah's Witnesses. Having an aversion to college education as they do, they tend to look for people who were already educated in those areas before they joined the religion.

Suppose there's a severe shortage that simply can't be made up by existing members. In that case, the Watchtower Society will hire companies run by Jehovah's Witnesses, which are encouraged but not required to use 100 percent Jehovah's Witness labor.

From time to time, non-Jehovah's Witnesses will find themselves working for the Watchtower Society through a series of contracts and cutouts. That's how I became a Watchtower spy for ten years in the payment processing and software engineering fields.

I worked as a software engineer for many years. I had a close friend within the religion, Darrin, who went to a neighboring congregation. Darrin and I only saw each other now and then as kids. He left the religion around the same time I did. We didn't reunite until years later. Darrin's dad, Bob, didn't speak to him much since Darrin was disfellowshipped. Despite limited contact, Darrin stuck his neck out for me by recommending me to his dad.

He told Bob I'd never had anything to do with the religion. He also told him I was the best in the business.

Bob, still an active Jehovah's Witness, hired me on a contract basis to help with server maintenance and administration. He is unaware of my affiliation with the religion to this day. I learned that he was responsible for the donation processing system used by Jehovah's Witnesses. Any time people attend a convention, brothers in good standing pace the arena with iPads equipped with credit card scanning machines. Those scanning machines were connected to software that I helped maintain for years.

He originally hired me for the project while transitioning to a new server system. I set up development and production servers for him, registered his name servers, maintained DNS, and configured the system with the latest versions of PHP and other software as required. I also assisted with penetration testing and preparation for PCI compliance, a standard certification required for any server that stores sensitive information like credit card numbers or private health data.

I never took advantage of my position in any way. Even if I had access to databases of Jehovah's Witnesses' credit cards, it would have been extremely unethical, illegal, and morally wrong to tamper with or even view the data. The only valuable thing I learned from the experience that could serve as any benefit to the ex-Jehovah's Witness community is how the payment processing system works, but it works the same way as every other system of that type, so that isn't of much use either.

To this day, the Watchtower Society is unaware of my role in their payment processing systems. With the release of this book, that may change.

———

In my judicial committee, around 2007, I told them I was repentant. I begged them not to disfellowship me. I told them I was at a cross-roads, and I desperately wanted to remain inside the religion. I meant it, too. They decided to disfellowship me despite my clear repentance and fervent requests to let me remain a part of the reli-gion. It didn't feel like a stroke of good luck at the time, and it led to years of pain and suffering, but when I came out the other side, I had been forged into something much different than I was before.

I told them I was at a crossroads, and I was correct. I could have conceivably become an active Jehovah's Witness to this day. I could be stuck in a terrible marriage because if we had both been members, neither of us would have felt empowered to divorce. I wouldn't have ever met the wonderful wife I have now. My daughter would have an unrecognizable personality. The only as-pect of my life I may prefer is the ability to have a relationship with my blood mother. I'm not certain that would be positive, given what I know about how conditional her "love" for me is.

My life is exactly where I want it to be. Yet another example of false Jehovah's Witness doctrine. I'm supposed to be miserable forever once I leave the religion. I should not be able to find joy. Jehovah's Witnesses do their best to force that to come true. Still, as soon as you find a stable, loving support network outside of the religion, you'll realize the thing causing your misery was the Jeho-vah's Witnesses themselves.

CHAPTER 11
MODERN CULTURE

THE HIERARCHY

Each congregation has between six and twelve elders. Each elder in the congregation is assigned a responsibility. The presiding overseer used to be the top-ranking administrator of the congregation. Now, the title is "Coordinator of the Body of Elders." The presiding overseer is still basically equal to all other elders. Elders can only be demoted or "deleted" by the circuit overseer. The circuit overseer is a traveling overseer who moves from congregation to congregation. There used to be a position titled "district overseer," Also called "district servants" or "regional servants." According to the Jehovah's Witness website, the position has been discontinued.

Elders can hold one or more of the following positions:

- Service overseer—organizes the preaching efforts.
- Public talk coordinator—arranges who will be speaking at the meetings.

- Operating committee members—responsible for taking care of the building.
- Watchtower study conductor—the elder who leads the watchtower study—the second half of the Sunday meeting.
- Life and ministry meeting overseer—an inferior replacement for the Theocratic Ministry School. This is after my time in the organization.
- Group overseers—handle groups of people responsible for various tasks, including shepherding calls.
- Coordinator of the body of elders—This role is assigned to one person. It used to be called Presiding Overseer, but that role has been discontinued. This person chairs meetings, assigns duties, and is considered the default speaker for introductions and announcements at most meetings. They also handle some financial matters.
- Congregation secretary—maintains records, sends updates to the headquarters, tells the congregation when conventions and other major events will occur, and oversees congregation accounts.

Ministerial servants are the next rung down in the hierarchy. Like deacons, they assist elders in their various tasks and roles.

Below ministerial servants are "privileged men" who are given the "privilege" of doing manual work for the congregation, such as setting up the sound system or administering certain things in very specific circumstances. Women are below the lowest-ranking male in the congregation.

CIRCUIT OVERSEERS

Circuit overseers are traveling ministers who go from congregation to congregation. The circuit is an area that commonly covers about

20 Kingdom Halls. If the Kingdom Hall doesn't have a place for the circuit overseer to stay, he and his wife are invited to stay with a local family.

The circuit overseer, also called the "CO," is a deeply revered member of the religion—and extremely powerful. The CO can delete elders, the organization's term for firing them. When I was in the religion, COs were given Buick cars to drive from place to place. I'm not sure why they picked Buick, but there's a fleet of them out there. The local Kingdom Hall typically covered their gas and food, but the Society covered what the Kingdom Hall didn't pay for. They were always on the road, always moving from place to place. They would show up to one of the 20-or-so Kingdom Halls in the circuit and give the Sunday morning talk while they were there.

The CO would also go in service with people in the congregation. Priority was granted to young children. The CO's goal was to encourage kids as much as possible—try to get them involved and excited about the religion. In my experience, circuit overseers were very nice, mild-mannered, kind people. Since leaving the religion, I've come to find that some circuit overseers abuse their power and take advantage of their position. If there's some problem that needs to be dealt with in the congregation, they might have an iron fist or a light touch. They're also given access to materials that the rest of the Jehovah's Witness world is not.

I remember going in service with my circuit overseer when I was about ten. He and I were walking up to a door together. I was dressed in my nicest suit, with my service bag at my side, prepared to impress the circuit overseer with my presentation. There was barking inside the house—not unusual.

Just then, we heard a garage door open. The circuit overseer said, "Move." He and I started quickly walking back to the car. We both arrived just in time to see a dog coming around the corner, ready to protect its property.

Somebody released a dog on a ten-year-old. I didn't want to be out there any more than anybody else. I was there because it was a requirement, and I was honored to have the opportunity to do it with a circuit overseer.

…and then somebody released a dog on us.

I know they're Jehovah's Witnesses, but please remember that they're also human beings. For all you know, they don't believe a word of it. They just feel they have to stay inside the religion to keep in contact with their friends and family. Don't release dogs on anybody. Don't mistreat them in any way. Simply ask them to put you on the "do not call" list.

Jehovah's Witnesses sometimes carry dog buzzers in their service bags. If a dog is attacking or about to attack, they pull the buzzer out and start playing a loud sound that irritates dogs' ears terribly, forcing them to stop attacking and flee.

THE ROLE OF WOMEN

Jehovah's Witnesses still believe that women should be in submission to the lowest-ranking man in a congregation, but surprisingly, a woman can be Anointed.

1 Timothy 2:12 says, "I permit no woman to teach or to have authority over men; she is to keep silent." The books were believed to be written by Paul, who named himself an apostle after the fact. He had never met Jesus and had known little about his life. He was only going off of Christian culture at the time.

That said, scholars widely accept 1 Timothy 2:12 as a forgery, added later by people who didn't want women involved in leadership. Jesus clearly included women in his ministry from the start. The role of women was different in different parts of the Bible. Sometimes, they were permitted to be involved; sometimes, they were not.

KINGDOM HALLS

Jehovah's Witnesses absolutely detest the term "church." They don't go to church; they go to meetings. They don't have those meetings at a church; they have them at Kingdom Halls. They're very persnickety about the vernacular.

Kingdom Halls have standardized designs. When a quick build is ordered, the blueprints are delivered to the congregation performing the quick build. Several different blueprints are used.

Each Kingdom Hall has a small kitchen with a sink (and sometimes a microwave). It will also likely have a refrigerator. In addition to the kitchen, depending on how large the Kingdom Hall is, they will have a single room they call a library containing a variety of Jehovah's Witness books, a set of Encyclopedia Britannica, other Bible translations, and other materials. It often has a large table in the middle of the room.

Judicial committees and study sessions also commonly take place in the library. For example, one-on-one meetings where somebody is "studying" Jehovah's Witness books with a baptized Jehovah's Witness in preparation for baptism are traditionally held in the library. The library has large windows showing the main hall and stage, but the windows are blinds.

Sometimes, Kingdom Halls will have a third large, empty room with the same chairs found in the main hall. The extra room and the library are commonly very useful for disabled people or parents with young children. The additional rooms will have a knob on the wall near the door to turn the sound up or down in the room.

There's a men's and women's bathroom at the back of the Kingdom Hall. I've only ever stepped inside a women's bathroom once, but when I was there, I saw an additional room built inside the bathroom with a day bed—presumably for nursing mothers. The men's bathroom simply has a few bathroom stalls and a sink.

Usually, each room will have a set of speakers connected to the sound system—even the bathrooms.

A small group of members meet at the Kingdom Hall and clean each week. They might meet after service or clean on Sunday after the meeting while everybody else is in service. They clean everything top-to-bottom. They wipe dust from every wall, clean the refrigerator and the microwave, and clean the bathrooms. Cleaning the Kingdom Hall is a display of humility and is considered an honor. There will also be a group that works outside the Kingdom Hall each week. They mow the grass, pull weeds from the mulch, power wash if necessary, and more.

Many Kingdom Hall blueprints don't have windows. One can only speculate why. I've looked for the answer but haven't found any. My best guess is that they believe they'll be persecuted in the end, so they don't want the secular authorities to be able to see if Jehovah's Witnesses are hiding inside.

BETHEL

Bethel is the name Jehovah's Witnesses give to its headquarters and other major properties. Colloquially, it refers to the location where upper leadership lives and works. Officially, Bethel locations are referred to as "branches." Jehovah's Witnesses self-reported 86 branches worldwide.[1] Branches include warehouses, book-binding locations, writing departments, and audiovisual production studios.

Normal Jehovah's Witnesses apply to join Bethel and, if accepted, move to the compound. The application process has changed over the years, but for some roles, it has required people to be in good health and have no underlying medical or dietary requirements, similar to the military.

Bethelites have no reason to leave the compound. Entry is strictly controlled, but Bethelites can leave the compound as they please. They have no reason to leave aside from door-knocking. Many branches are in the middle of nowhere—nothing around for miles. It would be considered suspicious if a Bethelite was leaving frequently and inexplicably. They need ID numbers to access the compound since it isn't open to the public. That implies that their coming and going is (or at least can be) monitored.

Living in the center of New York City required them to be reliant on society around them to some degree, but since they have built new properties in more secluded areas like Warwick, New York, they are entirely dependent upon their own systems.

The members built the property themselves, a volunteer effort. The Society simply supplied the property and the building materials and invited Jehovah's Witnesses to assist in the building effort, a process known as a quick build. Jehovah's Witnesses participate in the same process when they build a new Kingdom Hall.

KINGDOM MELODIES

The Jehovah's Witness songbook contains about 150 songs called Kingdom Melodies. As with everything said and done from the stage, the songs are pre-selected by Jehovah's Witness leadership before every service. The songs are originally performed by orchestra or piano and played through the Kingdom Hall sound system. The songbook has notes, words, and dashes to show word emphasis where appropriate.

Jehovah's Witnesses released a new songbook in 2016, including 19 new songs and excluding three old songs. The singer Prince was a Jehovah's Witness and became more fervent and involved near the end of his life. There were rumors among Jehovah's Witnesses that he assisted in writing ten of the 19 new songs, but as far as I can tell, it's not true.

SUNDAY MEETINGS

Jehovah's Witnesses have a weekend meeting and a midweek meeting each week. We arrive at the Kingdom Hall 30 minutes early to associate with our "brothers and sisters," the names they have for each other. Every meeting is dead silent except for the person on stage. A single baby making the slightest noise is piercing and obnoxious. Every cough or position adjustment is audible.

The Sunday meeting has two parts. At 10 AM, the music starts playing, and we start singing along with the songbooks. Modern congregations have two large TV screens on either side of the stage —words to the songs flash by as the congregation sings them. Sometimes, Bible verses are displayed on the screens during talks.

After the song, the man up front (called the conductor) says a prayer, and everybody sits down. The first portion of the meeting commences. "Conductor" is an appropriate term for the leader of these services. He has no say in what's said and done. The Governing Body chooses everything, from the songs to the outlines for the talks given.

Any free choice within the group is an illusion. Every word you hear from the stage, every word coming from a Jehovah's Witness mouth, whether at work or on your doorstep—it's always, always scripted by the Governing Body. They send outlines from headquarters for everything from watching R-rated movies to dating non-Jehovah's Witnesses to celebrating holidays. Just about every one of their doctrines is covered in this big list of outlines from which the elders can choose. They make you feel like you can ad-lib from time to time. In reality, you're just repeating what everybody else around you is saying, and they're repeating what they heard from the Governing Body.

Long ago, in the early days of the Watchtower Society, they used to provide mobile wind-up phonographs for members to take to people's doors and play a message from the leadership. It was a neat gimmick but served another purpose: individuals wouldn't communicate the information personally.

Everything communicated by a Jehovah's Witness comes from society. I suppose the conductor can ad-lib in his prayer, usually 30 seconds to 2 minutes long.

At the end of the prayer, the conductor says, "Good morning, brothers and sisters. We're so glad to have you here today. The name of the talk today is 'Stay Awake, Stand Firm, Grow Mighty'"—or something to that effect. He'll then say, "The talk will be given by brother [insert name here, sometimes local guest speaker]." Then, he invites the speaker on stage by saying his name in a questioning tone. "Brother [insert name here]?" Then he steps down.

Brother McFergleBergle or whoever it happens to be will walk up on stage. An up-and-coming young Jehovah's Witness man will adjust the microphone for the guest speaker and sit back down. The talk commences. It's about 50 minutes long. The additional ten minutes of the hour are devoted to singing the pre-determined song while "privileged," up-and-coming, particularly spiritual young men set up the sound system. They run the wires for the microphones, plug them in, flip switches to enable the loudspeakers, run the cords down the aisles, and back up again so there's plenty of slack and nothing is tangled.

Usually, the congregation is split into three sections of chairs. The chairs are very rarely moved, and they're typically very high quality and comfortable. My congregation had rows of five chairs lined up along the left side. Then, we had a big aisle wide enough to fit two or three wheelchairs side-by-side if needed. Then we have rows of 12 or so chairs lined up in the center, another big wide aisle, and a third set of chairs in rows of five chairs each on the far right side of the Kingdom Hall, just like on the left.

The society writes all sermon outlines—what they call "talks."

Each year, they have what they call a "special talk." The special talk takes place the weekend before the Memorial, around March or April. The Watchtower Society writes a new outline for a brand new 50-minute talk and sends it to the congregations. The talk is delivered for the first time in Kingdom Halls; then, it goes to the back of the bunch of outlines.

When the first half of the meeting ends, the speaker steps down and the meeting conductor goes up to the microphone. As he approaches, somebody in the front row is assigned to adjust the microphone to his height. He thanks the speaker for the good talk, which was really given by the Governing Body, and then he tells people which song they'll be singing. The elder gives a prayer after the song, and the next section of the meeting begins: the *Watchtower* portion.

They bring two people on stage for the second part of the meeting, each with a microphone. One stands at the main lectern in the center of the stage, and the other sits in a chair off to the side of the stage. The *Watchtower* magazine has a study edition and a public edition. The study version of the *Watchtower* has paragraphs that each make a specific point the Society wants its members to understand. There's a question under (or above) each paragraph. The answer can be found in the paragraph. The following text is a paragraph from a standard *Watchtower* about people who are critical of the Society.

6. What clear warning does the Bible give us about false teachers?

[6] How can we protect ourselves against false teachers? The Bible tells us exactly what to do. (Read Romans 16:17; 2 John 9–11.) The clear instruction in the Bible is: "Avoid them." That means that we have to stay away from them. The warning from the Bible is like a warning from a doctor who tells you to avoid a person who has a disease that may spread to others. The doctor knows that if you get this disease, you will die. His warning is clear, and you will do

what he says. The Bible says that apostates are mentally diseased and that they use their teachings to make others think like them. (1 Timothy 6:3, 4) Jehovah is like that good doctor. He clearly tells us to stay away from false teachers. We must always be determined to follow his warning.

> JEHOVAH'S WITNESSES. "WILL YOU PAY ATTENTION TO JEHOVAH'S WARNING?" *THE WATCHTOWER, STUDY EDITION (SIMPLIFIED).* JULY 15, 2011.

They start with paragraph one. The person on the side of the stage stands and reads the paragraph before sitting down. The conductor then reads the question. The audience is expected to have read these articles and underlined the answers to each question before showing up on Sunday. When the question is asked from the stage, some people raise their hands to answer.

The answer shouldn't be quoted from the magazine. It should be between 15 and 30 seconds long, somehow related to your life, or at the very least slightly reworded. However, every congregation has somebody who gives entirely too long and personal answers. In my congregation, that person was my mother. She revealed entirely too much personal information and just kept going for two or three minutes. It was painfully embarrassing when I was young. Answering at the meetings is considered a "privilege" to which everybody has access, including men and women(the only genders accepted by Jehovah's Witnesses).

It usually involves three or four people, and they are commonly the same people each time: elders' wives. Everybody is supposed to answer at least once throughout the month. The Watchtower conductor points to them and says their name— "Sister Morgan?" Then, one of the handlers walks down the aisle with the microphone. He stops at the row of chairs and passes it from person to person until the answerer receives the microphone.

Since I left the organization, I've noticed they use a different microphone style. The microphone handlers have the microphone attached to a long arm. They walk to the appropriate row and reach their arms out so the microphone is in front of the question answerer. I don't know if the arm is connected to Kingdom Hall crashers—if I had to guess, I would say no, they're completely unconnected—but I have no idea why they started using extended arms to reach the answerers directly.

MONDAY AND WEDNESDAY MEETINGS

The "Wednesday" meeting, as I'm calling it, is now called the midweek meeting by Jehovah's Witnesses. It wasn't always on Wednesdays for everyone. I'm referring to it as the Wednesday meeting because it was always on Wednesdays for me, and we always used that title in my family. Jehovah's Witnesses combined the Monday book study with the Wednesday meeting, and the book study groups became service groups.

Now, family worship is heavily promoted. Instead of having the book study every Monday night at the Kingdom Hall, families are supposed to sit together in their homes and go through the same process as the Monday night book study, except with fewer people. Jehovah's Witnesses are also expected to read from the daily text every morning as they have breakfast together.

Wednesday meetings are an hour and 45 minutes long, slightly different from how I grew up. The Theocratic Ministry School was intended to teach public speaking and doctrine. When I was younger, they allowed younger kids to read Bible sections in front of the congregation to start the meeting.

I was assigned talks from time to time—I went to the stage, somebody adjusted my microphone for me, and I stood in front of a crowd of hundreds of people while audibly reading the Bible. The lowest level in the Theocratic Ministry School is a five-minute Bible reading. If you approach the five minutes, you get tapped—they tap a pen on a book or table at the front of the Kingdom Hall. That's your cue to finish your thought and step down.

The Theocratic Ministry School was extremely valuable to me in my young life. I had a maroon book describing how to keep eye contact with a crowd, deal with nerves, build outlines, and various other useful public speaking tips. I still use some of those tips to this day.

The Theocratic Ministry School was a set of talks given by a few people in the Kingdom Hall. They were about pre-set subjects with pre-set outlines. Since I left, it's been discontinued and replaced with "Our Christian Life and Ministry Meeting." It's effectively the same as the Theocratic Ministry School. It starts with a question and answer section, like the second half of the Sunday meeting or the book study. Then, they have a Bible reading. I did these during the Theocratic Ministry School. It doesn't sound much different. People might read a chapter of a specific book and then step down after a short period.

Meetings taught me some valuable lessons. Although they weren't a net positive, they certainly included some positives. When I was young, however, no Jehovah's Witness event was as exciting to me as the conventions.

CONVENTIONS

Jehovah's Witnesses have three "conventions" per year, though they insist only one of these events be called a convention. When I was in the religion, they had a one-day "assembly" on Sunday and a two-day "assembly" on Saturday and Sunday. A convention happens once per year. Unlike assemblies, it comprises a much larger swath of congregations, and it's held over three days: Friday,

Saturday, and Sunday. The two assemblies throughout the year are called the circuit assemblies. The larger convention used to be called the district convention, but they renamed it when they eliminated the district overseer position.

The circuit assembly is a small grouping of local Kingdom Halls. The convention covers the state or the tristate area, depending on how many Jehovah's Witnesses are in any given zone. I can't speak to how large they are now, but when I was a member, they tended to hover around 10,000 attendees at conventions and 3,000 at assemblies in my area. Their size likely varies dramatically across different regions. Anybody can show up, find a seat, and listen for free.

Jehovah's Witnesses typically rent a local arena for all their assemblies because it's much cheaper than building their own. All assemblies generally work the same way. There will be a "theme" for the assembly, such as "Love Conquers All" or "Stay Awake, Stand Firm, Grow Mighty." Each day of assemblies lasts about eight hours, including a lunch break.

Concession stands are forbidden within the arena for the duration of the assembly, but Jehovah's Witnesses can't ban anybody from the street corner in front of the arena. When I was young, salesmen commonly waited in front of the arena to sell small, cheap binoculars and battery-powered fans. People selling things outside isn't standard practice at every convention, but when they did, my parents would let each of us kids buy one item.

When members walk in, they will find a convention program on tables nearby. The programs are usually printed on 4x6 cards and can vary from one to three pages, depending on the length of the convention. The program lists the talks for each day. Most talks are between 20 and 60 minutes long. The programs are the same for every assembly worldwide.

When I was on the inside, there was an event called The Drama. It was a kind of play performed by people within the circuit or district who were particularly spiritual—that is to say, the men were being given privileges regularly at the Kingdom Hall (and likely pioneering), and the women were only pioneering.

The Drama was very entertaining. The Watchtower Society would pick a random subject—the story of Noah, David and Goliath, or maybe Adam and Eve—and put on the play in front of everybody at the convention.

Luckily, drama performers didn't have to worry about a word slip. Nobody on stage had a microphone. They used a script written by the writing department and audio recorded by Jehovah's Witness leadership—all at Bethel. The "performers" on stage would simply dress up as the character they were playing, including glue-on beards—because beards were banned then.

It would fade out at the end of a scene, and the set would be moved around the same way a normal play would. The only difference is that the actors pretended to talk and make hand gestures like they were acting. They could have stuck anybody up there to move their hands around and react to the storyline. People could barely tell what they were doing from across an entire arena. Regardless, it was the highlight of the assembly for me.

Throughout the regular talks, I learned to take notes like a professional. I learned the different types of note-taking methods, and I got to the point where I could capture the idea in writing as quickly as somebody spoke. There was a great deal of Creme Savers. That candy is underrated. My mom used to have a humungous bag of them, which she'd bring to every assembly. I'd stop writing notes long enough to cram one in my mouth before returning to it.

Jehovah's Witnesses commonly encourage people to learn a second language so they can help convert foreign language speakers. If a congregation has enough foreign language speakers in an area, it will create an entirely new congregation for the foreign language. The Kingdom Hall staggers its hours so each congregation can use it several times per week.

The prospect of learning a new language excited me. Unfortunately, I lived in West Virginia, which is not exactly a state considered friendly to immigrants. There simply weren't many Spanish speakers in my area. So, I learned the next best thing: American Sign Language (ASL).

I used to sit on the assembly hall floor while an ASL translator translated the entire assembly for a deaf person. I was fascinated to learn that Jehovah's Witnesses created signs for things they only discussed, like the name Jehovah. I had great fun learning ASL at the conventions. It's one of the few things I valued after leaving the religion—that and my public speaking skills.

Circuit assemblies have baptisms directly before lunch. When I was in the religion, circuit and district assemblies had their baptism ceremonies on Saturdays, and Sundays had Drama. I understand Dramas have been deprecated and replaced with a 30-minute film produced by the Watchtower Society since I left, which is an absolute shame.

SIGNING THE CONTRACT

As I said, baptisms happen directly before lunch. They usually start around noon and last 30 minutes to an hour. Assemblygoers bring their lunches.

The ground floor is usually reserved for people with disabilities. People are encouraged to find seats in the bleachers. "Baptismal candidates," as they're called, sit directly in front of the stage for the first half of the assembly until the baptism takes place. Their families have seats elsewhere in the arena.

Baptism is a lifelong contract -- with a ceremony attached to it to make it spiritual -- between the individual and the organization.

There is no backing out of the contract. The consequence is shunning, no matter the age. Let's talk about signing the contract.

The convention talk given directly before baptisms is about the importance of getting baptized and showing dedication to Jehovah. When the talk is over, the conductor on stage asks two questions. These questions have changed over the years, but as of the writing of this book, they are as follows:

1. Have you repented of your sins, dedicated yourself to Jehovah, and accepted his way of salvation through Jesus Christ?
2. Do you understand that your baptism identifies you as one of Jehovah's Witnesses in association with Jehovah's organization?

After the conductor asks the first question, the baptismal candidates are expected to give a loud, audible "YES." The second question is asked, and a loud "YES" is again expected. The conductor dismisses the baptismal candidates, typically around 20–50 per assembly (depending on which assembly it is), and instructs them to get changed into swim gear in the nearby bathrooms.

Here's a quote from their website regarding the baptism questions:

Affirmative answers to these questions constitute a "public declaration" by the baptism candidates that they have put faith in the ransom and have unreservedly dedicated themselves to Jehovah. (Rom. 10:9, 10) Baptism candidates will want to give prayerful thought to these questions in advance so that they can answer in harmony with their personal convictions.

The term "public declaration" is doing some heavy lifting here. In the eyes of the Society, that term effectively means you've just signed a verbal contract with the organization. The consequences for breaking that contract are dire—they make sure of it.

I was so young that I barely really remember it. When I got baptized, I walked to the nearby bathroom, where my mother was waiting with a bag containing my swim gear. I walked into the bathroom and noted that older men were just whipping their junk out all over the place while changing into their swim gear. I took a stall. I changed into a swimming outfit—top and bottom required for all—and gave my mother my suit to hold, hung up on a hanger. I walked back to the main auditorium of the arena and got in line in front of the pool.

For women, an extremely modest one-piece swimsuit is expected. Women wouldn't want to be responsible for the downfall of an unsuspecting brother by having a nip slip or something like that. Usually, women wear plain white shirts over their swimsuits, just like others nearby. Logos of any sort are not allowed on any of the baptism clothing.

When I was baptized, three elders, wearing solid-colored swimming shorts and white shirts, stood in the pool. One stood on the other side of the pool, handing towels to newly baptized Jehovah's Witnesses, and two were in the water, baptizing two people at a time.

The pool is reasonably large. It could probably fit ten people at a time, but only four were ever in the pool. The elder tells you to hold your nose with your fingers and grab a wrist with your other hand. He puts one hand behind your head and another hand on the wrist your hand is holding, and he dips you completely under the water for a split second. You come back up, walk to the other side of the pool, and grab a towel—just like that, you're baptized as a Jehovah's Witness.

The process takes place in the exact same way for everybody and has for many years. The person holds their nose with one hand, grabs their wrist with the other, goes completely under for a split second, and is lifted back up by the back of their head and their wrist.

When I was young, I was told that gifts are inappropriate for baptisms. You are expected to get baptized—it's the bare minimum requirement. It shouldn't be celebrated; it should be met with an acknowledgment that the person did the right thing. I don't think that's official doctrine; it's simply part of the subculture among some Jehovah's Witnesses. With that context in mind, let me tell you about my baptism process.

CHAPTER 12
GOODBYE, LARRY

PREPARING FOR THE CONTRACT

Jehovah's Witnesses push children as young as eight years old to get baptized—effectively, a lifelong contract with the organization. Sixteen-year-olds can't fully consent to most situations because their brains aren't formed enough to fully understand the consequences of their actions. If even 16-year-olds can't consent to a contract, eight-year-olds certainly can't. If you can't get married or get a tattoo before a certain age, you certainly shouldn't be allowed to sign your life over to an organization that will pull the rug out from under you if you break that contract.

There is a lengthy period leading up to baptism, which they call studying the Bible. Generally, it starts with the person showing an interest in joining the religion. Whichever Jehovah's Witness is on the other side of that equation will meet with them each week and "study" one of their books—a chapter per week—just like they study the *Watchtower*.

I call them study buddies. Jehovah's Witnesses probably wouldn't appreciate that term. They'd probably view it as disrespectful. But I think my name is much better than theirs. They call them their "study" full stop. Anyway, the study buddy is expected to read the book and underline the answers in each paragraph the same way they underline answers in the *Watchtower* in preparation for the Sunday meeting. The two study buddies meet at one of their houses or the Kingdom Hall if they can access it. The Kingdom Hall is usually locked, and the lights are off between meetings.

The study buddies follow that process until the book is completed. During that time, the study buddy is viewed as dirty. Their lives are viewed as a complete mess, even if their lives aren't actually a mess. That's the perception. The moment they're baptized, that feeling changes. You're no longer afraid to hug them for fear of getting something on you. I'm being literal. That's how regular outsiders are viewed. Just imagine how they view apostates. Many Jehovah's Witnesses believe apostates like me are literally communing with Satan to find the best way of hurting God's people.

When I was involved, they had just switched to studying the *What Does the Bible Really Teach?* book with prospective witnesses. It was a long title, so they called it the "Bible Teach" book for short. The current book studied by prospective witnesses is titled *Enjoy Life Forever.* When they finish the first book, they can request to be an unbaptized publisher while they study the next book in line.

The entire process takes about a year from start to finish. I was born into the religion, so I didn't have to go through any additional steps. I was already an unbaptized publisher by about eight, and the long, arduous process of learning to fit into the culture seamlessly was already complete. When I told the elders I wanted to get baptized, one of them agreed to study with me to bring me to baptism. His name was Larry.

GOODBYE, LARRY

Before Larry was an elder, he came to our house and played Star Wars Trivial Pursuit with us. He and my family loved "Star Wars." When I was about ten, he would come over every week for a couple of months until, one day, he just stopped. When asked why he stopped coming, he told us that the current elders wanted to promote him to elder, but they felt that he worshiped "Star Wars." He loved it too much—maybe even more than he loved Jehovah. He had to eliminate everything he owned that had anything to do with "Star Wars." Then he could be an elder. And just like that, Larry never came over again.

He was married to a beautiful woman named Sherri for as long as I can remember. She was in the congregation with us when I was young. In her early 30s, she was diagnosed with cancer, and it quickly took her life.

Larry agreed to study with me shortly after her death. He was in his early 30s and still mourning his wife. He never spoke about Sherri, but I could see the pain in his eyes. I knew he was almost certainly thinking that he would never find another wife, not within the religion. Jehovah's Witnesses pair off between the ages of 18–20, largely because of the total ban on physical intimacy outside of marriage. There were almost no single Jehovah's Witnesses in their 30s. I felt terrible for him.

However, he agreed to study with me despite trying to cope with his wife's death. He picked me up from my house every week —even twice a week sometimes. He drove a little truck, and we opened the Kingdom Hall to prepare it for the congregation to attend the meeting. We turned the lights on, moved things around on stage, and shuffled papers—you know, the things elders do before meetings.

One day, we showed up to the Kingdom Hall and found the entire driveway snowed in. Larry said, "No study today. This is part of being a Jehovah's Witness. You help people wherever you can, whatever it takes." We spent an hour shoveling the driveway together before the meeting started. He was a truly good person and didn't deserve the bad hand he was dealt.

If you notice, I'm using past-tense language. I said "was a good man" instead of "is a good man" not because he died—he hasn't, as far as I know—but because *I* am dead to him. After getting disfellowshipped about six years later, he saw me in a store. He glanced at me, and we locked eyes for a split second. He looked away immediately and wouldn't look at me after that. He avoided me like I had a disease. But, of course, that is what he thought. He believed me to be mentally diseased. He thought if he spoke to me, it might rub off on him.

> The Bible says that apostates are mentally diseased and that they use their teachings to make others think like them. (1 Timothy 6:3, 4) Jehovah is like that good doctor. He clearly tells us to stay away from false teachers. We must always be determined to follow his warning.
>
> JEHOVAH'S WITNESSES. *THE WATCHTOWER, STUDY EDITION (SIMPLIFIED).* JULY 15, 2011.
> P. 11

When it was finally time to study the *Organized to Do Jehovah's Will* book, we started burning through the information about six months into the process. He knew I already understood it all. The most important part of that book, though, is what Jehovah's Witnesses call the 100 questions. They called it that in my Hall, anyway. The questions are at the back of the *Organized to Do Jehovah's Will* book. They're questions to affirm that you really do fully understand their doctrine. Before you're baptized, the elders have to sit down with you and test you. You must be able to answer the questions without hesitation, preferably with the cited Bible verses.

It's made up of two sets of questions. The first set has 27 questions, and the second set has 33 in the book's latest edition. The first set is titled "Christian Beliefs," and it primarily contains doctrine-based questions. Here are some examples:

Why is it important for you to use God's personal name?

You must pray, then, this way: "Our Father in the heavens, let your name be sanctified."

—Matt. 6:9

Everyone who calls on the name of Jehovah will be saved.

—Rom. 10:13.

Do you believe that the Governing Body of Jehovah's Witnesses is "the faithful and discreet slave" appointed by Jesus?

Who really is the faithful and discreet slave whom his master appointed over his domestics, to give them their food at the proper time?

—Matt. 24:45.

Why do people die?

Through one man sin entered into the world and death through sin, and so death spread to all men because they had all sinned.

—Rom. 5:12

How many people go to heaven to rule with Jesus?

Look! the Lamb standing on Mount Zion, and with him 144,000 who have his name and the name of his Father written on their foreheads.

—Rev. 14:1

If you've made it this far into the book, I'm sure you already know why this is absolutely absurd. Jehovah's Witnesses' use of God's name is just one example of the nonsense found within these questions. Yahweh wasn't used in the New Testament. The word used in the New Testament was "KURIOS," meaning Lord. By the time the New Testament was written and passed down, a superstition about using the holy name had already become firmly rooted in Jewish culture.

The second part is titled "Christian Living" and is about culture and expectations. Here are some examples:

Why do Jehovah's Witnesses not worship with other religious groups?

You cannot be partaking of "the table of Jehovah" and the table of demons.

—1 Cor. 10:21

"Separate yourselves," says Jehovah, "and quit touching the unclean thing"; "and I will take you in."

—2 Cor. 6:17

If there is a conflict between a human law and God's law, what would you do?

"We must obey God as ruler rather than men."

—Acts 5:29

What scriptures can help you to remain separate from the world when choosing a job?

Nation will not lift up sword against nation, nor will they learn war anymore.

—Mic. 4:3

Get out of her [Babylon the Great], my people, if you do not want to share with her in her sins, and if you do not want to receive part of her plagues.

—Rev. 18:4

The book concludes with the two questions you'll be asked immediately before being baptized:

1. Have you repented of your sins, dedicated yourself to Jehovah, and accepted his way of salvation through Jesus Christ?
2. Do you understand that your baptism identifies you as one of Jehovah's Witnesses in association with Jehovah's organization?

After answering "yes" to both of those questions, you're officially qualified to be baptized, and the elders will make a request to the Society. You'll be baptized at the very next assembly. After I qualified for baptism, I think I had to wait about three months until the next assembly rolled around.

That brings me to my final point. I have a few questions of my own for the Governing Body. I've included a list of 100 questions for Jehovah's Witnesses, not dissimilar to the 100 questions asked before baptism.

If Jehovah really is out there, he certainly isn't happy with the Watchtower Society. They changed his name and spoke on his behalf without his input. So, in that spirit, I hope you all appreciate the materials provided as Food at the Proper Time.

100 QUESTIONS FOR JEHOVAH'S WITNESSES

PREFACE

Jehovah's Witnesses pride themselves on being absolutely correct about a few religious beliefs prevalent in mainstream Christianity. For example, Jesus didn't believe in the doctrine of Hellfire or the Trinity—Jehovah's Witnesses are correct about that. The organization has done its research.

In the spirit of accuracy and understanding, I feel it's incumbent upon me to ask why Jehovah's Witnesses haven't adapted as new manuscripts have been unearthed and people have made new historical discoveries.

Jehovah's Witnesses are given a test colloquially called "The 100 Questions" when getting baptized. The questions can be found in the back of the Organized to Do Jehovah's Will book. Similarly, I've provided 100 questions for Jehovah's Witnesses—questions that go unanswered.

Please consider these questions in the spirit in which they're offered. I have no intention of hurting feelings, agitating, or attacking. I'm simply looking for the answers. Are Jehovah's Witnesses correct? Let's start at the beginning: the Holy Name.

CHAPTER 1
WORD TRANSLATION

1. Why use a warped version of the Holy Name, Jehovah, rather than the actual Holy Name, Yahweh?

The Tetragrammaton represents God's name: YHWH. As the name passed through Germanic regions, Y's were gradually replaced with J's because of regional pronunciations. Jews pronounced it Yahweh.

Jehovah's Witnesses consider God's name holy and believe it should be used in regular worship. Shouldn't the original be used since the name is so important to them?

2. Why does the New World Translation of the Bible replace the Greek words for "God" or "Lord" with "Jehovah?"

The Tetragrammaton does not appear in Greek scriptures. The word used to refer to God was KURIOS, meaning Lord. In some cases, THEOS was used, meaning God.

3. Why do Jehovah's Witnesses pay missionaries and Bethelites

so poorly? Can't they afford to pay the missionaries and Special Pioneers a living wage for full-time work?

Jehovah's Witnesses invite Bethelites to live and work on-site at various branches. Missionaries agree to get over 32 hours of preaching per week and receive a small stipend. What do they do when they have to enter the outside workforce? Many Bethelites don't have any marketable skills. For that matter, what are they supposed to do when it's time to retire? Why doesn't the Watchtower Society at least provide a retirement account?

4. Why do Jehovah's Witnesses believe Michael the Archangel is also Jesus?

According to the Bible book of Hebrews, no angel will ever sit at God's right hand.

> But to which of the angels has he ever said, "Sit at my right hand until I make your enemies a footstool for your feet?"
>
> *HEBREWS 1:13*

However, the Bible says that Jesus would sit at his right hand a few chapters later.

> But when Christ had offered for all time a single sacrifice for sins, "he sat down at the right hand of God," and since then has been waiting "until his enemies would be made a footstool for his feet."
>
> *HEBREWS 10:12–13*

The Bible book of Romans reaffirms that Jesus will sit at the right hand of God.

Who will condemn them? Christ Jesus is the one who died, yes, more than that, the one who was raised up, who is at the right hand of God, and who also pleads for us.

ROMANS 8:34

There is even more evidence against this claim, but that should already be sufficient.

5. Why does the Watchtower Society claim that the Archangel is a single individual rather than a class of angels?

Jehovah's Witnesses' book *What Does the Bible Really Teach?* mentions Jesus as Michael the Archangel in the appendix. The section titled "Who Is Michael the Archangel?" says the following:

God's Word refers to "Michael the Archangel." (Jude 9) This term means "chief angel." Notice that Michael is called the archangel. This suggests that there is only one such angel.

However, The New World Translation of the Bible says the following in the book of Daniel:

So Michael, **one of** the chief princes, came to help me, and I left him there with the prince of the kingdom of Persia.

DANIEL 10:13, NWT

The term "archangel" literally means "chief messenger."[1] Contrary to the Watchtower Society's claims, even the New World Translation of the Bible affirms that the Chief Messenger is a class of angels, not a singular angel.

6. Why would they insert their own additional interpretation on top of the interpretation provided within the pages of the Bible?

Does the Watchtower Society realize that apocalyptic writing was a genre of the time, no different than science fiction is today?

Why do Jehovah's Witnesses re-interpret apocalyptic literature when the writings were intended for that time and place in history?

Why isn't the interpretation given *within the same story* acceptable? Should we trust the Bible or not?

CHAPTER 2
FALSE PROPHECY

**7. Why does the Watchtower Society insist that the date
Solomon's temple fell was 606 BCE rather than 586 BCE?**

An ancient tablet cataloged as VAT4956, currently on display
in a Berlin Museum, tells us when it was written through
star charts.[1,2] The tablet is from the 37th year of
Nebuchadnezzar's reign. It provides 30 positions of the moon and
five positions of the planets for us to use as a timestamp reference.
By running calculations to find out when the planets and moon
would be in those locations, we have a precise time for when the
tablet was written.

The tablet VAT4956 shows star positions, which won't happen
for thousands of years. Beyond a shadow of a doubt, the tablet
reveals that the 37th year of Nebuchadnezzar's reign was in
568/567 BCE. The 37th year of Nebuchadnezzar's reign was in 567
BCE. According to Jeremiah 52:29, Solomon's Temple fell in the
eighteenth year of Nebuchadnezzar's reign.

This is the number of the people whom Nebuchadnezzar took into exile: in the seventh year, three thousand and twenty-three Judeans; 29 in the eighteenth year of Nebuchadnezzar he took into exile from Jerusalem eight hundred and thirty-two persons.

JEREMIAH 52:28–29

Since his 37th year was in 568 BCE, His 18th year was in 586 BCE. Solomon's temple fell in 586 BCE.

8. Why can't Jehovah's Witnesses accept that the Bible math used to calculate the year 1914 is wrong?

Jehovah's Witnesses' calculation to arrive in 1914 is based on Solomon's Temple falling in 606 BCE. It did not fall in 606 BCE. Why won't Jehovah's Witnesses acknowledge that fact and admit that the prophecy was wrong?

9. Why do Jehovah's Witnesses believe written history has accurately kept track of weeks, months, and even years?

Does the Watchtower Society account for the fact that Jews used a completely different calendar when calculating 1914? Exactly how many years were there between 606 BCE and 1914 BCE?

The Julian calendar was instituted in 45 BCE, and the Gregorian calendar in 1582. Before the Julian calendar, the world used many different calendars. Still, the most common and famous in the Middle East was the Hebrew/Jewish calendar. The Jewish calendar worked off lunar cycles and had varying numbers of days: sometimes 353, sometimes 354, and sometimes 355.

Did Jehovah's Witnesses account for leap years in their calculations? What about leap seconds? Why do they count from 606 BCE to 1914 BCE, 2,520 years, without accounting for missing days in the year? Are we counting revolutions around the sun? If we count lunar years, why don't we count lunar years from start to finish? Where is the consistency?

10. Why do Jehovah's Witnesses accept Charles Taze Russell's Bible math about the end coming in 1914 when the same Bible math was used to fail the Millerites only 75 years earlier?

In addition to calculating 1914 based on the false premise that Solomon's Temple fell in 606 BCE rather than 586 BCE, Charles Taze Russell used another method. He measured the Pyramid of Giza using pseudo-scientific measurements called "pyramid inches," which he used in more math equations.

Jehovah's Witnesses acknowledge the pyramidology of Charles Taze Russell in a Watchtower from May 15, 1956, pp. 297–300.[3] They named each participant in forming the idea but conveniently left Charles Taze Russell out of the article.

Proof of Charles Taze Russell's involvement and belief in pyramidology can be found in his own writings. He wrote a six-part series of books titled Studies in the Scriptures. The pyramidology can be found in "Series III – *Thy Kingdom Come*, p. 338

11. Why did they leave Charles Taze Russell out of the *Watchtower* article about pyramidology?

Are they ashamed of something? Why do Jehovah's Witnesses reject his pyramidology but accept the faulty date of 606 BCE? Why is Temple math more legitimate than pyramid math? How was Charles Taze Russell divinely inspired by Bible math but not divinely inspired by pyramidology calculations?

12. Why did the Watchtower Society claim that the end would

come before the year 2000, only to reverse that position by changing the wording later?

Jehovah's Witnesses released a *Watchtower* in 1989 that prophesied the end would come before the year 2000.[4] Later, they changed the wording, but the originals can still be found.

Previous wording:

> How thrilling that must have been for Paul and Barnabas—sailing to their first foreign assignment! The apostle Paul was spearheading the Christian missionary activity. He was also laying a foundation for a work that would be *completed in our 20th century.*
>
> JEHOVAH'S WITNESSES. *THE WATCHTOWER.*
> JANUARY 1, 1989. P. 12

Current wording:

> … He was also laying a foundation for a work that would be *completed in our day.*

13. How can Jehovah's Witnesses be trusted to know when the end will come after falsely prophesying that it would come in the autumn of 1975?

In November 1968, a district overseer gave a talk at an assembly in Texas. In his talk, he said, "Not really a full 83 months remains, so let's be faithful and confident and … we will be alive beyond the war of Armageddon…"[5]

Countless Jehovah's Witnesses publications prophesied the end would come in the autumn of 1975. A single incorrect prophecy makes the Governing Body false prophets and invalidates their mandate to lead, according to Deuteronomy 18:22.

14. Why do Jehovah's Witnesses continue to believe that the end will come within the generation of people alive to see the events of 1914 unfold when that generation is very clearly dead and gone?

In *The Watchtower* from May 15, 1984, pp. 4–7, Jehovah's Witnesses claimed that the generation anointed before 1914 would not die off before the end came. They commonly use Fred Franz as a gauge, claiming he was anointed in 1913. Why do they ignore that he said he was anointed in 1914?

When Fred Franz died in 1992, why didn't they admit that the Second Generation teaching was wrong? Why did they change the word "generation" to mean contemporary instead? We have a word for contemporary. The word is contemporary. Generation means something completely different.

15. What will the Governing Body do when the Second Generation teaching fails?

What is the Governing Body of Jehovah's Witnesses going to do when the end doesn't come by the time the second generation has passed away? Will the Watchtower Society do what they did for their 1975 prophecy? Will they try to cover it up? Will they try to erase it from history? Why can't they admit when they get things wrong and work to correct it?

CHAPTER 3
THE LGBT COMMUNITY

16. Why did Jehovah's Witnesses claim that touching yourself would turn you gay?

Jehovah's Witnesses have had a book for young people for years. Today, it's the Young People Ask book. In the 1970s, it was titled *Your Youth: Getting the Best Out of It*. Here's what the youth book had to say on the subject of homosexuality:

In fact, masturbation can lead into homosexuality. In such instances the person, not satisfied with his lonely sexual activity, seeks a partner for mutual sex play. This happens much more frequently than you may realize. Contrary to what many persons think, homosexuals are not born that way, but their homosexual behavior is learned. And often a person gets started when very young by playing with another's sexual parts, and then engaging in homosexual acts.

JEHOVAH'S WITNESSES. *YOUR YOUTH: GETTING THE BEST OUT OF IT.* 1976, P. 39

Why did Jehovah's Witnesses release that book? Why was it used for years after its release? Why did they quietly remove that sentiment from future editions of teen books? Do they not believe it anymore? Why not explicitly retract it?

17. Why isn't the majority of the human population gay?

Masturbation is very well studied. The scientific consensus is... it's completely normal and even offers health benefits. The population of straight or bisexual men in the UK should be 4% if we believe this article from Jehovah's Witnesses and a scientific survey from 2018. A 96% rate of gay men would have surely been reported everywhere.

18. Why do Jehovah's Witnesses think that being gay is wrong?

The Bible mentions homosexuality in any form in a total of 6 out of 31,102 verses. It seems clear to me that it wasn't an important issue. Three of those verses are in the Old Testament. Genesis 19, the story of Sodom and Gomorrah, and Leviticus 18 and 20.[1,2]

Some of the verses are based on Sodom and Gomorrah, so it's important to note that those cities weren't destroyed because gay people lived within their walls.

> Now this was the sin of your sister Sodom: She and her daughters were arrogant, overfed and unconcerned; they did not help the poor and needy.
>
> *EZEKIEL 16:49*

Sodom *was* found to have rapists within its walls when they arrived to investigate the city. Still, the reason for its destruction was the ill-treatment of the poor.

Leviticus 18 and 20 were part of the old law, which was invalidated when Jesus died. That's why we eat pork and shellfish today.

Three verses can be found in the New Testament. 1 Corinthians 6:9–10, 1 Timothy 1:10, and Romans 1:26–27

> Do you not know that wrongdoers will not inherit the kingdom of God? Do not be deceived! Fornicators, idolaters, adulterers, male prostitutes, sodomites, thieves, the greedy, drunkards, revilers, robbers—none of these will inherit the kingdom of God.

1 CORINTHIANS 6:9–10

This verse condemns male prostitutes specifically.

> …fornicators, sodomites, slave-traders, liars, perjurers, and whatever else is contrary to the sound teaching.

1 TIMOTHY 1:10

According to scholars who study this subject for a living, the act being condemned here was being the passive participant in the equation—that is, being a bottom.

> For this reason God gave them up to degrading passions. Their women exchanged natural intercourse for unnatural, and in the same way also the men, giving up natural intercourse with women, were consumed with passion for one another. Men committed shameless acts with men and received in their own persons the due penalty for their error.

ROMANS 1:26–27

In addition to talking about male prostitution and/or being the passive participant in the equation, the verses also referred to pederasty. Older men would take young boys as pupils and sexually assault them regularly. That was considered a sexual sin. Being gay was not considered a sin at the time.

Paul wrote those Bible books. He converted to Christianity about three years after Jesus had already died. He never met Jesus personally. Paul's goal was to form Christian culture in its early days. For example, Paul caught wind of a man in the Corinth congregation bragging about sleeping with his stepmother. He worried that would make Christianity look bad, so he ordered them to expel him from the congregation. He reversed course in 2 Corinthians, but the point is that Paul was overly worried about image. Prostitution, pederasty, and sleeping with one's stepmother were out.

Not only did Paul never condemn long-term gay relationships, but more importantly, Jesus didn't condemn them, either. Jesus didn't say a single word about being gay. Jesus cared most about helping the poor. If you could help the poor and give his family (aka any human) something to drink when they were thirsty or eat when they were hungry, you were considered a sheep rather than a goat (Matthew 25:31–46).

19. Why do Jehovah's Witnesses add expectations for Christians on top of what Jesus outlined?

Jesus said two new commandments sum up all others: Love your neighbor as yourself and love God with your whole heart, soul, and mind (Matthew 22:37–39).

Jesus said there was one requirement to enter the kingdom of God besides those two commandments. He explained this in the sheep and goats parable in Matthew 25:31–46: "You gave me water when I was thirsty. You gave me clothes when I was naked." The sheep said, "Lord, when did we do those things for you?" Jesus said, "What you did to the least of my family, you did for me."

The message is clear: Love your neighbor as yourself. That includes caring for the poor, which was Jesus' primary focus. It had nothing to do with knocking on doors, talking to disfellowshipped family, attending a non-believing parent's funeral, or hating gay people:

> The Bible's stand is not unreasonable. It simply directs those with homosexual urges to do the same thing that is required of those with an opposite-sex attraction —to "flee from fornication." The fact is that millions of heterosexuals who wish to conform to the Bible's standards employ self-control despite any temptations they might face. Those with homosexual inclinations can do the same if they truly want to please God.[3]

20. Why do Jehovah's Witnesses avoid birthdays? The Bible doesn't say anything about Jesus celebrating them.

Then again, they hate gay people, though he didn't say anything about that either. Jehovah's Witnesses don't celebrate birthdays *because* Jesus didn't say anything about birthdays. In fact, there's no record of Jesus ever mentioning birthdays, good or bad. Jehovah's Witnesses use that as the basis for avoiding birthday celebrations:

> The Bible never refers to a servant of God celebrating a birthday. This is not simply an oversight, for it does record two birthday celebrations by those not serving God. However, both of those events are presented in a bad light.[4]

But they have a problem with gay people, even though he

didn't say anything about that either. This is yet another example of Jehovah's Witnesses unevenly applying principles.

21. Why do Jehovah's Witnesses act like they're the victims of persecution when they are the ones persecuting others?

Jehovah's Witnesses tell a story about persecution in a 2023 *Watchtower*. The story is farfetched at best, but it clearly portrays how Jehovah's Witnesses feel about gay people. The organization is desperate to convince people that they "love everybody," as they claim being gay is tantamount to child molestation. Take a look at the 2023 *Watchtower* article:

Some even try to bully our young ones into breaking their loyalty to Jehovah. Note, for example, what happened to a young man named Graeme, who lives in Australia. He faced a challenging situation when he attended high school. The teacher asked the class how they would react if a friend confided in them about being a homosexual. The teacher said that all in the class who would support a friend in pursuing such a lifestyle must stand on one side of the room; those who would not, on the other side. Graeme says, "The entire class stood on the side that supported that lifestyle except for me and another Witness." What happened next was a real test of Graeme's loyalty to Jehovah. "For the rest of the hour-long class," he says, "the other students and even the teacher taunted and insulted us. I did my best to defend my faith in a calm and reasonable way, but they didn't listen to a word I said." What effect did this test of loyalty have on Graeme? He says, "I did not like being the target of such verbal attacks, but I felt incredibly happy that I was able to defend my beliefs without compromise."

JEHOVAH'S WITNESSES. *THE WATCHTOWER*. AUGUST, 2023. P. 6

There are still many anti-gay people around. The Jehovah's Witness wouldn't be the only one to do so in this scenario.

The point of the article, though, is to make Jehovah's Witnesses feel like they're persecuted at every turn. The world is against them, and this fabricated story from the Watchtower only reinforces that perception.

CHAPTER 4
THE MANDATE OF HEAVEN

22. Are Governing Body members prophetic or not?

The Governing Body members claim to be prophets of God.

Those who do not read can hear, for God has on earth today a prophetlike organization, just as he did in the days of the early Christian congregation.

JEHOVAH'S WITNESSES. *THE WATCHTOWER.* OCTOBER 1, 1964, P. 601

For an answer, people should listen to the plain preaching by the remnant prefigured by Jeremiah, for these preach to men the present-day fulfillment of Jeremiah's prophecies. Who made them a prophet to speak with the authority that they claim? Well, who made Jeremiah a prophet?

JEHOVAH'S WITNESSES. *THE WATCHTOWER.* JANUARY 15, 1959. PP. 39–41

In part 2 of Jehovah's Witnesses' annual meeting, released January 2024, at the 44-minute mark, Governing Body member Geoffrey Jackson revealed "new light," which is what they call new doctrine that replaces or adds to existing doctrine, that people could rejoin Jehovah's Witnesses after the Great Tribulation starts. The previous position was that the metaphorical "door of the ark" would close after the Tribulation begins, and membership would be closed to everybody. Jackson said the following:

> If they change their hearts and joined us, would we be disappointed? Now, we can't be dogmatic. But, we don't want to be like Jonah.

Jonah was a prophet of God who refused to prophesy. As punishment for refusing to deliver prophetic information, he was swallowed by a big fish. By comparing themselves to Jonah, they are tacitly claiming to be prophets.

The Governing Body often claims not to be prophets. In the 2023 annual meeting, Jeffrey Winder, a member of the Governing Body, outright states that God does not inspire him in any unique way. However, the Governing Body constantly offers prophecy—1914, 1925, 1975, 2000, and the Second Generation teaching, to name a few. They talk about being prophets and offer prophecies fairly regularly—1914, 1925, 1975, 2000, and the Second Generation teaching, to name a few.

Deuteronomy Chapter 18 outlines the expectations of prophets. It says that prophets should be tested. They should be ignored and distrusted if what they say doesn't come true. What they said did not come from God.

Not only have prophecies described by the Governing Body of Jehovah's Witnesses not come true, but some have been proven false.

23. Why do Jehovah's Witnesses believe only a specific subset of Christians should follow one of Jesus' most important commands before his death?

Matthew 26 describes Jesus' final night on earth. He was with his disciples at the Last Supper. He instructed them to eat bread and drink wine in remembrance of him. The key word to note in Matthew is the word "disciple."

Apostles were leaders, but disciples were students of Jesus. In Matthew 26:26, Jesus instructs disciples to take communion.

While they were eating, Jesus took a loaf of bread, and after blessing it he broke it, gave it to the disciples, and said, "Take, eat; this is my body." Then he took a cup, and after giving thanks he gave it to them, saying, "Drink from it, all of you; for this is my blood of the covenant, which is poured out for many for the forgiveness of sins."

MATTHEW 26:26–28

Mark's account reaffirms that disciples were instructed to participate in the ceremony to remember Jesus.

While they were eating, Jesus took bread, and when he had given thanks, he broke it and gave it to his disciples, saying, "Take it; this is my body." Then he took a cup, and when he had given thanks, he gave it to them, and they all drank from it.

MARK 14:22–23

Jesus clearly stated that his disciples should do this in remembrance of him. In Luke, the scene described only included his apostles. Even so, he didn't say the observance was exclusive to leadership. It seems clear that Jesus wanted people to *remember* him. That was the point of the ceremony. Why do Jehovah's Witnesses limit who is allowed to remember Jesus by taking communion?

24. Do anointed brothers who've been jailed have to drink toilet wine for the Memorial?

Will Jehovah understand if they choose not to partake? Is it okay if they partake in their hearts, or must they drink the toilet wine in prison? Is leavened bread okay, or should they find a way to un-leaven their sandwich bread? Is yeast the issue, or is it the air?

Does Jehovah think peoples' best efforts are reasonable enough in this case? If so, why doesn't Jehovah think people's best efforts are reasonably sufficient in other areas of their lives? How can people "fall short," and who can judge whether they've fallen short, aside from Jehovah himself?

25. Geoffrey Jackson, under oath before the entire world, stated that it would be presumptuous to think Jehovah's Witnesses are God's only spokespeople. Does he truly believe that, or was he lying?

Geoffrey Jackson was called to testify in front of the Australian Royal Commission for their mishandling of child sexual abuse cases.

While testifying, the Australian Royal Commission asked Governing Body member Geoffrey Jackson the following question: "Do you see yourselves as Jehovah God's spokespeople on earth?"

Geoffrey Jackson responded, "That, I think, would certainly be quite presumptuous to say that we are the only spokesperson which God is using."

Is this an example of a Governing Body member lying under oath to avoid bad press? It's unacceptable for a Jehovah's Witness to lie to protect their own lives. Do the rules only apply to the followers but not the leaders?

26. Why do Jehovah's Witnesses use the Two Witness Rule even in heinous criminal situations from which the Two Witness Rule is specifically Biblically exempted?

Deuteronomy 22:25–27 outlines exemptions from the Two Witness Rule:

> If, however, the man happened to meet the engaged girl in the field and the man overpowered her and lay down with her, the man who lay down with her is to die by himself, and you must do nothing to the girl. The girl has not committed a sin deserving of death. This case is the same as when a man attacks his fellow man and murders him. For he happened to meet her in the field, and the engaged girl screamed, but there was no one to rescue her.

> *DEUTERONOMY 22:25–27*

Why do Jehovah's Witnesses ignore that set of verses to the detriment of so many children within the organization?

27. Why do Jehovah's Witnesses believe the Two Witness Rule has modern-day relevance since the invention of the video camera and DNA testing?

The Bible outlines a system of governance, but society has advanced technology that renders the old method obsolete today.

Jehovah's Witnesses are not investigators. As a body, elders cannot access DNA testing, databases, or other advanced technology to solve crimes. Why, then, do Jehovah's Witnesses have a history of encouraging members of the religion to handle things internally instead of calling the police?

Why has the Watchtower Society lost so many lawsuits for their mishandling of child sexual abuse cases?

After the Governing Body recognized that more child abusers could be caught by means other than the Two Witness Rule, why did they stubbornly refuse to explicitly instruct elders to report cases of child sexual abuse to the police? Why won't they, at the very least, advise elders to instruct victims' parents to call the police? How can a system possibly be called moral when it explicitly leaves room for predators to escape justice?

28. Why was Tony Morris fired from the Governing Body?

What happened to Tony Morris? Why was he fired? He shaped a lot of doctrine while on the Governing Body. He claimed members wouldn't enter the new system if they didn't knock on doors often enough. Is that still valid? Are any of his "new light" claims still active? If so, how was it determined which parts were from Jehovah and which were from his brain?

29. Why were Tony Morris's morning worship videos removed from the Jehovah's Witness website?

Why were Tony Morris's videos removed from the website? Are his videos no longer considered spiritual food? If his messages were being given to us as spiritual food, but we found that they weren't spiritual food after all, how can we trust that we're receiving it now? Are Jehovah's Witnesses starving people's spirits?

30. Who can decide if one of the Governing Body members isn't providing spiritual food after all?

How do we know the people currently on the Governing Body have Jehovah's mandate? Maybe Tony Morris had Jehovah's Mandate, and the other Governing Body members didn't. How can we tell?

I remember a test presented to God's people in Deuteronomy 18:22. If their prophecies fail, they aren't prophets. They're liars.

CHAPTER 5
INCORRECT BELIEFS

31. Why do Jehovah's Witnesses believe that Jesus died on a stake instead of a cross?

Jehovah's Witnesses' reasoning rests upon the word used to describe it: the Greek word *stauros*. Stauros means an upright pole. However, we have descriptions of crosses used to execute people. One such description can be found in the epistle of Barnabas. In that book, it's likened to somebody standing upright with outstretched arms or like a ship's mast. It was a cross. Not a stake.[1]

Scholars universally accept that Jesus died by the cross, not by torture stake. Jehovah's Witnesses are the only ones who deny this. Bart Ehrman, for example, goes into detail about why we know it was a cross rather than a stake.

Not only does the epistle of Barnabas describe a cross, but it was *the* common method of execution at the time. It was a cross. It just was.

32. Why do Jehovah's Witnesses ignore the verse that says

multiple nails were used to hold Jesus' hands to his torture device?

John 20:25 indicates that multiple nails were used to execute Jesus. Why would multiple nails be used if his hands were crossed one over another? Were his hands comically large?

> So the other disciples told him, "We have seen the Lord!" But he said to them, "Unless I see the nail marks in his hands and put my finger where the **nails** were, and put my hand into his side, I will not believe."
>
> *JOHN 20:25*

Coupled with the fact that the cross was simply the standard method of execution at the time, the conclusion is undeniable. Jesus died by the cross, not by the stake. The Watchtower Society got downright indignant about the subject in the *Watchtower* from April 1, 1984, pp. 30–31.

> Much time and trouble have been wasted in disputing as to whether three or four nails were used in fastening the Lord. Nonnus affirms that three only were used, in which he is followed by Gregory Nazianzen. The more general belief gives four nails, an opinion which is supported at much length and by curious arguments by Curtius. Others have carried the number of nails as high as fourteen.
>
> JEHOVAH'S WITNESSES. *THE WATCHTOWER.*
> APRIL 1, 1984. PP. 30–31

If you notice, the last sentence uses weasel words, meaning they don't specify their source. "Others have carried the number"—

what others? Who? Which people specifically say that? Do they have the credentials to make that kind of claim? If these "others" really did claim that, why didn't Jehovah's Witnesses simply give their name like they gave the names of their other sources?

33. Why do Jehovah's Witnesses use the JW.ORG logo as an idol?

Another complaint from Jehovah's Witnesses is that the cross is used as an idol. I could agree with that assessment, but Jehovah's Witnesses use their JW.ORG logo similarly.

They use the logo on their books, pens, magazines, stickers, buttons, pins, necklaces, and even earrings. Jehovah's Witnesses might say they're just using it to advertise the religion. I would argue that Christians are just using the cross to advertise their religion, too. Some don't, certainly—but many do.

Jehovah's Witnesses lay out the argument against the cross in their *Watchtower* from November 1, 1950, pp. 425–427.

> Reference to the original languages in which the Bible was written will show beyond a question of doubt that Christ was never hung on any pagan cross. Hence, the use of the word "cross" in the English-language Bibles is a mistranslation.

The *Watchtower* quotes its own Bible translation to back up the claim. The article continues:

> On this, the New World Translation of the Christian Greek Scriptures, in its appendix, on pages 768–771, in commenting on Matthew 10:38, where the Greek word σταυρός (stau·ros') first appears and which is translated "cross" in most Bibles, states: "This is the expression used in connection with the execution of Jesus at Calvary. There is no evidence that the Greek word stau·ros' meant here a 'cross' such as the pagans used as a

religious symbol for many centuries before Christ to denote the sun-god. [sic]"

This article is still considered valid doctrine and is referenced on the Jehovah's Witness website. The article cites a publication they wrote as evidence of their claim about the cross.

34. Why do Jehovah's Witnesses cite their own literature as evidence of their claims?

If you'll notice, I haven't quoted a single publication as evidence in one of my other publications. It's circular. Why did Jehovah's Witnesses cite their own publication as evidence of their claim that the original language says "stake" instead of "cross?"

Do Jehovah's Witnesses believe that their own publications are equivalent, or even superior to the Bible? Do they think the Bible can't be understood without the assistance of the Watchtower Society's publications? This is the definition of "source: I made it up."

35. Who worked on the translation effort for The New World Translation of the Bible?

The world has no idea who translated Jehovah's Witnesses' translation of the Bible. They haven't released the names of the translators. That's a big deal within scholarly communities. If a Bible translation is released, the translators' names should be, too. I don't know of any other Bible translation that doesn't list its translators.

36. Why should we trust the organization to give us honest and complete interpretations of works they don't cite?

In many instances, Jehovah's Witness literature doesn't even name the source, let alone properly cite a source. Why should we believe a word out of the mouths of the Governing Body or the writing department when they consistently get it wrong?

37. Why do Jehovah's Witnesses bend the New World Translation to support the belief that Jesus created the world instead of God creating the world?

Jehovah's Witnesses believe that God created Jesus, and Jesus created everything else. In a way, Jesus is the actual divine creator.

Here's the NRSVA translation of Colossians 1:17:

He himself is before all things, and in him all things **hold together**.

COLOSSIANS 1:17, NRSVA

Take a look at Jehovah's Witnesses version, the New World Translation:

Also, he is before all other things, and by means of him all other things **were made to exist.**

COLOSSIANS 1:17, NWT

Why did Jehovah's Witnesses translate it that way? No other major translation interpreted the language to mean that everything was "made to exist" using Jesus.

38. Why do Jehovah's Witnesses add another layer of prophecy on top of what's already described in Daniel regarding the King of the North?

Daniel, Chapter 11 is an example of a messenger explaining a fantastical vision of a King of the North and a King of the South to the writer.[2] At the time, the Ptolemaic Empire (King of the South) and the Seleucid Empire (King of the North) engaged in a vicious war, and Jerusalem was caught in the middle. The battle is widely accepted to be the sixth Syrian war.

An angel already explained the apocalyptic vision within the text. How can Jehovah's Witnesses read a text that God already interpreted through an angel and claim that there's an additional interpretation that God didn't see fit to describe in the Bible?

Why would God give a secret interpretation to the Governing Body and provide the rest of the world no way of independently verifying what they claim? Why is the angel's interpretation included at all if it isn't the correct one?

39. Why do Jehovah's Witnesses reject God's prophetic interpretation of the book of Daniel? Why do Jehovah's Witnesses think they're more qualified than Daniel to interpret the prophecy?

Daniel, Chapter 2 contains an apocalyptic vision of a statue of Nebuchadnezzar. Daniel explains that each section of the statue represents a world empire. Daniel uses the same pattern in Chapter 8 in his apocalyptic vision about beasts coming from the sea.

In Daniel, Chapter 8, an angel lists those empires as Babylon, Persia, and Greece. Then the angel says the Greek Empire will shatter into four kingdoms. That's exactly what happened. The Seleucid Empire was the kingdom that ruled over Jerusalem. In the statue prophecy from Daniel 2 and the beasts of the sea prophecy from Daniel 8, Daniel was prophesying that the Seleucid Empire would be destroyed for persecuting God's people.

After the Seleucid Empire was described as one of four broken pieces of a larger empire in Chapter 8, Daniel gives us absolutely no clues as to what the next empire will be. That's because the Roman

Empire wouldn't exist for another 100 years after the Book of Daniel was written.

The angel in Daniel 8 says the empires are Babylon, Persia, Greece, and the Seleucid Empire. Jehovah's Witnesses take an extra step to interpret prophecy beyond what the Bible explains. To Jehovah's Witnesses, the legs represent Rome instead of the Seleucid Empire, and the feet of clay and iron represent the Anglo-American Empire instead of the Roman Empire.

Why do Jehovah's Witnesses skip over the Seleucid Empire, which was next to rule Jerusalem? America has existed for as long as the Seleucid Empire: between 200 and 300 years.

40. How can Jehovah's Witnesses ignore multiple empires that came after the Roman Empire but before the Anglo-American Empire?

The Muslim world controlled modern-day Israel and Jerusalem for centuries. Even ignoring the Ottoman Empire, shouldn't Jehovah's Witnesses at least consider the other Muslim empires that came before?

41. Why do Jehovah's Witnesses believe that the British Empire was a remnant of the Roman Empire?

The *Daniel's Prophecy* book, published by the Watchtower Society, says that the Roman Empire eventually became the British Empire. This belief justifies ignoring every other empire to control Jerusalem since Jesus' day.

What makes them think the Roman Empire turned into the British Empire? The Western Roman Empire became the Byzantines, and the Eastern Roman Empire became Rome, Italy.

The belief that the Western Roman Empire eventually became the British Empire is necessary to accept Jehovah's Witnesses' interpretation of Nebuchadnezzar's statue prophecy from Daniel 2.

Suppose Jehovah's Witnesses believe the Western Roman Empire became the British Empire. Why don't they also believe that the Babylonian Empire became the Persian Empire and count both empires as the statue's golden head?

Why did Jehovah's Witnesses skip over Britain's historical rival, France, before America even existed?

42. Why do Jehovah's Witnesses believe that demons possess objects, such as Smurf dolls?

In the 1980s, an urban legend swept through congregations of Jehovah's Witnesses. It was based on the Smurfs. Jehovah's Witnesses heavily demonized the Smurfs. They didn't outright ban the TV show, but the culture controlled people more effectively than doctrinal commands ever could.

The urban legend changes from person to person, but my version describes a girl with a Smurf doll in her meeting bag. She showed up to the Kingdom Hall, and during the meeting, the Smurf doll stood up out of the purse and exited the Kingdom Hall, speaking obscenities on its way out the door. The legend claims that Jehovah's light was just too bright for it.

The urban legend seems bizarre, but Jehovah's Witnesses believe that objects can be possessed and animated by demons. It's the same reason they encourage people to be cautious about shopping at yard sales. You never know what the previous owner was up to. With those premises, is it such a leap to believe it could happen to a Smurf doll?

In recounting this myth, I've found a workaround—if you purchase something at a yard sale, simply bring it into the Kingdom Hall. If it doesn't run away swearing, it should be demon-free. Right?

43. Why don't Jehovah's Witnesses allow women to be involved in the teaching process, just like men?

1 Timothy 2:12 discusses women's involvement in the church.

I permit no woman to teach or to have authority over a man; she is to keep silent.

1 TIMOTHY 2:12

Jehovah's Witnesses are aware of deeply complex scholarly information. For example, they're aware that Jesus didn't believe in the Trinity or the Hellfire doctrine. Scholars weren't always aware of that fact. That means Jehovah's Witnesses did their research. They're *very* well-versed in some of these biblical subjects. How are they unaware that 1 Timothy 2:12 and 1 Corinthians 14:34–35 are not original to Paul?[3]

Is the Watchtower Society unaware that the verses were added later, or is it uninformed about the Bible and early Christianity? Although they seem informed in other areas, I can only assume they intentionally ignore the Bible's history.

44. Why do women have to wear hijabs in some cases?

Jehovah's Witnesses base their hijab doctrine on 1 Corinthians 11:11–15:

Nevertheless, in the Lord woman is not independent of man or man independent of woman. For just as woman came from man, so man comes through woman; but all things come from God. Judge for yourselves: is it proper for a woman to pray to God with her head unveiled? Does not nature itself teach you that if a man wears long hair, it is degrading to him, but if a woman has long hair, it is her glory? For her hair is given to her for a covering.

1 CORINTHIANS 11:11–15

This Bible verse seems to imply that women are equal to men. It also seems to say that women should wear a veil when they *pray*. Why do Jehovah's Witnesses insist women wear head coverings when leading the congregation in some way?

The verse also implies that the veil is the woman's hair. Is the verse saying that women should have long hair and men should have short hair? Should women wear a hijab only if they have short hair?

Of course, the governing body will provide us with all of this information. They have an excellent track record of correctly interpreting the Bible—if we ignore their hundreds of mistakes.

CHAPTER 6
SHUNNING

45. Why do Jehovah's Witnesses mandate that members shun people? Why is it codified in their rules?

The Watchtower Society justifies its shunning policy with the following verse:[1]

But now I am writing to you not to associate with anyone who bears the name of brother or sister who is sexually immoral or greedy, or is an idolater, reviler, drunkard, or robber. Do not even eat with such a one.

1 CORINTHIANS 5:11

Paul wrote that letter to the congregation in Corinth. A man in the congregation had slept with his stepmother and was bragging about it in church. Paul instructed the Corinthian congregation to shun the man for his behavior, fearing it would make the early Christian church look bad.[2]

The Corinthian congregation responded negatively to Paul's

command. They shunned the man but, in the process, discovered that shunning is deeply painful. Human beings are simply not supposed to shun other humans. In response, Paul sent another letter to the Corinthian congregation and reversed his shunning policy.

> But if anyone has caused pain, he has caused it not to me, but to some extent—not to exaggerate it—to all of you. This punishment by the majority is enough for such a person; so now instead you should forgive and console him, so that he may not be over-whelmed by excessive sorrow.

> *2 CORINTHIANS 2:5–7*

Why do Jehovah's Witnesses selectively choose to read Paul's first letter to the congregation in Corinth but completely ignore his response? How can they justify the excessive sorrow they spread to thousands of shunned ex-members?

46. Did Jehovah's Witnesses lie on their website and in a Norway courtroom by claiming that the religion does not mandate shunning?

One Jehovah's Witness article titled "Do Jehovah's Witnesses Shun Those Who Used to Belong to Their Religion?" heavily implies they don't shun people:[3]

> Those who were baptized as Jehovah's Witnesses but no longer preach to others, perhaps even drifting away from association with fellow believers, are not shunned. In fact, we reach out to them and try to rekindle their spiritual interest.

That conveniently says nothing about disfellowshipped people.

This paragraph is about inactive people who've stopped going in service. Why didn't they unequivocally denounce shunning as an evil practice that is never done in any form by Jehovah's Witnesses? They go on to address disfellowshipped people a few paragraphs down:

> Disfellowshipped individuals may attend our religious services. If they wish, they may also receive spiritual counsel from congregation elders. The goal is to help each individual once more to qualify to be one of Jehovah's Witnesses. Disfellowshipped people who reject improper conduct and demonstrate a sincere desire to live by the Bible's standards are always welcome to become Jehovah's Witnesses again.

Are Jehovah's Witnesses ashamed of their practice of shunning? Why aren't they stating plainly what God supposedly instructed them to do? The elder's handbook has a list of disfellowshipping offenses. Chapter 12, paragraph 17, subsection 1 of the *Shepherd the Flock of God Elder's Manual*, 2021 edition, says the following:

> Unnecessary Association With Disfellowshipped or Disassociated Individuals: Willful, continued, unnecessary association with disfellowshipped or disassociated nonrelatives despite repeated counsel would warrant judicial action.

The elder's handbook clearly lists conditions under which Jehovah's Witnesses should be shunned. Even if this isn't explicitly stated in the handbook, it's widely practiced culturally. Additionally, the Watchtower Society encourages an alarming view of outsiders.

47. Why does the Watchtower Society teach that anybody critical of the religion to any degree is mentally diseased?

A 2011 *Watchtower* clearly outlines how Jehovah's Witnesses are supposed to feel about anybody critical of the religion. That includes me, and that now includes you after having read this book:

> The Bible says that apostates are mentally diseased and that they use their teachings to make others think like them. (1 Timothy 6:3, 4) Jehovah is like that good doctor. He clearly tells us to stay away from false teachers. We must always be determined to follow his warning.
>
> JEHOVAH'S WITNESSES. *THE WATCHTOWER, STUDY ED. (SIMPLIFIED).* JULY 15, 2011. P. 11

What kind of atmosphere does the Watchtower Society think they're fostering by saying that to their members? How can they justify brazenly twisting the truth by claiming they don't shun?

48. Why do Jehovah's Witnesses forbid members from attending the funeral or wedding of a friend or family member who isn't a Jehovah's Witness?

This rule falls under the apostasy category, which refers to participation in interfaith activities. Why is it a disfellowshipping offense, as outlined in the Elder's Handbook, *Shepherd the Flock of God?*

49. Why did Jehovah's Witnesses release a *Watchtower* article condemning shunning in 1947 and subsequently codify the practice in 1952?

Jehovah's Witnesses released Awake! in 1947, which talks about excommunication. It says the following:[4]

If you are one of the 138,000,000 people in the world that were born and raised as "Protestants," then you are already excommunicated by the Roman Catholic Hierarchy. This means that you are looked upon with the blackest contempt by the Vatican, being cursed and damned with the Devil and his angels.

> JEHOVAH'S WITNESSES. "ARE YOU ALSO EXCOMMUNICATED?" *AWAKE!.* JANUARY 8, 1947, P. 27

The organization seemed to understand why shunning was so damaging five years before implementing it. If Jehovah's Witnesses were picked as Jesus' chosen organization in 1919, why did Jesus inspire them to release anti-shunning material up to 1947?

50. Why did Jehovah's Witnesses defend and speak highly of Freemasons in 1947?

Jehovah's Witnesses also seemed to defend Freemasons in the 1947 *Awake!* article on ex-communication:

> All those belonging to such lodges as the Masonic, Fenians, Independent Order of Good Templars, Odd Fellows, Sons of Temperance, or the Knights of Pythias, are also excommunicated.

What changed? Jehovah's Witnesses were supposedly chosen by Jesus as his representative on earth in 1919. Why did they both defend Freemasonry and condemn shunning after being selected by Jesus? Is Jehovah unsure of his feelings on any given subject? If He changed His mind about which organization should represent him, would that organization tell us?

51. Why is selling lottery tickets at a gas station a disfellowshipping offense?

I understand that Jehovah's Witnesses aren't allowed to smoke cigarettes, chew tobacco, or play the lottery. I don't understand why they aren't allowed to work in a position where they would be expected to sell those items to people. Just how divorced from society should we be, according to Jesus? Is it okay to be in a store where cigarettes are sold?

Is it okay for a Jehovah's Witness to invest in the stock market, knowing that some of the money they make will come from Philip Morris, the cigarette company? It's unacceptable to make any money from tobacco sales. Why do Jehovah's Witnesses earn revenue from the H. M. Riley Trust, which is invested in cigarette companies?[5]

52. Why are cannabis gummies banned in legal areas, but alcohol is not banned?

Cannabis is arguably less harmful than alcohol by a wide margin. Consuming anything through combustion, like smoking a cigarette, can be very damaging to a person's health. However, consuming cannabis gummies is not using combustion and is not damaging to a person's health in any way. Why is alcohol allowed, but cannabis within legal states and countries is not?

53. Why is it a disfellowshipping offense to get remarried after divorcing an abusive partner unless that partner cheated?

As a young Jehovah's Witness myself, I had to deal with a terribly abusive father. My mother left with me repeatedly, but the elders encouraged her to return. She wasn't allowed to remarry even when she finally permanently escaped from him. She was permanently linked to him. He had cheated on her years earlier, but she forgave him for it. After forgiving him, she wasn't allowed to leave.

My mother was stuck with my dad to the bitter end unless he cheated. Why do Jehovah's Witnesses command women and men to stay linked to abusive partners, no matter what?

54. Why are Jehovah's Witnesses so determined to prevent members from having outside relationships?

In their 2016 convention, Jehovah's Witnesses presented a video colloquially called "the Bunker Video." It portrays Jehovah's Witnesses sitting together in a locked basement, hiding from authorities. They're in the Great Tribulation. Each one tells a story about how they remained loyal to Jehovah.

One of the older women present tells a story about her coworkers. She said they were trying to be friendly with her. They invited her to get coffee with them. She took pride in the fact that she didn't give in to associating with them. She separated herself and stopped her friendly attitude.

Why do Jehovah's Witnesses view the outside world this way? Why is it important for the Society to prevent members from having outside friendships?

CHAPTER 7
PAGANISM

55. Why did Jehovah's Witnesses label shunning as a pagan practice in 1947?

The 1947 *Awake!* article is a perfect example of the organization's hypocrisy. They spent a fair bit of it opining about shunning practices. This *Awake!* Alone has sparked multiple questions I'd love to have answered by the leadership. The second column of the 1947 Awake! says shunning is of pagan origin. They make the same argument about Christmas.

Where, then, did this practice originate? The Encyclopaedia Britannica says that papal excommunication is not without pagan influence, "and its variations cannot be adequately explained unless account be taken of several non-Christian analogues of excommunication." The superstitious Greeks believed that when an excommunicated person died the Devil entered the body, and therefore, "in order to prevent it, the relatives of the deceased cut his body in pieces and boil them in wine."

There doesn't seem to be a citation for the quote from Encyclopedia Britannica. I have no idea if it accurately represents what was said in the 1947 edition.

56. What do Jehovah's Witnesses mean when they say "pagan?"

Jehovah's Witnesses have a long list of things that are banned for having pagan roots. As far as I can tell, "paganism" could mean anything. The Olympics are banned because the opening ceremony includes torch lighting, and the Olympics started in Greece. By that logic, anything that's not explicitly of Christian origin is pagan. Even explicitly Christian practices can have pagan roots in their eyes.

Here is a short list of things banned within the religion for having some ties to paganism. I'll be asking specific questions about some of these things later. As of when this book was published, the list stands as follows:[1]

- Christmas, Easter, birthdays, New Year's Eve, Valentine's Day, Mother's Day, Father's Day, Halloween, Dia de los Muertos (a Mexican tradition), and every other holiday for their own reasons
- Carnivals—Jehovah's Witnesses. *Awake!*. March 8, 1973, pp.5-8
- Olympics—Banned for the reasons mentioned above.
- Throwing Rice, Throwing the Bouquet, Wedding Marches
- Rosary, Star of David, Astrology
- Symbols on graves such as fish, anchor and dove, peacock
- Democracy
- Mazes and Labyrinths—Jehovah's Witnesses. *Awake!*. December 22, 1999. pp.20-24

- The Cross
- Jehovah's Witnesses think Jesus died on a stake driven into the ground instead of a cross.
- Hell
- Immortality of the Soul
- Jehovah's Witnesses think only angels and anointed people have immortal souls. Normal Jehovah's Witnesses will still be able to die after Armageddon.
- Clerical Celibacy, Trinity, Mary the mother of God, Saying "Bless you."
- Philosophy
- Specifically, Taoism, Confucianism, Greek Philosophy, Materialism, and Platonic philosophy.
- Throwing Soil into a grave, Throwing flowers into a grave.
- Drawing Halos on religious figures
- The Twist and certain other forms of dancing[2]

57. Why are some things acknowledged as pagan but acceptable anyway?

List of things that have pagan roots but are acceptable anyway:[3]

- Veil on bride
- Bridesmaids have the same color as the bride, or even white.
- Wedding Ring.
- The Watchtower Society acknowledges pagan roots, but they're deliberately ignored.
- Wedding cakes, Calendars, using flowers at a funeral.
- Piñatas.
- Piñatas aren't technically banned but heavily discouraged.

- Disfellowshipping.
- Originally believed to have pagan origins, the practice was implemented within five years of releasing an article condemning it as pagan.

Jehovah's Witnesses acknowledge that they believe the veil has a connection to paganism in a Watchtower from 1969:

To some in Germany, a white gown signifies virginity. Others there believe that it prevents evil spirits from recognizing the bride. In Japan, some view the white gown as a symbol of mourning; the bride 'dies' to her parents and remains with her husband until death.

JEHOVAH'S WITNESSES. *THE WATCHTOWER*. JANUARY 15, 1969. PP. 57-61.

In the following sentence, they excuse the wedding veil as acceptable anyway. "However, to many persons throughout the earth, the white dress is simply a quaint tradition with no meaning. A Christian bride need not think that a white gown is essential, nor that it is universally forbidden."

58. Why is the Twist banned as a dance with pagan roots?

In the 1960s, there was a fear-mongering campaign over dancing. The fear swept through traditionalist communities the same way anti-LGBT sentiment has swept through modern traditionalist communities. Here's what Jehovah's Witnesses had to say about dancing:

Many of the news reports will likely have a few words about the origin of a new dance, and this is true of the twist. Time magazine, for instance, commented:

"The Twist at first was an innocent enough dance; it has since been largely discarded in favor of such refinements as 'The Roach' and 'The Fly.' But the youngsters at [a certain New York nightclub] [sic] have revived The Twist and parodied it into a replica of some ancient tribal puberty rite. The dancers scarcely ever touch each other or move either feet. Everything else, however, moves. The upper body sways forward and backward and the hips and shoulders twirl erotically, while the arms thrust in, out, up and down."

> JEHOVAH'S WITNESSES. "HOW SHOULD CHRISTIANS VIEW DANCING?" *THE WATCHTOWER.* JULY 1, 1962. PP. 409–414

Later in the article, they use the Twist as an example of an unacceptable dance because of its connection to paganism.

In this example we have found that the dance craze mainly involves bodily gyrations and that the words used to describe them are "frantic," "sensual" and "erotic." You have also learned what kind of persons developed the dance and that it is basically an imitation of some pagan tribe's dance, involving gestures of a sexually suggestive nature.

59. Why are mazes and labyrinths labeled as pagan by Jehovah's Witnesses?

Mazes and labyrinths are also of pagan origin in the eyes of Jehovah's Witnesses. Here's a quote from a 1999 issue of the *Awake!:*

Large floor mazes were laid in other medieval French and Italian cathedrals and churches, including those at Amiens, Bayeux,

Orléans, Ravenna, and Toulouse. The one at Reims was destroyed 200 years ago, and the Mirepoix Cathedral's maze features a central Minotaur.

Regarding the incorporation of labyrinths into prominent religious buildings, one authority writes: "The pagan labyrinth was adopted by the medieval Christian church and adapted for its own use by including Christian symbolism in the design."

JEHOVAH'S WITNESSES. AWAKE!.
DECEMBER 22, 1999 PP.20-24

Based on this magazine, the mazes and labyrinths they describe are of Christian origin, not pagan. Why do Jehovah's Witnesses believe that things of Christian origin are pagan?

60. Why can't Jehovah's Witnesses celebrate birthdays?

Jehovah's Witnesses strictly forbid birthdays. Here are their reasons:

- Birthday celebrations have pagan roots.
- Early Christians didn't celebrate birthdays.
- Christians aren't required to celebrate birthdays.
- The Bible never refers to a servant of God celebrating a birthday.

Let's ask about each reason in detail.

61. Birthday reason 1: Why are pagan roots ignored for wedding rings or brides' veils, but not for birthday celebrations?

The first reason listed on Jehovah's Witnesses' website as to why they can't celebrate birthdays is because birthday celebrations have pagan roots.

When asked why Jehovah's Witnesses are allowed to wear wedding rings, which is another explicitly pagan practice, the response from the Watchtower Society was the following:

> Moreover, the wedding ring at one time had religious significance. Yet, most people today do not know that, considering a wedding ring a mere evidence that someone is married.

> JEHOVAH'S WITNESSES. *THE WATCHTOWER.* FEBRUARY 15, 2007. P. 30

Paganism is a problem for Jehovah's Witnesses, but only in certain circumstances. Jehovah's Witnesses addressed the "pagan roots" of wind chimes in a 1981 *Watchtower* article.

> If one's motive in putting up a wind chime has nothing to do with false religion, superstition or demonism, and there is little possibility of others getting the wrong impression regarding its use in the home, it is a simple matter for personal decision.

> JEHOVAH'S WITNESSES. "QUESTIONS FROM READERS." *THE WATCHTOWER.* JUNE 1, 1981. P. 31

According to that *Watchtower* passage, pagan roots aren't a problem for Jehovah's Witnesses if the intent is not to participate in a pagan practice and it's not perceived as pagan worship. Birthdays are not perceived as pagan worship. Additionally, as with wedding rings, the pagan roots of birthdays are so far removed from paganism that most people don't know they have pagan roots.

Again, what constitutes "pagan roots?" It now appears to be anything that isn't of Jehovah's Witness origin.

62. Birthday reason 2: We have no accounts of early Christians celebrating birthdays—So what?

The second reason listed on the Jehovah's Witness website for not celebrating birthdays is that early Christians didn't celebrate birthdays.

I'm not sure I understand the connection between what ancient people did or did not do and what we should be doing today. Ninety percent of ancient people were illiterate. Should modern Christians also mirror that aspect of culture and society?

63. Birthday reason 3: Christians aren't required to celebrate birthdays—So what?

The third reason listed for avoiding birthday celebrations is that Christians aren't required to celebrate them. They're only required to celebrate Jesus' death.

There are many things Christians aren't required to do, but they do them because they enjoy them. For example, Christians aren't required to keep cats in their homes, and the Bible doesn't require Christians to attend a religious service twice weekly. The lack of a requirement is not the same as a requirement *not* to do something.

64. Birthday reason 4: The Bible never refers to a servant of God celebrating a birthday—So what?

The fourth and final reason listed on the Jehovah's Witness website for refusing to celebrate birthdays is that the Bible never refers to a servant of God celebrating a birthday. Here's what the website said on the subject:

This is not simply an oversight, for it does record two birthday celebrations by those not serving God. However, both of those events are presented in a bad light.

When I was a Jehovah's Witness, I was told it was because somebody lost a head at every birthday celebration mentioned in the Bible. That's a funny observation I hadn't noticed before, and it's effectively the logic being used in their fourth reason for avoiding birthdays.

I simply don't accept that justification. If that's the reason why Jehovah's Witnesses don't celebrate birthdays, then they shouldn't keep dogs, either. Every time the Bible mentions dogs, it's in a negative light.[4] Despite that fact, Jehovah's Witnesses aren't forbidden from keeping them. Jehovah's Witnesses' rules are unevenly applied.

65. Why is toasting at weddings banned for Jehovah's Witnesses?

Jehovah's Witnesses are banned from toasting at weddings because of—you guessed it—its possible connection to paganism.

A common practice at weddings and on other social occasions is toasting. The 1995 International Handbook on Alcohol and Culture says: "Toasting . . . is probably a secular vestige of ancient sacrificial libations in which a sacred liquid was offered to the gods . . . in exchange for a wish, a prayer summarized in the words 'long life!' or 'to your health!'

True, many people may not consciously view toasting as a religious or superstitious gesture. Still, the custom of lifting wine glasses heavenward might be viewed as a request to "heaven"—a superhuman force—for a blessing in a way that does not accord with that outlined in the Scriptures.

JEHOVAH'S WITNESSES. "CHAPTER 13:
CELEBRATIONS THAT DISPLEASE GOD".
KEEP YOURSELVES IN GOD'S LOVE. 2008.

Toasting, The Olympics, and carnivals are just as removed from paganism as wedding rings and wind chimes. Despite that, wind chimes and wedding rings are allowed while the others are not.

The Governing Body claims to receive guidance from God himself. They claim that the Watchtower Society has been Jesus' chosen representative on earth since 1919. Why would Jehovah apply rules unevenly?

66. Why do Jehovah's Witnesses believe Hell is of pagan origin?

Hell is a Christian creation, though Jesus didn't believe in it. Christianity didn't adopt it until hundreds of years later. Many believe our modern concept of Hell was shaped by Dante's poem "The Divine Comedy." The Christian concept of Hell was described in great detail in the book The Apocalypse of Peter, written around the same time as the Book of John.[5]

The words "apocalypse" and "revelation" mean the same thing in different languages. Apocalypse can also mean "explaining.". There was debate over whether the Apocalypse of John (the book of Revelation) or the Apocalypse of Peter should be in the Bible. Obviously, the Apocalypse of John won at the end of the day.

The Apocalypse of Peter contains graphic descriptions of Hell as the reader is taken on a tour to see the most horrific punishments imaginable. Some of those punishments include the following:

- Liars whose lies caused the death of martyrs have their lips cut off, with fire in their bodies and entrails.

- Rich people who neglected the poor are clothed in rags and pierced by a sharp pillar of fire.
- Women who had premarital sex have their flesh torn to pieces.
- Mothers who committed infanticide have their breast milk congeal into flesh-devouring animals that torment both parents (their dead children are delivered to a caretaking angel called Temlakos).

67. When Jehovah's Witnesses use the term "pagan," is it intended to apply to anything that's not of Jehovah's Witness origin?

Jehovah's Witnesses seem to believe that even things of Christian origin are of pagan origin. Just because non-Christians had a similar concept doesn't mean it was lifted directly from non-Christians. If it only applies to anything of non-Christian origin, why are the cross, Hell, mazes, and labyrinths banned?

CHAPTER 8
EVIL LEADERS

68. Why did Joseph Rutherford have a mansion built and deeded to Bible characters?

n 1929, Joseph Rutherford had a mansion built and deeded to Bible characters. It was named Beth Sarim, meaning House of Princes. He decided to stay in the mansion until the Bible characters arrived. You know, to keep it warm for them.

Finding out about this fact finally caused all of my doubts about the religion to coalesce. If there was any possible explanation for this besides greed and exploitation, I believe I would have found it already.

69. Why did Jehovah's Witnesses seemingly erase the mansion from their history?

Why did Jehovah's Witnesses remove mentions of Beth Sarim from their literature? Are they ashamed of their past? As of 1919, the Watchtower Society was Jesus' chosen organization on Earth.

Why would they be ashamed of anything that's happened since that point? If this was only a case of a man doing something selfish and hiding behind Jehovah's Witnesses, why hasn't he been denounced as a fraud, and had the doctrine he introduced reversed?

70. Why did the Watchtower Society still celebrate Christmas after being chosen by Jesus in 1919?

Was Jesus okay with Christmas at the time? Did he change his mind? For that matter, why did the Watchtower Society still use the cross at the time? Why were blood transfusions still acceptable? Are those things okay now, or were they wrong back then?

71. Why did Joseph Rutherford write a letter to Hitler endorsing his beliefs about Jews?

Jehovah's Witnesses are strictly forbidden from having any involvement in political matters. Why did Joseph Rutherford, the second president of the Watchtower Society, express his support for Hitler? The letter to Hitler and the supportive "Declaration of Facts" document were referenced in Jehovah's Witnesses' 1975 yearbook.[1]

The letter to Hitler expresses distinctly pro-German positions. Joseph Rutherford took a political stand and respected and admired Hitler.

Dear Reichskanzler,

...

The Brooklyn headquarter of the Watchtower Society is pro German in an exemplary way and has been so for many years. For that reason, in 1918, the president of the Society and seven members of the board of directors were sentenced to 80 years in prison, because the president refused to use two of the magazines published in America under his direction for war propaganda against Germany. These two magazines, "The Watchtower" and "Bible Student" were the only magazines in America which refused to engage in anti-German propaganda and for that reason were prohibited and suppressed in America during the war.

RUTHERFORD, JOSEPH. *LETTER TO HITLER.*
1933

A few paragraphs down, the letter continued to put a puff in Hitler's petticoat.

The Bible Researchers of Germany are fighting for the very same high ethical goals and ideals which also the national government of the German Reich proclaimed respecting the relationship of humans to God, namely: honesty of the created being towards its creator.

RUTHERFORD, JOSEPH. *LETTER TO HITLER.*
1933

We don't even need to reference the Declaration of Facts or the letter to Hitler to see how Joseph Rutherford felt about Jews.

72. Why did Joseph Rutherford hate Jews so much?

In 1927, he published this statement in the Watchtower Society's publication *The Golden Age:*

Be it known once and for all that those profiteering, conscienceless, selfish men who call themselves Jews, and who control the greater portion of the finances of the world and the business of the world, will never be the rulers in this new earth. God would not risk such selfish men with such an important position.

JEHOVAH'S WITNESSES. THE GOLDEN AGE. FEBRUARY 23, 1927. P. 343

73. How can Jehovah's Witnesses believe that Jesus chose the Watchtower Society as his representative on earth while somebody as vile as Joseph Rutherford was in charge in 1919?

Why is this still doctrine? How could Jehovah's Witnesses possibly believe that Jesus picked Joseph Rutherford as the leader of his representation on earth?

74. Why lie about the reason Joseph Rutherford banned beards?

In December 2023, beards were unbanned for the first time since 1925. Governing Body member Stephen Lett spoke on the subject. He explained that beards were banned because they were associated with a rebellious political attitude.

Except that's not why they were banned. The real story is still available on the Jehovah's Witness website.[2] The story was originally told in 1971 by William J. Schnell in his book titled *30 Years a Watchtower Slave.* Four years later, Jehovah's Witnesses published the story in their 1975 yearbook.

Rutherford engaged in a fierce power struggle to regain control of the Watchtower Society from the Bible Students. When he won, he banned members from wearing beards to stamp out the challenge to his power.

An amusing incident took place at the time of the Judge's visit. The Director of our German branch, as had many before him, had grown a large beard, patterned after Charles T. Russell's beard. The Judge did not want anything at all to remain which might remind him of Russell—not even the cultivation of a beard. So, sitting at the table for dinner one night within my earshot, the Director asked the Judge for one more large rotary press. The Judge said nothing for a while, merely ate. So, suddenly he looked up, his eyes pinned severely on the Director's huge beard and said, "I will buy you the press if you take that thing off," pointing to the beard. It surely shocked the Director's sensibilities, but he meekly heeded the warning and soon shamefacedly appeared minus the beard.

SCHNELL, WILLIAM J. 30 YEARS A WATCHTOWER SLAVE. 1971. PP. 51–52

That story was told in Schnell's book in 1971. A similar story was told a few years later in the Jehovah's Witnesses' 1975 yearbook. Here's what their website says about it:

But more equipment was needed. For that reason Brother Balzereit asked Brother Rutherford for permission to buy a rotary press. Brother Rutherford saw the necessity and agreed, but on one condition. He had noticed that over the years Brother Balzereit had grown a beard very similar to the one that had been worn by Brother Russell. His example soon caught on, for there were others who also wanted to look like Brother Russell. This could give rise to a tendency toward creature worship, and Brother Rutherford wanted to prevent this. So during his next visit, within hearing of all the Bible House family, he told Brother Balzereit that he could buy the rotary press but only on the condition that he shave off his beard. Brother Balzereit sadly agreed and afterward went to the barber. During the next few days there were several cases of mistaken identity and some funny situations because of the "stranger" who was sometimes not recognized by his fellow workers.

JEHOVAH'S WITNESSES. 1974 YEARBOOK. PP.
97–98

That's a little more charitable, but effectively the same situation. And again, it's still on their website. Why did Stephen Lett lie about the reason when it could be found on Watchtower Online Library?

Stephen Lett claimed it was because hippies wore beards and didn't want to be associated with a political movement. That was easily disproven by reading their website. The Watchtower Society claimed beards were banned because they wanted to prevent people from idolizing Charles Taze Russell. Why didn't they just ban that specific style of beard? If they're worried about creature worship, why do rooms in the headquarters have paintings of the Watchtower Society presidents? Isn't that a clearer example of idolatry? Either way, wearing a similar beard is mimicry, not idolatry. Did the Governing Body members or presidents between 1925 and 2023 not understand the difference?

75. Why do Jehovah's Witnesses pretend Joseph Rutherford's beard ban event didn't happen, even though it can be found on their website today?

Why aren't the Governing Body members just honest about their past? In the 2023 annual meeting, Jeffrey Winder described the process of changing doctrine. The Governing Body has the research staff dig up everything the Watchtower Society has ever said on a subject. The Governing Body then debates the issue. Doctrine changes if the decision is unanimous.

76. Did Stephen Lett lie when he claimed beards were banned because of their association with a rebellious political attitude?

Did the Governing Body's research staff overlook the story in the 1974 yearbook? Is the Governing Body genuinely completely oblivious to the *real* reason why beards were banned? Did they just make up a reason when reversing the decision? Why would they make up a reason rather than being honest with their members?

77. Why do Jehovah's Witnesses believe the United Nations is the Great Beast of Revelation? By whose authority do they make that declaration?

If we examine the Bible verses used by Jehovah's Witnesses to determine that the UN is the Great Beast, many other organizations or people could fit the bill. Why didn't Jehovah's Witnesses pick the European Union instead?

78. Why was the Watchtower Society registered as an NGO of the United Nations from 1992 to 2001?

Jehovah's Witnesses believe the United Nations to be the Great Beast of Revelation. They believe the UN will destroy religion during the Great Tribulation.

The Watchtower Society agreed to the UN pledge to uphold the goals and interests of the United Nations.

When The Guardian caught the Watchtower Society, it denied that it had agreed to the pledge. It claimed that the pledge wasn't on the application form when they joined when, in fact, it was.[3]

79. Why did the Watchtower Society pull out of the United Nations within days of *The Guardian* news article being published? Were they ashamed?

The Watchtower Society claims their writing staff registered the Watchtower Society as an NGO to gain access to the UN library, but the same books were available without being registered as an NGO of the United Nations.

CHAPTER 9
DEADLY DECISIONS

80. Why are blood transfusions banned for Jehovah's Witnesses?

Jehovah's Witnesses base their blood transfusion doctrine on one specific verse in the Old Testament. The verse is in Leviticus, which is part of the Old Law that Christians *aren't* required to follow.

And anyone of the people of Israel, or of the aliens who reside among them, who hunts down an animal or bird that may be eaten shall pour out its blood and cover it with earth.

For the life of every creature—its blood is its life; therefore I have said to the people of Israel: You shall not eat the blood of any creature, for the life of every creature is its blood; whoever eats it shall be cut off.

LEVITICUS 17:13–14

81. Why do Jehovah's Witnesses follow the old law regarding blood but ignore it regarding shellfish and pork?

Jehovah's Witnesses believe the old law was fulfilled and no longer necessary when Jesus came to earth. Why did they pick that one verse out of Leviticus and decide to follow it? Why do they ignore all the rest?

82. Why do Jehovah's Witnesses interpret the phrase "don't eat blood" as "don't take a lifesaving medical treatment?"

The word used in the Bible literally means "to eat." I thought using the word "eat" was an odd choice, so I looked deeper. The Hebrew word looks like this: "אֹכְלָיו" It's pronounced *'ō·ḵə·lāw*.

The word means explicitly to eat, to devour through your mouth and into your stomach. It doesn't relate to using blood in a lifesaving medical procedure. Why did Jehovah's Witnesses interpret the word as "to use in a medical procedure" instead of what it really means? Isn't that changing the Bible?

83. If God is all-knowing, why didn't he have Jesus mention blood transfusions even once?

The concept of a blood transfusion didn't exist when the book of Leviticus was written. However, God is all-knowing and all-wise. Why didn't Jesus mention it at least once if he wanted us to avoid blood transfusions? Wasn't Jesus sent to earth to set the standard for how the Christian religion is supposed to operate? Couldn't Jesus have condemned using blood in medical procedures specifically? That would have made it pretty clear.

84. Did the fourth president of the Watchtower Society, Fred Franz, ban blood transfusions to get attention?

After Joseph Rutherford's death, Nathan Knorr became the Watchtower Society president in 1942. Fred Franz became Knorr's vice president in 1945 and remained vice president until he became president in 1977.

In 1994, Jerry Bergman wrote a book about the history of objections to blood transfusions. Transfusions were heavily discouraged starting in 1945 and fully banned by 1961.

> After the Judge's [Joseph Rutherford's] death, as World War II was ending and persecution against the Witnesses began declining, along with the attendant drop in news-media publicity, Hayden C. Covington told the author [of THE FOUR PRESIDENTS] that Fred Franz saw the prohibition against blood transfusions as a way to accomplish two things: to continue to publicize the religion, and to create an uproar in the community.This reaction would convince the membership they were being "persecuted" and "suffering for righteousness sake," a sure sign they were "in the truth."

> BERGMAN, JERRY. *BLOOD TRANSFUSIONS: A HISTORY AND EVALUATION OF THE RELIGIOUS, BIBLICAL, AND MEDICAL OBJECTIONS.* 1994. P. 5

85. Why was it acceptable to receive an organ transplant from 1949 to 1961?

Jehovah's Witnesses allowed organ donation in 1949 but seemed to have a very strange view of the process.

> Have your teeth or hair fallen out? Has arthritis frozen your joints? Have a hole in your skull that needs plugging up? Need a new roof in your mouth? Or do you need a replacement for your lungs, kidneys or heart? If so, you will be interested to know that there are many shops around the country that are now in the business of

supplying "spare parts" for the human body, both natural and artificial.

JEHOVAH'S WITNESSES. *AWAKE!.*
DECEMBER 22, 1949. P.17

I didn't know they were doing roof-of-mouth transplants in 1949.

86. Why did the Watchtower Society decide that organ donation was a conscience matter in 1961?

Determining that a procedure or behavior is a conscience matter is a subtle way of telling members not to do it without explicitly stating it. Dating an outsider, having non-Jehovah's Witness friends, and taking certain medicines produced with blood fractions are all considered conscience matters.

The Watchtower Society listed organ donation as a "conscience matter" in 1961. It's not technically wrong, but it's very questionable. "God might decide to kill you in Armageddon. We just don't know." Look at the 1961 *Watchtower* article on the subject:

Is there anything in the Bible against giving one's eyes (after death) to be transplanted to some living person?-L. C., United States. The question of placing one's body or parts of one's body at the disposal of men of science or doctors at one's death for purposes of scientific experimentation or replacement in others is frowned upon by certain religious bodies. However, it does not seem that any Scriptural principle or law is involved. It therefore is something that each individual must decide for himself.

JEHOVAH'S WITNESSES. "QUESTIONS FROM

READERS." *THE WATCHTOWER.* AUGUST 1,
1961. P. 480

Reading these words would certainly be enough to prevent many Jehovah's Witnesses from getting organ donations. "The new system" is a term used by Jehovah's Witnesses to refer to where they believe they'll go after Armageddon. 144,000 anointed Jehovah's Witnesses go to heaven; every other Jehovah's Witness goes to a kind of Garden of Eden 2.0—the new system.

How many Jehovah's Witnesses needlessly died because they rejected organ donations for fear they wouldn't make it into the new system?

87. Why did the Watchtower Society ban organ donation in 1967, claiming that it's tantamount to cannibalism?

In 1967, the Watchtower Society released an article explicitly condemning organ donation as scripturally wrong. They said it was tantamount to cannibalism.

Sustaining one's life by means of the body or part of the body of another human...would be cannibalism, a practice abhorrent to all civilized people...It is not our place to decide whether such operations are advisable from a scientific or medical standpoint...Christians who have been enlightened by God's Word do not need to make these decisions based simply on the basis of personal whim · or emotion. They can consider the divine principles and use these in making personal decisions as they look to God for direction, trusting him and putting their confidence in the future that he has in store for those who love him.

JEHOVAH'S WITNESSES. *THE*

WATCHTOWER. NOVEMBER 15, 1967. PP. 702–
704

If the number of Jehovah's Witnesses who died for rejecting an organ donation was high before, it certainly spiked dramatically after it moved from "conscience matter" to outright ban. Why did Jehovah change his mind? According to Jehovah's Witnesses, he's all-knowing, all-wise, and never changing.

88. Why did the Governing Body change the organ donation policy *again* in 1980?

The Watchtower Society once again reversed course in 1980.

There is no Biblical command pointedly forbidding the taking in of other human tissue. It is a matter for personal decision.

JEHOVAH'S WITNESSES. *THE WATCHTOWER*.
MARCH 15, 1980. P. 31

Will there ever be an apology for people who needlessly died between the years of 1961 and 1967 when it was banned?

89. Why did Jehovah's Witnesses believe that the recipients of an organ donation inherited the personality of the donor in 1975?

The 1975 *Watchtower* had this to say about organ donation five short years before it was unbanned again:

A peculiar factor sometimes noted is a so-called 'personality trans-plant.' That is, the recipient in some cases has seemed to adopt certain personality factors of the person from whom the organ came.

JEHOVAH'S WITNESSES. *THE WATCHTOWER.*
SEPTEMBER 1, 1975, P. 519

Why did Jehovah's Witnesses claim that people could inherit the personality of people from whom organs were donated? Where is the basis for this idea in the Bible?

CHAPTER 10
CHILD ABUSE

90. Why aren't elders explicitly instructed to call the police when they find out about a possible case of child sexual abuse?

Since the 1960s, involving secular authorities in anything has been frowned upon socially. The codified rules have fluctuated in many ways, but the culture dictates much of Jehovah's Witnesses' lives. To this day, no official instructions have been given to the elders to involve authorities when an assault occurs. As I show in the next question, the current handbook recommends elders "neither encourage nor discourage" parents from calling the police.

91. Why are elders instructed to work closely with the police in some circumstances but not others?

The elder's handbook instructs elders to meet with local police in case of a fire or burglary.

Communication with Local Law Enforcement: The elders should have up-to-date phone numbers for the police. Two elders (or a capable ministerial servant along with one elder) should be designated to visit the police station to promote good relations, expressing appreciation for their assistance if called upon. It may be advisable to ask the local authorities for security suggestions. Where several congregations are in the vicinity of the same police station, there should be good coordination as to how this contact with the police will be maintained.

JEHOVAH'S WITNESSES. *ADDENDUM TO SHEPHERD THE FLOCK OF GOD ELDER'S HANDBOOK.* 2022. P. 11, PARA. 26

Why are Jehovah's Witnesses explicitly instructed to connect with police in that case, but they aren't explicitly instructed to call the police in cases of child sexual abuse?

Child abuse is a crime. Never suggest to anyone that they should not report an allegation of child abuse to the police or other authorities. If you are asked, make it clear that whether to report the matter to the authorities or not is a personal decision for each individual to make and that there are no congregation sanctions for either decision. Elders will not criticize anyone who reports such an allegation to the authorities. If the victim wishes to make a report, it is his or her absolute right to do so.

JEHOVAH'S WITNESSES. "CHAPTER 12: CHILD ABUSE". *SHEPHERD THE FLOCK OF GOD.* SECTION 18–21, PP. 131–133

I appreciate that they eventually inserted that final line in the 2021 edition of the Elder's handbook. Next, I'd love it if they instructed elders to call the police. If the elders aren't instructed, maybe parents should be mandated to do so. Ambiguous language like this has allowed loopholes to be exploited over the years.

92. Does the Watchtower Society think that indoctrinating children is okay?

Jehovah's Witnesses have a series of children's cartoons called Caleb and Sophia. The cartoons teach children to be Jehovah's Witnesses. Why do Jehovah's Witnesses indoctrinate children instead of letting them choose their religion freely?

Do Jehovah's Witnesses believe that children are capable of fully grasping the consequences of their actions at 12 years old? If not, why would they allow children as young as eight to be baptized, effectively signing a lifelong contract with the Society?

93. Why does the Watchtower Society encourage children to get baptized as young as possible?

Do Jehovah's Witnesses think children can understand the consequences of signing a lifelong contract? Would Jehovah's Witnesses believe it's acceptable for two 12-year-olds to be married? If not, why do they think baptism, a much more serious decision, is acceptable?

CHAPTER 11
WRATH AND HATE

94. Why do Jehovah's Witnesses judge people?

omans 2 condemns judging people. It clearly states that God will judge what's in people's hearts. Nobody on earth has the authority to fill that role in God's place.

Therefore you have no excuse, whoever you are, when you judge others; for *in passing judgement on another you condemn yourself*, because you, the judge, are doing the very same things. You say, "We know that God's judgement on those who do such things is in accordance with truth." Do you imagine, whoever you are, that when you judge those who do such things and yet do them yourself, you will escape the judgement of God?

ROMANS 2:1–4

95. Why don't Jehovah's Witnesses exercise patience and kindness?

Romans 2:4-5 says that God shows patience and kindness to people to bring them back to the fold.

> Do you imagine, whoever you are, that when you judge those who do such things and yet do them yourself, you will escape the judgement of God? Or do you *despise the riches of his kindness and forbearance and patience*? Do you not realize that God's *kindness is meant to lead you to repentance*? But by your hard and impenitent heart you are *storing up wrath for yourself on the day of wrath*, when God's righteous judgement will be revealed.
>
> *ROMANS 2:1–5*

Why do Jehovah's Witnesses think that shunning people is an effective way of bringing people back into the fold? Why do they completely ignore Romans 2:1–5 and show wrath and judgment anyway?

96. Why are Jehovah's Witnesses excited at the thought of critics being snuffed out like a flame?

Ex-Governing Body member Tony Morris gave a public talk about apostates. After describing a vivid scene where their bodies will burn and whatever doesn't burn will be eaten by maggots, he says the following:

> Not a pleasant sight. But, what a fitting picture of the final end of all of god's enemies. Sobering, yet something we look forward to. However, the apostates and the enemies of Jehovah would say, "oh, that's gruesome. That's despicable. You teach your people these things?" No, *God* teaches *his* people these things. This is what he's foretelling. And frankly, for friends of Jehovah God, how reassuring, that they're finally going to be gone—all these despicable

enemies that have just reproached Jehovah's name—destroyed, never ever to live again. Now, it's not that we rejoice in someone's death, but when it comes to god's enemies…finally, they're out of the way. Especially these despicable apostates who at one point had dedicated their life to god and then…they joined forces with Satan the Devil, the chief apostate of all time.

He quotes from a Bible verse next. He says,

But the wicked will perish. The enemies of Jehovah will vanish like glorious pastures. Particularly, they will vanish like smoke. So…I thought this would be a nice memory aid [to help] this verse stay in the mind. Here's what Jehovah is promising.

He lights a match, holds it in front of him for a moment, and blows it out. He looks back up from the match and smiles as he chuckles. The crowd laughs.

He says, "That's Jehovah's enemies. They're going to vanish like smoke."

Are these the actions of a godly man? Would Jesus ever be excited at the thought of a single person suffering, as Tony Morris did in his film about apostates?

97. Why do Jehovah's Witnesses *hate* gay people?

Jehovah's Witnesses would deny this charge. "We don't hate gay people," they say, "we love everybody. We just want them to meet God's moral expectations." We've already spoken about God's moral expectations, but I claim that Jehovah's Witnesses *do hate* gay people. Look at this quote from a 1995 *Awake!*

A youth who desires to please God must therefore conform to His moral standards and shun immoral behavior, though doing so may be agonizingly difficult. True, some individuals may very well be prone to homosexuality, just as some individuals are, according to the Bible, "prone to wrath." (Titus 1:7) But the Bible still condemns displays of unrighteous anger. (Ephesians 4:31) Similarly, a Christian cannot excuse immoral behavior by saying he was "born that way." Child molesters invoke the same pathetic excuse when they say their craving for children is "innate." But can anyone deny that their sexual appetite is perverted? So is the desire for someone of the same sex.

> JEHOVAH'S WITNESSES. "WHY DO I HAVE THESE FEELINGS?" *AWAKE!* FEBRUARY 8, 1995, P. 16

Jehovah's Witnesses view gay people the same way they view child molesters. They view them as morally depraved, dangerous to everybody around them, and believe that "their sexual appetite is perverted." Gay people wouldn't exist in a government set up and controlled by Jehovah's Witnesses. If that's not hate, I don't know what is. They can claim they don't hate them all they want, but it's a hard conclusion to avoid.

98. Why isn't it a disfellowshipping offense for a parent to abandon their children?

The Catholic Church controlled entire towns centuries ago. If a member of the town broke a Catholic rule, they wouldn't be able to rent a room anymore. They couldn't buy food or hang out with friends. The hope was that they would wander into the woods and die. Excommunication, or disfellowshipping, effectively marks a person as dead in the eyes of the shunners.

That is the punishment for being gay. That's the punishment for being critical of the religion, having a girlfriend, or smoking a cigarette. It's the punishment for a nearly endless list of supposed "sins."

When I was disfellowshipped in eleventh grade, my mother kicked me out of my home, and I had to drop out of high school. Jehovah's Witnesses seemed to think my mother made the right decision. Not only was she not punished, but her status and respect within the congregation seemed to rise.

Why is abandoning a child not viewed negatively? Why isn't it a disfellowshipping offense? Forget Jehovah's Witnesses' false claims that they don't shun. Why don't they ban shunning? If they're so desperate to convince the outside world that this isn't part of their core doctrine, why not guarantee it doesn't happen by creating a mandate?

99. Why do Jehovah's Witnesses have wrath in their hearts rather than love?

My last conversation with my mother ended with her telling me I was repulsive to her because I was critical of the Watchtower Society. After being kicked out of my house in eleventh grade, I was taken in by a Methodist woman named Sue. She was my daughter's great-grandmother.

Sue knew I believed in Jehovah's Witnesses doctrine, but she loved me anyway. When I realized that Jehovah's Witnesses were wrong and walked away from the whole thing, Sue still loved me. When I became addicted to heroin to cope with the loss of everything I ever knew, Sue let me live with her. When I was too destitute to buy Christmas presents for my own wife and daughter, Sue bought presents for them, addressed from me.

Sue never called me repulsive. No matter how low I got, she was still with me. Even after divorcing her granddaughter, she allowed me to live with her and loved me as if I were her own son. She was the perfect embodiment of the qualities Jesus expected from his followers. She took care of the poor and loved everybody, no matter what. Sue was my real mother, for all intents and purposes.

Sue died on September 21, 2022. She had nothing but love in her heart.

Every Jehovah's Witness I've ever known has disowned me. They look at me with disgust. They even call me repulsive. They hate me. They persecute me. They do not follow Jesus' example as Sue did.

Why do Jehovah's Witnesses have hate and wrath in their hearts instead of love, as Jesus commanded? Why do they pretend to love everybody while being selective about the love they show? How can someone claim to be a good person when the only love they ever show—even to their own children—is conditional? Why do they believe God will save them when they are the embodiment of the goats described in Jesus' sheep and goats parable in Matthew 25:31–46?

100. Why do Jehovah's Witnesses take good-faith criticism as a personal attack?

Criticism is how we all get better. How are we supposed to know God chooses the Governing Body if we can't point out the occasional flaw without being shunned? The Bible specifically instructs God's people to constantly question the leadership to ensure they speak for God (Deuteronomy 18:22). Does the Governing Body expect us to ignore that verse selectively?

———

We are each individually responsible for the decisions we make. Only God can judge (Romans 2:1–5). In that spirit, I will wait for

God's condemnation of my actions—not a group of men who obviously have a flawed interpretation of the Bible.

As Deuteronomy 18:22 instructs, I applied the test for a false prophet to the Watchtower Society. I've determined that they've spoken presumptuously, so I will no longer be frightened by them.

> If a prophet speaks in the name of the Lord but the thing does not take place or prove true, it is a word that the Lord has not spoken. The prophet has spoken it presumptuously; do not be frightened.
>
> *DEUTERONOMY 18:22*

NOTES

1. A HISTORY OF MISTAKES

1. Marina, Marko. "Where Was Jesus Born? Unraveling the Birth Narratives of Jesus." Bart D. Ehrman - New Testament Scholar, Speaker, and Consultant, 16 Oct. 2023, www.bartehrman.com/where-was-jesus-born/#:~:text=Based%20on%20Matthew%20and%20Luke,between%207%20and%204%20B.C.E. Accessed 3 Feb. 2024

2. "The Great Pyramid of Giza—Watchtower ONLINE LIBRARY." Jw.org, WOL, 2024, wol.jw.org/en/wol/d/r1/lp-e/1956362. Accessed 9 Jan. 2024.

3. Grundy, Paul. "Facts about 607 B.C.E., 587 B.C. And Whether Jesus Started Ruling in 1914." Jwfacts.com, 2022, www.jwfacts.com/watchtower/607-587.php. Accessed 3 Feb. 2024.

4. Ehrman, Bart. "The Fear of Hell, Good Debaters, and the Name of God: Mailbag April 22, 2016 | the Bart Ehrman Blog." The Bart Ehrman Blog, 2016, ehrmanblog.org/the-fear-of-hell-good-debaters-and-the-name-of-god-mailbag-april-22-2016/. Accessed 7 Jan. 2024.

5. Ehrman, Bart. "YHWH and Jehovah: Same? Different? Where's Jehovah Come From? | the Bart Ehrman Blog." The Bart Ehrman Blog, 2021, ehrmanblog.org/yhwh-and-jehovah-same-different/. Accessed 7 Jan. 2024.

6. Jehovah—the Meaning of God's Name and Its Use | Bible Teach." Jehovah's Witnesses. jw.org, 2024, www.jw.org/en/library/books/bible-teach/jehovah-meaning-of-gods-name/. Accessed 7 Jan. 2024.

7. Ehrman, Bart. "Were Ancient Israelites Actually Monotheists? | the Bart Ehrman Blog." The Bart Ehrman Blog, 2021, ehrmanblog.org/were-ancient-israelites-actually-monotheists/. Accessed 7 Jan. 2024.

8. "Syrian and Palestinian Religion | Definition, Mythology, Sites, & Facts | Britannica." Encyclopædia Britannica, 2024, www.britannica.com/topic/Syrian-and-Palestinian-religion. Accessed 7 Jan. 2024.

9. Wikipedia contributors. "Yahweh." Wikipedia, The Free Encyclopedia. Wikipedia, The Free Encyclopedia, 5 Jan. 2024. Web. 7 Jan. 2024.

10. Ehrman, Bart. "Is 'Jehovah' in the Bible? | the Bart Ehrman Blog." The Bart Ehrman Blog, 2015, ehrmanblog.org/is-jehovah-in-the-bible/. Accessed 7 Jan. 2024.

11. "Heaven and Hell Are 'Not What Jesus Preached,' Religion Scholar Says." NPR, 31 Mar. 2020, www.npr.org/2020/03/31/824479587/heaven-and-hell-are-not-what-jesus-preached-religion-scholar-says#:~:text=Live%20Sessions-,Heaven%20And%20Hell%20Are%20'Not%20What%20Jesus%20Preached%2C'%20Religion,in%20the%20teachings%20of%20Jesus. Accessed 3 Feb. 2024.

12. Wikipedia Contributors. "Apocalypse of Peter." Wikipedia, Wikimedia Foundation, 27 Jan. 2024, en.wikipedia.org/wiki/Apocalypse_of_Peter. Accessed 3 Feb. 2024.

13. Hur, Unsok. "The Disciples' Lack of Comprehension in the Gospel of Mark - Unsok Hur, 2019." Biblical Theology Bulletin, 2019, journals.sagepub.com/doi/10.1177/0146107919827483#:~:text=It%20is%20reasonable%20to%20see,of%20Jesus%20predicting%20his%20crucifixion. Accessed 7 Jan. 2024.

14. Ehrman, Bart. "The Return of Jesus (Rapture?) in 1 Thessalonians | the Bart Ehrman Blog." The Bart Ehrman Blog, 2015, ehrmanblog.org/the-return-of-jesus-rapture-in-1-thessalonians/. Accessed 7 Jan. 2024.

2. THE 144,000

1. Ehrman, Bart. "Paul's Letter to the Thessalonians | the Bart Ehrman Blog." The Bart Ehrman Blog, 2015, ehrmanblog.org/pauls-letter-to-the-thessalonians/. Accessed 7 Jan. 2024.

2. Ehrman, Bart. "A Bit of a Shocker: Jesus and the Son of Man | the Bart Ehrman Blog." The Bart Ehrman Blog, 2020, ehrmanblog.org/a-bit-of-a-shocker-jesus-and-the-son-of-man/. Accessed 7 Jan. 2024.

3. Hur, Unsok. "The Disciples' Lack of Comprehension in the Gospel of Mark - Unsok Hur, 2019." Biblical Theology Bulletin, 2019, journals.sagepub.com/doi/10.1177/0146107919827483#:~:text=It%20is%20reasonable%20to%20see,of%20Jesus%20predicting%20his%20crucifixion. Accessed 7 Jan. 2024.

4. Ehrman, Bart. "A Bit of a Shocker: Jesus and the Son of Man | the Bart Ehrman Blog." The Bart Ehrman Blog, 2020, ehrmanblog.org/a-bit-of-a-shocker-jesus-and-the-son-of-man/. Accessed 7 Jan. 2024.

5. Grundy, Paul. "Watchtower Doctrine Regarding the 144,000 Being a Literal Number." Jwfacts.com, 2014, www.jwfacts.com/watchtower/144000.php. Accessed 21 Jan. 2024.

6. Ehrman, Bart. "The Number 666 in the Context of the Book of Revelation | the Bart Ehrman Blog." The Bart Ehrman Blog, 2020, ehrmanblog.org/the-number-666-in-the-context-of-the-book-of-revelation/. Accessed 8 Jan. 2024.

3. HOSTILE TAKEOVER

1. Wikipedia Contributors. "Watch Tower Society Presidency Dispute." Wikipedia, Wikimedia Foundation, 11 Oct. 2023, en.wikipedia.org/wiki/Watch_Tower_Society_presidency_dispute. Accessed 20 Jan. 2024.

2. Grundy, Paul. "1925 and the Watchtower Teaching That Millions Now Living Will Never Die!" Jwfacts.com, 2017, www.jwfacts.com/watchtower/1925.php. Accessed 20 Jan. 2024.

3. Grundy, Paul. "1919 - How the Watchtower Arrives at This Being the Year

Jehovah Chose Them." Jwfacts.com, 2018, jwfacts.com/watchtower/1919-derived.php. Accessed 20 Jan. 2024.

4. "Part 1—Germany—Watchtower ONLINE LIBRARY." Jw.org, WOL, 2024, wol.jw.org/en/wol/d/r1/lp-e/301974004#h=163. Accessed 24 Jan. 2024.

5. What Does the Bible Say about Dinosaurs?" Jehovah's Witnesses. jw.org, 2024, www.jw.org/en/bible-teachings/questions/dinosaurs-in-the-bible/. Accessed 18 Jan. 2024.

6. Grundy, Paul. "Beth-Sarim - Rutherford's House of Princes & Beth Shan." Jwfacts.com, 2017, www.jwfacts.com/watchtower/bethsarim.php. Accessed 20 Jan. 2024.

7. Bundy, Trey. "Jehovah's Witness Abuse Files Remain Secret after Court Settlements." March 21, 2018, revealnews.org/blog/jehovahs-witness-abuse-files-remain-secret-after-court-settlements/. Accessed 24 Jan. 2024.

8. Grundy, Paul. "The Different Standards Applied to Brothers in Malawi, Mexico and the Oath of Allegiance." Jwfacts.com, 2014, www.jwfacts.com/watchtower/malawi-mexico-oath-allegiance.php. Accessed 20 Jan. 2024.

9. Grundy, Paul. "Rutherford and the Watchtower's Support of Hitler." Jwfacts.com, 2015, www.jwfacts.com/watchtower/hitler-nazi.php. Accessed 20 Jan. 2024.

10. Browning, Christopher R. Ordinary Men : Reserve Police Battalion 101 and the Final Solution in Poland. New York :Harper Perennial, 1998

4. PAGANISM

1. Grundy, Paul. "Watchtower Quotes Regarding Pagan Practices." Jwfacts.com, 2016, www.jwfacts.com/watchtower/quotes/pagan-practices.php. Accessed 20 Jan. 2024.

2. Wikipedia Contributors. "Apocalypse of Peter." Wikipedia, Wikimedia Foundation, 27 Jan. 2024, en.wikipedia.org/wiki/Apocalypse_of_Peter. Accessed 3 Feb. 2024.

3. Ehrman, Bart. "How Were People Crucified? | the Bart Ehrman Blog." The Bart Ehrman Blog, 2020, ehrmanblog.org/how-were-people-crucified/. Accessed 9 Jan. 2024

4. Evans, Lloyd. "Traumatized by a Cupcake: The Latest Caleb & Sophia Monstrosity." YouTube, YouTube Video, 7 Jan. 2021, www.youtube.com/watch?v=e50ORAmICgA. Accessed 6 Jan. 2024.

5. ReligionForBreakfast. "Did Christmas Copy the Sun God's Birthday?" YouTube, YouTube Video, 15 Dec. 2021, www.youtube.com/watch?v=mWgzjwy51kU&t=960s. Accessed 9 Jan. 2024.

6. ReligionForBreakfast. "The Very Recent Origins of the Christmas Tree." YouTube, YouTube Video, 14 Dec. 2023, www.youtube.com/watch?v=m41KXS-LWsY. Accessed 21 Jan. 2024.

7. How Did Christmas Trees Become so Popular? | Britannica." Encyclopædia Britannica, 2024, www.britannica.com/video/252609/christmas-tree-decoration-holiday. Accessed 22 Jan. 2024.

8. Fox. "Michael's first Christmas". 1993

9. Stern, Marlow. "Donald Glover on Spider-Man, Stripping in 'Magic Mike XXL,' and a Possible 'Community' Return." *The Daily Beast*. February 20, 2015.

5. THE PREACHING WORK

1. Service-Year-Report-of-Jehovahs-Witnesses-Worldwide/2022-Grand-Totals/. Accessed 8 Jan. 2024.

2. "Jehovah's Witnesses—2018 Grand Totals." Jehovah's Witnesses. jw.org, 2018, www.jw.org/en/library/books/2018-service-year-report/2018-grand-totals/. Accessed 21 Jan. 2024.

6. THE SHUNNING BEGINS

1. Grundy, Paul. "Jehovah's Witnesses, Disfellowshipping and Shunning, Including Family Members." Jwfacts.com, 2015, www.jwfacts.com/watchtower/disfellowship-shunning.php. Accessed 25 Jan. 2024.

2. Ehrman, Bart. Paul and that Peculiar Church in Corinth | The Bart Ehrman Blog. The Bart Ehrman Blog. Published 2021. Accessed January 6, 2024. https://ehrmanblog.org/paul-and-that-peculiar-church-in-corinth/

3. Grundy, Paul. "Jehovah's Witnesses, Disfellowshipping and Shunning, Including Family Members." Jwfacts.com, 2015, www.jwfacts.com/watchtower/disfellowship-shunning.php. Accessed 12 Jan. 2024.

4. "Should a Christian Choose to Use Birth Control? | Bible Questions." Jehovah's Witnesses. jw.org, 2024, www.jw.org/en/bible-teachings/questions/contraceptives-bible-view/. Accessed 25 Jan. 2024.

5. Wikipedia Contributors. "Gary Gygax." Wikipedia, Wikimedia Foundation, 22 Jan. 2024, en.wikipedia.org/wiki/Gary_Gygax#Advanced_Dungeons_&_Dragons_and_Hollywood. Accessed 26 Jan. 2024.

6. McCarthy, Justin. Gallup.com, Gallup, 5 June 2023, news.gallup.com/poll/506636/sex-marriage-support-holds-high.aspx. Accessed 20 Jan. 2024.

7. Jones, Jeffrey M. Gallup.com, Gallup, 17 Feb. 2022, news.gallup.com/poll/389792/lgbt-identification-ticks-up.aspx. Accessed 26 Jan. 2024.

8. Put on and Keep on the New Personality | Study." Jehovah's Witnesses. jw.org, 2017, www.jw.org/en/library/magazines/watchtower-study-august-2017/put-on-keep-on-new-personality/. Accessed 20 Jan. 2024.

9. Am I Gay? Is It Wrong to Have Homosexual Urges? | Teenagers." Jehovah's Witnesses. jw.org, 2024, www.jw.org/en/bible-teachings/teenagers/ask/pressure-to-be-gay/. Accessed 26 Jan. 2024.

10. Grundy, Paul. "Jehovah's Witness Watchtower Doctrine Regarding Homosexuality - Jw.org." Jwfacts.com, 2016, www.jwfacts.com/watchtower/homosexuality-gay-jehovahs-witnesses.php. Accessed 20 Jan. 2024.

7. THE TWO WITNESS RULE

1. Evans, Lloyd. "Elder Leaks Jehovah's Witness Child Sex Abuse Form - Episode 42 - JW Watch." YouTube, YouTube Video, 18 Jan. 2024, www.youtube.com/watch?v=VOaMVdq3IRo. Accessed 23 Jan. 2024.
2. Grundy, Paul. "Watchtower Child Abuse Paedophile Policy and Related Court Cases." Jwfacts.com, 2015, www.jwfacts.com/watchtower/paedophilia.php. Accessed 23 Jan. 2024.
3. Dateline. Anderson, Barbara. "Witness fro the Prosecution.", YouTube Video, 1 Mar. 2017, www.youtube.com/watch?v=asQ2Rl9xeQY. Accessed 23 Jan. 2024.

8. EVEN MORE FALSE PROPHECY

1. Ehrman, Bart. "Jesus on Gehenna | the Bart Ehrman Blog." The Bart Ehrman Blog, 2018, ehrmanblog.org/jesus-on-gehenna/. Accessed 20 Jan. 2024.
2. Gehenna | Judgment, Punishment, Hellfire | Britannica." Encyclopædia Britannica, 2024, www.britannica.com/topic/Gehenna. Accessed 2 Feb. 2024.
3. Ehrman, Bart. "666: The Number of the Beast | the Bart Ehrman Blog." The Bart Ehrman Blog, 2015, ehrmanblog.org/666-the-number-of-the-beast/. Accessed 29 Jan. 2024.
4. Grundy, Paul. "Watchtower Society - United Nations NGO Status 1992." Jwfacts.com, 2022, www.jwfacts.com/watchtower/united-nations-association.php. Accessed 29 Jan. 2024.

9. JEHOVAH'S WITNESSES' BELIEFS ABOUT "THE END"

1. Ehrman, Bart. "The First Apocalypse: The Book of Daniel | the Bart Ehrman Blog." The Bart Ehrman Blog, 2017, ehrmanblog.org/the-first-apocalypse-the-book-of-daniel/. Accessed 9 Jan. 2024.
2. Ehrman, Bart. "The Famous Short Stories about Daniel | the Bart Ehrman Blog." The Bart Ehrman Blog, 2022, ehrmanblog.org/the-famous-short-stories-about-daniel/. Accessed 9 Jan. 2024.
3. Ehrman, Bart. "Background to the Christian Afterlife: The Maccabean Revolt: A Blast from the (Recent) Past! | the Bart Ehrman Blog." The Bart Ehrman Blog, 2017, ehrmanblog.org/background-to-the-christian-afterlife-the-maccabean-revolt-a-blast-from-the-recent-past/. Accessed 9 Jan. 2024.
4. Martin, W. J. "The Hebrew of Daniel." Notes on Some Problems in the Book of Daniel 30 (1965).
5. Ehrman, Bart. "The First Apocalypse: The Book of Daniel | the Bart Ehrman Blog." The Bart Ehrman Blog, 2017, ehrmanblog.org/the-first-apocalypse-the-book-of-daniel/. Accessed 31 Jan. 2024.
6. Ehrman, Bart. "Analyzing the Prophecies in Daniel 7, 2 and 9. Platinum Guest Post by Omar Abur-Robb | the Bart Ehrman Blog." The Bart Ehrman Blog, 2023,

ehrmanblog.org/analyzing-the-prophecies-in-daniel-7-2-and-9-platinum-guest-post-by-omar-abur-robb/. Accessed 31 Jan. 2024.

7. "Who Is Michael the Archangel? Is Jesus? | Bible Teach." JW.ORG, JW.ORG, 2024, www.jw.org/en/library/books/bible-teach/who-is-michael-the-archangel-jesus/. Accessed 13 Feb. 2024.

8. When Was Jesus Created, and Why Is He Called God's Son?" Jehovah's Witnesses. jw.org, 2024, www.jw.org/en/library/magazines/wp20130301/when-jesus-created-why-son/. Accessed 1 Feb. 2024.

9. Diagram from Daniel 2: World Powers Foretold by Daniel's Image | NWT." Jehovah's Witnesses. jw.org, 2024, www.jw.org/en/library/bible/nwt/appendix-b/daniel-2-image/. Accessed 9 Jan. 2024.

10. "How This World Will Come to an End | Study." Jehovah's Witnesses. jw.org, 2024, www.jw.org/en/library/magazines/w20120915/world-end/. Accessed 1 Feb. 2024.

11. The Scarlet Beast of Revelation 17—What Is It?" Jehovah's Witnesses. jw.org, 2024, www.jw.org/en/bible-teachings/questions/scarlet-beast-of-revelation-17/. Accessed 1 Feb. 2024.

12. What Is Babylon the Great? | Bible Questions." Jehovah's Witnesses. jw.org, 2024, www.jw.org/en/bible-teachings/questions/babylon-the-great/. Accessed 1 Feb. 2024.

13. What Is the Great Tribulation? | Bible Questions." Jehovah's Witnesses. jw.org, 2024, www.jw.org/en/bible-teachings/questions/great-tribulation/. Accessed 1 Feb. 2024.

14. What Is the Battle of Armageddon? | Bible Questions." Jehovah's Witnesses. jw.org, 2024, www.jw.org/en/bible-teachings/questions/battle-of-armageddon/. Accessed 1 Feb. 2024.

15. Online Video Library | JW.ORG Videos English." Jehovah's Witnesses. jw.org, 2024, www.jw.org/en/library/videos/#en/mediaitems/VODPgmEvtAnnMtg/pub-jwb-108_8_VIDEO. Accessed 1 Feb. 2024.

16. Ehrman, Bart. "Jesus' Teaching about the Kingdom of God | the Bart Ehrman Blog." The Bart Ehrman Blog, 2017, ehrmanblog.org/jesus-teaching-about-the-kingdom-of-god/. Accessed 7 Jan. 2024.

17. Ehrman, Bart. "The Birth of Purgatory | the Bart Ehrman Blog." The Bart Ehrman Blog, 2018, ehrmanblog.org/the-birth-of-purgatory/. Accessed 12 Jan. 2024.

10. IN HIDING

1. "One Room Schoolhouse – College of Education and Professional Development." Marshall.edu, 2023, www.marshall.edu/coepd/one-room-schoolhouse/. Accessed 15 Mar. 2024

11. MODERN CULTURE

1. "What Is Done at a Branch Office of Jehovah's Witnesses?" JW.ORG, JW.ORG, 2024, www.jw.org/en/library/books/jehovahs-will/branch-office-of-jehovahs-witnesses/. Accessed 20 Jan. 2024.

1. WORD TRANSLATION

1. Cooke, William. The Methodist New Connexion Magazine and Evangelical Repository, Volume XXXV., Third Series. 1867, p.493

2. FALSE PROPHECY

1. Grundy, Paul. "Facts about 607 B.C.E., 587 B.C. And Whether Jesus Started Ruling in 1914." Jwfacts.com, 2022, www.jwfacts.com/watchtower/607-587.php. Accessed 6 Jan. 2024.
2. Ehrman, Bart. "Background to Apocalypticism: The Maccabean Revolt | the Bart Ehrman Blog." The Bart Ehrman Blog, 2016, ehrmanblog.org/background-to-apocalypticism-the-maccabean-revolt/. Accessed 6 Jan. 2024.
3. "The Great Pyramid of Giza—Watchtower ONLINE LIBRARY." Jw.org, WOL, 2024, wol.jw.org/en/wol/d/r1/lp-e/1956362. Accessed 9 Jan. 2024.
4. Grundy, Paul. "Watchtower Quotes Regarding ..." Jwfacts.com, 2024, www.jw-facts.com/watchtower/quotes/20th-century-2000.php. Accessed 6 Jan. 2024.
5. Grundy, Paul. "1975 - Watchtower Quotes to Show What Really Was Predicted." Jwfacts.com, 2017, www.jwfacts.com/watchtower/1975.php. Accessed 2 Feb. 2024.

3. THE LGBT COMMUNITY

1. Siker, Jeff. "Homosexuality in the Bible (and the Christian Church) | the Bart Ehrman Blog." The Bart Ehrman Blog, 2019, ehrmanblog.org/homosexuality-in-the-bible-and-the-christian-church/. Accessed 3 Feb. 2024.
2. Siker, Jeff. "Homosexuality and the New Testament. Guest Post by Jeff Siker. | the Bart Ehrman Blog." The Bart Ehrman Blog, 2019, ehrmanblog.org/homosexuality-and-the-new-testament-guest-post-by-jeff-siker/. Accessed 3 Feb. 2024
3. "Am I Gay? Is It Wrong to Have Homosexual Urges? | Teenagers." JW.ORG, JW.ORG, 2024, www.jw.org/en/bible-teachings/teenagers/ask/pressure-to-be-gay/. Accessed 26 Jan. 2024.
4. "Why Don't Jehovah's Witnesses Celebrate Birthdays? | FAQ." JW.ORG, JW.ORG, 2024, www.jw.org/en/jehovahs-witnesses/faq/birthdays/. Accessed 3 Feb. 2024.

5. INCORRECT BELIEFS

1. Ehrman, Bart. "How Were People Crucified? | the Bart Ehrman Blog." The Bart Ehrman Blog, 2020, ehrmanblog.org/how-were-people-crucified/. Accessed 9 Jan. 2024.

2. "The King of the North" in the Time of the End | Watchtower Study. JW.ORG. Published 2020. Accessed January 6, 2024. https://www.jw.org/en/library/magazines/watchtower-study-may-2020/The-King-of-the-North-in-the-Time-of-the-End/

3. Ehrman, Bart. "The Non-Pauline Oppression of Women | the Bart Ehrman Blog." The Bart Ehrman Blog, 2020, ehrmanblog.org/the-non-pauline-oppression-of-women-for-members/. Accessed 3 Feb. 2024.

6. SHUNNING

1. Grundy, Paul. "Jehovah's Witnesses, Disfellowshipping and Shunning, Including Family Members." Jwfacts.com, 2015, www.jwfacts.com/watchtower/disfellowship-shunning.php. Accessed 9 Jan. 2024.

2. Ehrman, Bart. Paul and that Peculiar Church in Corinth | The Bart Ehrman Blog. The Bart Ehrman Blog. Published 2021. Accessed January 6, 2024. https://ehrmanblog.org/paul-and-that-peculiar-church-in-corinth/

3. Do Jehovah's Witnesses Shun Those Who Used to Belong to Their Religion?" JW.ORG, JW.ORG, 2024, www.jw.org/en/jehovahs-witnesses/faq/shunning/. Accessed 3 Feb. 2024.

4. Grundy, Paul. "Watchtower Quotes Regarding Pagan Practices." Jwfacts.com, 2016, www.jwfacts.com/watchtower/quotes/pagan-practices.php. Accessed 9 Jan. 2024.

5. "Henrietta M. Riley Trust - Jehovah's Witnesses." Jehovah's Witnesses, 18 Oct. 2022, avoidjw.org/donations/usa/hmrt/. Accessed 3 Feb. 2024.

7. PAGANISM

1. Grundy, Paul. "Watchtower Quotes Regarding Pagan Practices." Jwfacts.com, 2016, www.jwfacts.com/watchtower/quotes/pagan-practices.php. Accessed 20 Jan. 2024.

2. Jehovah's Witnesses. Watchtower. July 1, 1962, pp.409-414

3. Grundy, Paul. "Watchtower Quotes Regarding Pagan Practices." Jwfacts.com, 2016, www.jwfacts.com/watchtower/quotes/pagan-practices.php. Accessed 20 Jan. 2024.

4. Evans, Lloyd. "Traumatized by a Cupcake: The Latest Caleb & Sophia Monstrosity." YouTube, YouTube Video, 7 Jan. 2021, www.youtube.com/watch?v=e50ORAmICgA. Accessed 6 Jan. 2024.

5. Wikipedia Contributors. "Apocalypse of Peter." Wikipedia, Wikimedia Founda-

tion, 19 Jan. 2024, en.wikipedia.org/wiki/Apocalypse_of_Peter. Accessed 20 Jan. 2024.

8. EVIL LEADERS

1. Grundy, Paul. "Rutherford and the Watchtower's Support of Hitler." Jwfacts.com, 2015, www.jwfacts.com/watchtower/hitler-nazi.php. Accessed 6 Jan. 2024.
2. "Part 1—Germany—Watchtower ONLINE LIBRARY." Jw.org, WOL, 2024, wol.jw.org/en/wol/d/r1/lp-e/301974004#h=163. Accessed 24 Jan. 2024.
3. Grundy, Paul. "Watchtower Society - United Nations NGO Status 1992." Jwfacts.com, 2022, www.jwfacts.com/watchtower/united-nations-association.php#fn1. Accessed 6 Jan. 2024.